J. BABI

W9-CHQ-145

HOW THE UNIVERSE WORKS

Dear Michael —
To see for yo-
inside. To acquire
wisdom never let yourself
walk alone. ♡ Kath

HOW THE UNIVERSE WORKS

BY

Laeh Maggie Garfield

CELESTIALARTS
Berkeley, California

Cover and text design by David Charlsen
Typeset by Recorder Typesetting Network

Illustrations by Gabrielle Gern

Library of Congress Cataloging-in-Publication Data

Garfield, Laeh Maggie.
    How the universe works / Laeh Maggie
    Garfield.
        p.   cm.
    ISBN 0-89087-534-0
    1. New Age movement.   I. Title.
    BP605.N48G37   1991
    130—dc20   90-24154
                                                   CIP

First Printing, 1991
Printed in the United States of America
1 2 3 4 5 — 95 94 93 92 91

*To my daughters Lianne and Kari
And to all the change makers, those willing to grow with the times,
and to the medicine women and men of this planet*

ACKNOWLEDGEMENTS

Gratitude beyond mere words goes to Bob Wachtel for his years of brainstorming, feedback, and instinctive atunement with the teachings contained in this book. Without his valuable counsel and encouragement this work would not be as informative and clear.

Although he rarely leaves Sonoma County, Rio Olesky is a world class astrologer. His insight into human nature, gained from years as a counselor, and his astrological knowledge continue to amaze me. Thank you, Rio.

My apprentices and students deserve credit for asking me all the questions an accomplished person forgets the novice doesn't know.

In spite of being non-writers Edmée Gern, Bonnie Ronzio, and Edwin Knight know how to midwife a book.

To Gabrielle Gern, the artist, graduate apprentice, and friend whose creativity has enlivened this book and others of mine.

Always in the past the penalty for revealing knowledge was death. If this is so, it means the successful completion of my journey. I contracted with the Universe to write this book and I am glad to have done it.

The material on these pages is serious. Misuse and dabbling can create unfortunate, unwanted results. Every technique and method explained in *How the Universe Works* ought to be treated with the respect due any deep body of knowledge. Take no shortcuts. Do no harm. Proceed with good intentions. Fabricate nothing new until you've done and redone every step to perfection and have fully mastered the section you've undertaken.

May the Truth always be with you, imbuing you with courage, faith, and trust in your own Mission. The love sent to you through this manuscript is unconditional. Take it and share it with all who walk beside you.

CONTENTS

SECTION ONE: THE OTHER WORLDS

The Mansion of Sound, Mature Souls, The Mansion of Knowledge, Old Souls, The Mansion of Wisdom, Your Mansion, Overview

SECTION ONE
THE OTHER WORLDS

The Mission

It's a journey with my soul that I am taking, one that only goes from the cradle to the grave.

Kate Wolf

Magic is eternal. It rests inside your fundamental nature, dormant until you summon it. Miracles occur when you break through outworn beliefs and let the power and love of the moment guide you. Like love, magic is a renewable resource, not the property of one person who takes it all to the grave. And it enables you to reach the goal—enlightenment in a multitude of ways.

No one can stop you from knowing the secrets of the Universe. However, organized religion and the financially powerful have done as much to deny or demean the credibility of those who do know and are willing to teach. Occasionally the dominant institutions allow true knowledge to flourish, but solely as a part of a formula that permits the social order to continue unchanged.

A sense of humor is essential when cultivating any sort of wisdom. Without it, you're sunk. No matter how wise or learned you may be, you cannot know everything in a single lifetime. Everyone operates according to fragments of knowledge based on personal or professional areas of interest.

While studying outer space, you might well become aware of the connection between science and mysticism, although you will discover little about human nature. By working as a gardener you

5

come to understand the natural world and may also build comprehension of the spiritual realm, yet you'll learn little about outer space. As a professional in the psychoanalytical arts, you may not have time to talk to plants or delve into comparative cosmology, but you might come to a broad overview of the human condition and a deep appreciation for life's challenges.

Every path taken seriously can lead you to true knowledge and wisdom. How you interpret your experiences, how well you listen to your inner voice, how swiftly and sensibly you are able to rearrange your life to accommodate the next step on your path, is an indication of how fruitfully your Mission will be accomplished. The secret of personal success is to be true to yourself.

Life is a mission with a beginning and an end. It's not a competition to see how many years you can accumulate. The measure of its worthiness is that it gives you pleasure and allows you to serve your society, your planet, your Creator, and provides a sense of purpose. To that end you must find your Mission in life, the one contracted for before you were born.

During a short illness when I was twelve, my Life Vision occurred and I was told what to do with my life. Although I wanted a big family, I curbed that desire in order to fulfill my Mission. Material goods, friends, family, all paled next to my desire to fulfill my contract with the Universe, which in essence, is the contract with my soul. By degrees I learned to trust that if human beings were to share our spiritual core, a unified cosmology would become self-evident, and from this would emerge a worldwide religion. I saw clearly that most religions promote a high birthrate and suppression of other faiths in order to achieve dominance, that interfaith coexistence is an uneasy, guarded truce; and that religious xenophobia has far too many times led to war and other violence unworthy of spiritual seekers.

In my youth, the prevailing religions refused to teach women their inner mysteries. As a result I went directly to the Source, who sent spirit guides to help. Along the way there came into my life a teacher of great skill, Native American master Shaman Essie Parrish.

There is a true dependency of men upon women. Yet society knows little of how to honor womanly qualities, which are not weak nor subservient. Compared to men women are hardier, better at adapting, and have a built in facility and capacity for compassion. Since we are again moving into a time of the matriarchal religions any lasting change has got to be done in a balanced way, enabling us to blend and recognize the maternal and paternal aspect of the Creator in everything sacred and profane.

Many so-called alternative spiritual groups justify societal misconceptions about womanly nature to suit their own agendas. Confused men and women, with little information about historic or aboriginal matriarchal societies have expounded incorrectly from the pulpit on the feminine nature of spirituality basing their conclusions on a three generation comparison dating back to our grandmothers' time and restricted to our particular culture.

As a consequence this book includes the actual and mythic spiritual gifts and achievements of women. The Universe itself is balanced with respect to male and female energies. When I discovered the holy spirit to be the feminine component of the Trinity and that the Hebrews have male and female names for the Source it confirmed my faith in all of Creation as equal and unbiased.

Throughout the text there are references to the terms yoga, dZog Chen, the Kabbalah and terms some Native American tribes use for the same phenomenon. Yoga predates the Hindu religion for which it forms the central mystical pathway. DZog Chen is the shamanic way in Tibetan Buddhism and the Kabbalah is the core of Jewish mysticism. All are equivalent traditional shamanic ways for reaching enlightenment. Each form leads to the same wisdom although each system has its structural dogma.

The Universe is a mirror. If you stare into it long enough, you'll see every tiny detail and the overview simultaneously.

1

Secret Stairways

Out yonder there is a huge world, which exists independent of us human beings and which stands before us like a great, eternal riddle, at least partially accessible to our inspection and thinking. The contemplation of this world beckons like a liberation.

Albert Einstein

By concentrating on ways we can live in cooperation with the Creator, we send signals that make our world work smoothly rather than helping it to become an intolerable mess. By resolving our underlying conflicts and living out our destiny with courage and insight, we can attune ourselves with the Universe. Being born on earth is an exceptional opportunity to live in beauty and harmony by serving the highest good for all Mother Nature's inhabitants, including plants and minerals.

For a spiritual journey to work for you, it must match up with your individual path. You construct a mosaic of the philosophical ideas you are exposed to, the cultural beliefs of your generation, and the religious concepts and practices you espouse. As you mature, you chip away layers of beliefs and values you once lived by, or aspired to live by, and embrace new ones. Certain beliefs will remain at your core, unshakable regardless of how chic or passé they may be.

As a global villager, exposed to a multitude of spiritual ideals, philosophies and intercultural practices, Eastern, Western, and tribal in origin, it may be difficult for you to sort out what fits and what doesn't. Irrespective of who you learn from, however impeccable your sources, test whatever is presented. Follow nothing blindly. Keep only what works, and hold the rest in abeyance.

Seekers of enlightenment try one path and then another, often finding they're not in total agreement with the religion or guru they've attached themselves to. Every pathway has a language all its own in which to couch the acceptable mystical experiences. Should you grow beyond the dogmatic terminology, your vision and feelings may be shoehorned into a tighter mold to fit the religion, rather than be recognized as part of a greater picture, one that goes beyond culturally accepted criteria.

It is most difficult to live in the world yet not be of it. As householders, parents, job holders, students, you cannot leave your day-to-day existence to take up a hermit's lifestyle, as a way through the mysteries. Your seeking is the strongest kind because you test what you've learned against the backdrop of the life you are living.

It's no good to be told something, for then it's not really yours. You have to practice it to make it yours. The exercises in this book are for you to do. Knowing by head never equals the depth of experience and full wisdom that come with knowing by heart. A spiritual life journey is a marriage between intellect and experience.

The Way Through:
Moon, Sun, and Stars   Enlightenment is divided into three separate tiers. Each contains a body of knowledge that builds a sound foundation for the next. Although you may explore a few aspects of all layers simultaneously, only competence and mastery of the beginning strata will allow you to go forward. Your dynamic energy and skill at remaining mentally

intact throughout the tests devised by your teachers, both living and spiritual, will show whether you are ready to be welcomed into the second circle of illumination. Glimmers of cognition concerning the final stage of enlightenment can filter down to you, and you may grasp the universal truth behind it. However, actual insight is withheld until your proficiency at moving through the second spiral of knowledge has been proven.

Change your deep down beliefs and your life will change. Change your surface beliefs and only the exterior, your image and material world, will change.

MOON SPIRAL

Knowledge is gained, especially the discovery of the self, in the transition through the first stage represented by the moon. Uncovering your unconscious and your own godly potential is the sole way to ascend the stairs to the next level. Once you are unblocked you can manifest anything within reason and occasionally beyond reason. The skills associated with the moon spiral, or the first degree, are healing, visioning, journeying, working with spirit allies, simultaneously applying the knowledge gained to everyday life.

The moon level is extremely practical. Everything can be tested against the maxim of whether or not it works. The moon level is feminine and intuitive. Therapeutic methods, healing, ritual, the subconscious, and the shadow side all fall into this category. Some well known forms that epitomize the moon level of developing enlightenment are: meditation, self-help programs, dreamwork, dance therapy, psychodrama, bodywork, psychoanalysis, and yoga or Tai Chi.

The Raven in legend brings this knowledge by taking you through the underworld, or the tunnel, to the super-conscious. Ravens are one of the few birds that interact cooperatively to keep the species alive, sharing food sources and the work of locating dead meat. The Raven, a bird that eats carrion to keep the earth clean, serves as the guardian of the moon.

Symbolically it acts upon your psyche to clean up your carrion, the outmoded (dead) belief systems and values you carry around. As you work towards enlightenment in the primary degree, doing the practices associated with it, you become emotionally and mentally freer, even peaceful, able to let love come into your life. This is the way of the gentle warrior, who uses no outward weapons, fighting only with clarity and with peace of mind and heart.

The bridge from the lunar to the solar mysteries is consistent interaction with Rootman and Rootwoman as described in detail in Chapter 6.

SUN SPIRAL

The second degree of enlightenment is the solar level represented by the Sun. Six areas of wisdom and illumination are contained within this step: Death, Decay, Love, Birth, Time, and Truth.

The entryway is through the barriers of time. Knowledge of time comes through meditations on the element of water.

There are two types of time in the real sense. Eternal or Cosmic time, and World or Passing Time. The latter is the one we are most familiar with. Once you understand these basic formats for time, death becomes your ally and you can see beyond this single incarnation you are committed to.

Knowledge of true time allows you access to the Truth and absolves you from fear of death. You come to know the angel of death without dying yourself. Birth and sex are two other areas of wisdom that unfold to the active and sincere seeker journeying towards enlightenment on the solar pathway.

Love, a mystery that seems beyond our comprehension, is possible to unveil to great or small extent, depending upon the risks you are willing to take to expose yourself to its magic. Love, from neighborliness to deepest friendship, from romantic love to marriage, and the most profound human love of all—parenthood, can be revealed to you. Love's allies: loyalty, intimacy, respect, and honesty also loosen their secrets as you circle higher and higher on the second spiral of enlightenment. Your love of the Creator . . . All That Is . . . will be tested. And you will experience the Eternal's endless love for you.

The sun level includes journeying into the higher mind, inner wisdom, and inspiration. On a practical level it is the merging of science and mysticism, compassion and wisdom. Inspired scientific explorer Stephen Hawking exemplifies this type of Renaissance person for our time.

Eagles, especially white ones, are the spirit animals that lead dedicated people to knowledge and awareness. The Eagle is also a fire god associated with lightning. It is the single living creature that can look directly into the sun without damaging its sight. This accounts for the Eagle's veneration as a sun god in many cultures. Eagles eat small creatures of the earth that would otherwise overrun fields and woods with their fecundity, destroying all other forms of life. As the guardian spirit of the second tier of enlightenment, the Eagle keeps you from going overboard with what you're learning.

STAR SPIRAL

The star level is the entryway to "The Great Mystery," the wisdom known in all times and in all places. This level is represented by the stars. Through this doorway space becomes an integral part of your knowledge. Here you work with transformation, electromagnetism, gravity (and lack of gravity called vacuums), and nuclear and molecular structure.

Electromagnetism is first encountered in the moon spiral of enlightenment where it heals or injures people, plants, and animals. At the star level, electromagnetism keeps the constellations in orbit and regulates galaxies.

A gentle, beautiful, graceful water bird, the Swan, is the traditional guardian of the star spiral or transmigration of the soul. The rarest of these special birds is the black Swan, whose presence indicates your complete acceptance into the third ring of enlightenment. The Swan, big as it is, eats algae, keeping rivers flowing and lakes clear.

Contact with beings from other planets is one way to learn about the third tier; astrology is another way to become familiar with the star level's energetic dynamic. Only esoteric astrology will work. Stargazing* on a starry night will teach you to make accurate predictions. Contact with the earth is essential to keep yourself grounded as you feel your way through. You will need all the skills you have developed during the years you were in the moon and solar spirals. The ocean is one of the most potent

---

*Stargazing is covered in Sound Medicine by Laeh Maggie Garfield.

forces to assist your development within the star spiral. By going into mysticism unreservedly, you can enter the star spiral of enlightenment. Once you begin to travel along this path, the realm of the Source becomes accessible.

Advice to the Traveler   If you want to enter Universal consciousness via a more effective pathway than the one you usually use, you will have to meditate every day at the same time. According to the Tibetans, who have studied meditation extensively, there are thirty-nine types—each one with seventeen sub-forms. Your psyche will automatically pick the technique you need most day by day. The important thing is not to follow your thoughts. Let them float by.

Another potent method, useful throughout each of the three stages, is to follow your dreams. Dreams cut across the barrier of death. Do active and creative dreaming. Keep a dream diary and draw pictures of the images that have been especially powerful for you.

Good books for lucid dreaming are listed in the bibliography.

In addition, mastery of the four elements will lead you up the ladder step by step until you become a sage. The meditations by which you may ascend are taught in Chapter 11 of my book *Sound Medicine*. A synopsis of the practical application of the elements is: water to control the emotions, fire to facilitate transformation and communication, wind to know the universe, and earth to institute survival skills and ascend to the stars.

Sound, and the inner knowledge of how it works in healing and visioning worldly reality through each of the Realms of being, is a major pathway of the journey along the levels of enlightenment.

Underlying each element is an essential sound. That sound can tell you more about the Source than anything ever written. Finding the individual seed sounds, mantras, and names of guardian spirits for fire, water, air, or earth, leads you through the spiral of wisdom and enlightenment. Do not stop when you get the rhythm of an element. There is still more sound beyond whatever you are hearing.

Initially the hidden sound beyond the ocean waves is the same sound as the wind makes, as fire's innermost wind makes, as the Creator makes. Go deeper and you will hear the sound dividing into the elements and all other components of life. And beyond that exists another unifying sound.

Interrelationships between the levels of your own soul, spirit guides, past lives, archangels, your male and female selves, the Witness, your Advisors, and The Creator are fundamental. Techniques for accurately gathering information, discerning your baseline belief system, and reconnecting with the four components of your own soul aid your progress.

It takes nine years for a proficient and dedicated person to traverse a spiral of enlightenment. The majority require between fourteen and twenty-two years to complete the moon level. Aping the trappings, alleged manners, or behavior of a higher level of spiritual prowess won't get you there any faster. In fact, it may slow you down. Pretending to have a gentle nature only masks your real but suppressed energy. Pretense always shows; it is best to continually refine your own nature without resorting to spiritual gimmicks. Besides, you tend to fool yourself more than you fool anyone else. Therefore you miss out on your real development irrespective of how grand your material or spiritual position in the world becomes.

Be prepared to divest yourself of outmoded concepts and vexing rules that have haunted you and diverted you from yourself. Dropping excess baggage you've acquired on the long journey toward enlightenment, as well as elusive yet *true* sounding information from well meaning authorities, allows you to know the truth. The journey you are about to embark upon has some guideposts, but you must continue to clear and follow your own pathway, no matter where you are on your path, no matter how well or poorly you've done with your life's Mission so far.

2

Realms of Existence

There may come a moment when a flaming arrow pierces your heart and sets it on fire. You see everything the way it really is; you are frightened and tempted to hold back, to be safe. If you do the experience ends. But if your time of quiet has taught you a tolerance for uncertainty, you will let go. You will spin in wildness. Tears and laughter will be the same. You will want to burst. There is no time. There is no space. There is no life. There is no death.

Tolbert McCarroll

THE REALMS

Every human being is on a journey to become divine, as wise and as pure as our Creator, The One. For a real seeker, outer-world events are unimportant compared to discovering how the Universe works. The cosmos is an orderly, organized, well-thought-out, well-executed design. As a living entity, you have your place in it, neither lowlier nor more important than any

17

other ensouled being. Each mineral, plant, animal, and thinking individual has a part to play in the mosaic, in this world and in the worlds beyond our earth. Your soul's journey winds its way from naivete to wisdom and accomplishment.

The world of nonphysical beings is much more friendly than the major religions describe it. Fear of negative entities makes you a receptacle for them, thus a balanced state is the best way to experience the other Realms.

Physical Realm   The Physical Realm on earth is the one we recognize and identify with most readily. The Physical Realm is also known as the manifesting realm, or realm of motion, which encompasses every point, element, molecule, chemical, and geophysical location in the Universe. There are other planets which support life forms similar to our own. Filmmakers have used imagination and intuition to bring us lively portrayals of extra-terrestrials. Humanoids on other planets need not resemble us to have equally valid lifetimes, filled with mental and emotional exploration. Sometime in the future you, too, may look something like E.T. or Jyota and live hundreds of years in a single body. No matter where you are incarnated, you inhabit the Physical Realm, the world of action, the world of living things.

Planets resembling our Earth in some way afford technological and mental development, including telepathy. Each planet is a learning place for different types of data. All have limits imposed by the physical bodies that intelligent entities are able to carry on that orbiting globe.

We each have our own impression of the Physical Realm on earth. In shamanic practice a human being can take possession of a bird and fly. This is not the reality common to everyone. There is the customary perception that we agree upon as reality; however there is also our private experience that provides every person with a unique cosmology.

Our habitat in the galaxy has certain physical limitations that you might want to work at overcoming. Some of the things children are taught early on not to attempt, like Tumo, are usually accessible to them. To levitate, walk on water, live on air, or keep warm by applying inner fire (Tumo) rather than use an external heat source, are special abilities accomplished by the extraordinarily motivated. Defying gravity occurs in altered states of consciousness. It can be brought about by years of meditation, a powerful ritual, or a life threatening event like a hurricane. In your ordinary state of mind you know that without proper winches and cables, you cannot right a car once it's overturned and gone off the road. However, at the superconscious level you're aware it could be done with the mind, if only you knew how to reset your thought boundaries.

Physical reality is based on a set of limitations imposed on you by the culture you live in. In this realm you feel separate. However, this is a learned position. Babies, until age two-and-a-half, cannot separate their emotions and feelings from those around them. Nor do they show any differentiation between self and other. Some lucky souls retain a portion of that telepathic gift from childhood to adulthood, and are able to tune into the vibration of anyone they're interested in around the globe or beyond the gate of life.

Formation Realm   The Realm of Formation is home to immaterial guardians who oversee the development and the safety of land formations such as mountains or sacred places. These guardians serve for prolonged periods of time, epochs rather than the relatively shorter spans served by the guardians of trees.

The guardians of Formation differ greatly from the entities who oversee Knowledge. Guardians of the teachings are of a superior order, handling more diverse and complex projects than those who work on physical projects, whether terrestrial or pertaining to the stars.

Elves, devas, fairies, leprechauns, tree spirits, animal spirits, all belong to the Formation Realm. The world of Formation is static; its beings manifest a single vibrational harmonic. They represent a limited dimensional progression, holding that energy open and fixed in the Universe. Operating in synchronicity, they mass for Missions lasting as long as a particular quality or condition is required anywhere in the cosmos.

Desires of angelic beings or planetary gods to create species and phyla, minerals and geographic landmarks, are taken into account. There are Devas and devas*—other entities who cooperate with humans, discarnates, and others to achieve the climate,

---

*There are two types: Devas who are Godlike divine beings, and devas who are nature spirits.

topography, vegetation, and the exact chemical and alchemical balance that supports our unique spinning globe. Other planets, stars, asteroids, and moons are also governed by the Realm of Formation. An elderly avid gardener I know considers a set of elemental spirits from the Realm of Formation to be her gardening buddies. She spoke of gnomes (underground elves), who help the roots of her plants, and of undines or nereids (water sprites), who oversee the plant parts above ground. With puckish delight she recounted how salamanders (fire elementals) activate the pollination process and how sylphs (air spirits) carry seeds and scents through the air. These are just one set of names for some of the elementals who perform assignments in the Realm of Formation. The familiar names are Swiss, taken from the old science of the elements in hermetic and neo-Platonic doctrines, and popularized by Rudolph Steiner's followers. The elementals were first written about by Paracelsus (1493–1531) in his *De Nymphis*.

Much of the information you get from the Realm of Formation can readily be tested. Suppose a patch of chamomile flowers tells you to brew them into a tea to calm your nervous system as an aid to sound sleep. You could look up chamomile in a medicinal herbal and verify its effects. Herbs have been used since antiquity to heal. A plant may telepathically tell you it doesn't like a particular section of the garden. You ignore it, and the plant gets a blight. You move it, sick as it is, to the spot where it seems to want to be; where it recovers and thrives.

But there is other information that isn't as simple to prove. In general trees, minerals, plants, and animals tell us what they need. For example, "Plant trees to attract more rain," is a message you get while sitting in a grove of trees. The trees gave you a hint. They didn't tell you how to go about it, although you realize it'll take thousands of new trees. Whether you do grassroots organizing, or gather national or local government sponsorship to plant them is up to you. And, it will take years until the trees have grown enough to see if their message was accurate.

Occasionally a scientist will corroborate the mystic's point of view that sea mammals and humans are not the sole intelligent earthly life forms. Like other living things, trees talk to one another. The Oregon physicist Ed Wagner calls their language W-waves. He measured the speed of W-waves at 3 feet per second through trees, and about 15 feet per second through the air.

"They travel much too slowly for electrical waves and seem to be an altogether different entity," Wagner wrote in the Washington State University magazine *Northwest Science*. When a tree is being chopped down, it puts out "a tremendous cry of alarm, while adjacent trees put out smaller ones."

In every grove there is a head tree that communicates with the spirits (devas) for that species, and with the forces of nature. That tree "speaks" to the other trees and takes their message back. In this way trees request rain which is one sound reason to keep many healthy forests, as clear cutting damages the weather pattern in an area. Lack of adequate trees also means insufficient clean air.

Animals as well as plants communicate with us. Pets are a connection with the Realm of Formation, which may account for their increasing popularity. Your dog, for instance, cannot tell you that he has a foxtail imbedded in his eye. Even after the eye has stopped tearing, the hound continues to appear rundown. You have a dream indicating there's a problem in your dog's eye. Whether you call on the veterinarian, have acupuncture done, or treat it yourself, the choice is yours. The dog only wants care. If you listen carefully to your pets, you'll know what their needs are, as well as and what kind of help they can provide to you.

Rocks and mountains may look inert, but we are discovering that they are far from it. They are alive, and a person who is attuned to the earth element can see their aura and watch them breathe. An underlying intelligence runs through every *living* thing. We misjudge it because so few modern, urbane, so-called "civilized" people take the time to talk to the animals or stones. The wisdom of another life form isn't human-centered and care must be taken not to suffocate its responses. Careful listening is the watchword for those who wish to know the magical Realm of Formation.

Realm of Creation   The Realm of Creation is where you dwell when you are not in a living, breathing, physical body. It is the place that you come from, and it is where you return when you die. The Clans, the Mansions, spirit guides, Oversouls and every non-living relation or acquaintance of yours resides here. Creation Realm governs the human sphere of life on earth. Births, politics, marriages, and chance meetings are arranged there. This is the realm of existence wherein thoughts, unformed fears, and mass visions become situations, climatic changes, new species and phyla, or devastation, in manifested reality.

The Realm of Creation is the world of pure mind, mind beyond intellect. This quality of mind is the power to grasp and express with genuine inner understanding, to create as well as to register and absorb knowledge.

In this realm you come to know less of separateness and more of connectedness. Your affiliations and friendships are based on more loving cooperative motives than those you make in the Physical Realm.

To become wise in the ways of the Realm of Creation, you must willingly enter it again and again. An unbelievably complex web is woven between it and our physical world. Families, friends, cultures, mass migrations, belief systems, and skills are all intertwined from generation to generation and era to era to allow every living being's full potential to surface. Families are brought together over and over again, not only by birth, but in marriage and circles of friendship, to play out required steps in each participant's growth.

An aunt of yours, long dead, turns out to be your new sister-in-law's spirit guide. It seems odd, because your mate's family lives thousands of miles from where you were raised. Even more puzzling, your mother, her brothers and sisters, believe your newborn daughter is a reincarnation of their lost sister. Can she be alive in your child and also the guide of someone you know? Yes, it is possible to be alive in one body yet simultaneously be a spirit guide whose appearance and manners are from another one of your incarnations.

A friend whom you casually meet in Arizona, and become closer to as the years pass, turns out to be the granddaughter of some people your grandfather built a house for. Her uncle was your family's attorney in the latter part of the last century in upstate New York. Is this only coincidence? A nurse in the California hospital where you work, grew up in the same house in Vancouver, B.C., where your great-grandmother raised her children. Your family album is filled with photos of the house.

The boy who sits behind you in your history class has the same last name as you do and with a small amount of investigation you find you are second cousins, once removed. Phenomena such as these are reported to spiritual practitioners with relative frequency, so much so that they seem commonplace.

In the Old Testament, the Realm of Creation is called "the world of the throne." You have access to it through dreams, meditation, visualizations, prayer, and contact with spirit guides, Source Self, and the Oversoul. Your own soul is a member of the Creation Realm, and as a result you are permitted to cross the gate to it from the land of action at will.

In the Creation Realm, seraphs (highest of the nine orders of angels) and others who no longer take incarnate bodies fulfill tasks as teachers, Oversouls, Oversoul's Oversoul, Advisors, and Archangels. The seraphim's inner knowledge is multidimensional. They know all the individual lifetimes of those they caretake and the exact order of the Universe. The sephroth's vibrational force and intelligence incorporates all ten emanations or attributes of the Creator, which they gained through uncounted lifetimes. They will remain unsinkable elevated consciousness ever after.

As an illustration, if miserly industrialist John D. Rockefeller could have become a seraph upon his death, he would be the guardian of stinginess and abundance coupled together because in his lifetime he hadn't acquired the twin positives of abundance and generosity.

Plenty is a gift of the Creation Realm. You have access to it in every lifetime. What is it you want plenty of? You can have an abundance of whatever you want: clothes, intelligence, madness, starvation, cash, love, war, intuition, talent. First, however, you must decide. Once you know what you're after, it will come to you.

Although the Source Self's residence, the Realm of Creation interacts with the Realm of Formation, people seldom comprehend that they are free to communicate with, or enter and leave these Realms while serving in the Physical Realm. The Realm of Formation and the Realm of Creation react, co-exist, and influence one another in the Physical Realm.

The Realm of the Source   The Realm of the Source is the dwelling place of the Almighty, ruler of our Universe. It is the home of planetary gods, of ascended beings, and of Star-level enlightenment. Everything known and unknown in the entire cosmos emanates from the Source. Prophets take their knowledge of events to come from the World of Emanation, unlike channels who get theirs from beings inhabiting the Realm of Creation.

The Creator does not abide alone. Archangels and gods of planets, solar systems, and galaxies also reside in the Realm of the Source. All advanced beings can merge their energies to appear as a pulsating, glowing ball, emanating one sound and one color (dazzling blue-white light), in order to preserve every level of existence.

If you are in a battle for your life and truly want to send the Angel of Death away empty-handed, you will have to contact and communicate with the Realm of the Source. Fortunately, nearly everyone has had some practice with prayer and can cross the borders while engaged in fervent, heartfelt prayer.

Except in prayer, most people never have the courage to go directly to the Realm of the Source, believing erroneously that to do so is to die. I also held this belief until desperation forced me to volunteer to enter the "forbidden place." I found that the door to the Source is no more shut and bolted than is the gate to the Realm of Creation. The Source is not a nasty, vituperative godling; on the contrary it is a really open, kindly, loving, accepting energy.

Although it is true that the Source is not fully intelligible to those of us locked in the body, we can approach and understand its realm to some degree. True: we merely glimpse it until we are advanced souls. In the Realm of the Source there is no separateness, only unity.

3

Who's Who

Reality is nothing but a collective hunch.
Lily Tomlin

You are a living being, infinitely complex. It is nearly impossible for you to understand your own motivations, beliefs, values, or reasons, let alone those responsible for the actions of another individual. Examining environmental factors or heredity can only provide limited insight into your own or anyone else's penchant to conform, or the sudden display of eccentric behavior. People are made up of more than one single mind, and have an aggregate personality. You and every other living soul have quite a few sub-personalities, which may include components from past lives. An incarnated soul itself isn't a single blended unit.

The Human Soul A human soul has four components, each of which serves a separate function, together forming a distinct one-of-a-kind self. The four components, assembled at your prenatal request, are the Source Self, the Witness, the Personality, and the Creator. The primary portion of your soul is the Essence Self or Source Self. This is the part of you that sets the stage for the blending of the components that you call "myself". Carl Gustav Jung described the different parts of the soul as a quaternity that expresses the wholeness of self. Ancient people throughout the world held that the human soul consists of four interwoven yet separate selves, each with a different function.

Essence or Source Self Your Source Self is your essential nature and the essential nature of all the other lifetimes you have been privy to. The Source Self lives on other planes of existence and is always near the body. In the body it resides in the pineal gland.

Other names for the Source Self are the Essence Being, Higher Self, or simply the Essence. It is the part of you that originally decides to incarnate. To reincarnate it must create a personality, interest two distinctly separate souls to join the project as Rootman and Rootwoman (Chapter 6), obtain help from the Advisors, engage one or more entities as spirit guides, notify the Witness who usually oversees their incarnations, and obtain the Creator's blessing.

The Source Self is the part of you that has experienced all the separate incarnations of you and your co-beings. While it is true that you shall never again be the same as you are now, your Source Self will reincarnate, in other forms, at other times. Your unique personality, as distinct from your Source Self, may or may not choose to live again in another body. But even if your Source Self generates future co-beings, you shall always continue to exist as "you" and to evolve at your own best pace. Once created, you cannot be dismissed or uninvented. You can, if you wish, modify your character and gain abilities in the body you've formed for this incarnation. Your personality can continue to grow, but more slowly after you die.

Your Source Self contains and transmits your consciousness of both universal and earthly time, in addition to your intellect, your memory, your five senses, your imagination, creativity, and intuition. You can use the visionary power of this part of your soul to expand your potential and help you wield your talents effectively.

You never see your Source Self face to face, although you may sense its presence in dreams, visions, or apparitions.

Occasionally, people report hearing someone walking around their house while home alone. You may have felt the sensation of someone breathing behind you. If you hold your breath it stops breathing also and when you exhale again the Source Self exhales. On rare occasions your Source Self may appear as your double, and you'll come upon it with its back to you. It might even touch you. These contacts are meant as warnings, to take care, or as a gift of extra protection when you need it most.

Early one morning when I'd dropped back to sleep for an extra few minutes before arising, my Source Self appeared in my deep dream state and told me something in language so specific that I woke with a start. The visual imagery in an appealing unanticipated color implanted itself in my brain forever. The message my Source Self brought was to further help my own enlightenment.

Co-Beings   Co-beings are souls from the same Source Self. (See the upper diagram on page 28.) Once a co-being's life is lived, the personality does not reincarnate. Sometimes two to four co-beings are concurrently alive in different countries, social classes, or cultures; yet they remain in spiritual contact. The personalities of your co-beings do not die with them, nor do their skills, talents, and intellect. All are available to you as the need arises.

An Oversoul and several Source Selves may agree to undertake a series of incarnations for the purpose of doing something important in the world. In the lower diagram on page 28 you will see four Source Selves and an Oversoul undertaking a series of incarnations within a decade. All are male. All speak English dialects as a mother tongue; some are of African ancestry, some of European. The majority undertook the immigrant experience, as all but one wound up living in the same English-language country where only one of them was born. Can you surmise the lesson, and their collective Mission? Clue: Peter's parents sent him abroad to live so that he wouldn't be incarcerated for his politics.

Peter, Ian, George, and James have come to me at one time or another as students and clients. To have seen their Mission and their common Oversoul was a lesson for me arranged by my guides. Ian's trance work allowed him to meet his co-beings Henry and Charles and the Liberian and to name Peter and George whom I already knew.

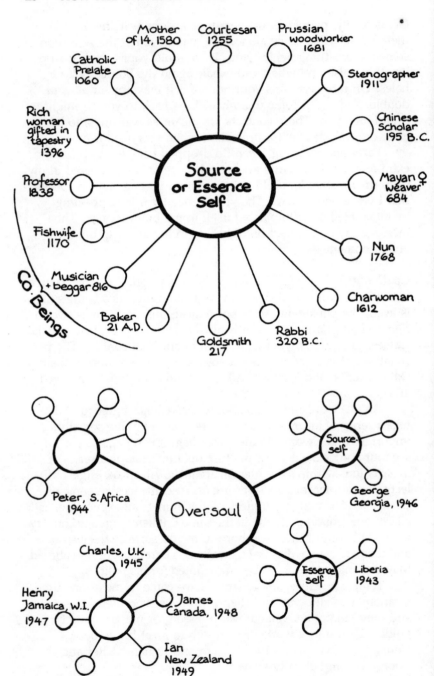

Witness   Although a Witness often serves the same Source Self continuously, the Source Self may freely request another Witness for a single incarnation or for a series of lifetimes. Depending on its own developmental needs, a Witness can serve a different Clan for the purpose of aiding a given lifetime, or a Witness can choose to join only Source Selves from its own Clan. The service isn't altruistic; the Witness is also growing from level to level in its own system of Mansions.

A Witness is an archangel. Archangels form a ring of power on inner levels and they are a council unto themselves. Each one who chooses the assignment oversees a particular Clan.

A Witness serves hundreds of incarnated beings simultaneously on the earth and on other planets. On multiple levels of consciousness, it remains continuously alert to the needs of any of its charges, aware of a myriad of details at once. One is reminded of the ancient legend of the all-seeing eye.

A Witness enters a forming infant through the placenta in the fourteenth week of pregnancy. One's insight, visionary prowess, and capacity for prophesy are conveyed through contact with the Witness. The stronger your communication with your Witness, the more strongly your spiritual powers can manifest.

Witnesses are not indwelling. They are available, as if on threads connected to their charges, but they do not have a permanent place within the body. Whenever the Witness enters your body it can be found in the throat chakra. Your Witness serves as the recording angel or clerk, noting in the Akashic Records all that occurs in your life.

The Witness is the part of you that shows you the overview of each situation, and the potential moves and activities that would benefit you. When you're out of contact with the Witness you have hindsight. Active contact promotes foresight, and reveals the absurdities of life at the very moment they've happened. A prime example is, being overcome by sudden laughter in the midst of a heated argument as you recognize your own bullheadedness and calculating nature. When you first meet your Witness, the amount of unconditional love and acceptance you feel can be overwhelming. The Witness does not sit in judgement of you.

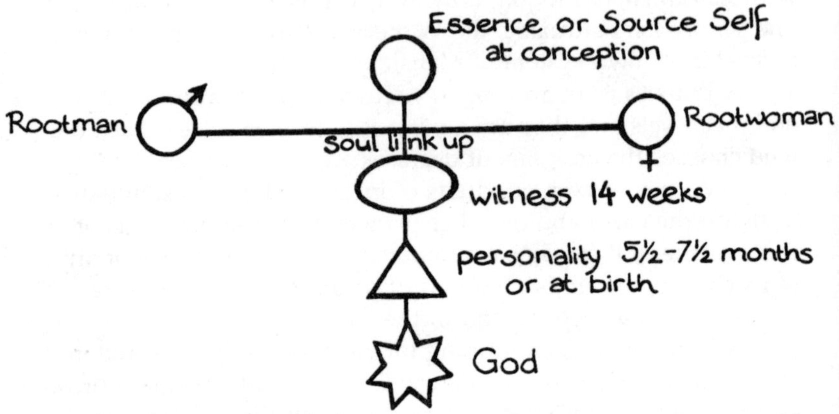

Essence or Source Self
at conception

Rootman

Soul link up

Rootwoman

witness 14 weeks

personality 5½-7½ months
or at birth

God

The Personality   Around the seventh month of gestation, the personality formulated by the Source Self and its Advisors enters the body permanently. Some personalities arrive on
the scene earlier, about the same time the mother feels her baby
quicken. Others become indwelling shortly after birth. If more
than a month has elapsed and an infant's personality fails to
bond sufficiently with the body, the child often becomes autistic
or suffers personality disorders. The lack of a personality has
been noted in some infants who succumbed to crib death.

A mother who sees the vacant look of an infant whose personality has failed to become indwelling should bathe her baby
in lukewarm water several times a day for a minimum of fifteen
minutes each session. Cradling the child in her arms the whole
time will encourage the personality to enter and remain.

Most of us have traits we wish we had not developed. Popular psychology blames them on parental training. It is clear,
however, that this is not so. In infancy, irrespective of future influences in the home, each person is already more than half-
formed. Soul age is the main determining factor in the ability of

individuals to overcome the patterns of the family that raised them and the family that gave them their genetic codes.

The underlying code of your personality is a string of thought forms, requirements of your Source Self for developing its overall character. As a series of thought forms, characteristics can remain dormant or become dominant as you choose. Upbringing can accent one trait over another, but each of us has some traits that are so deeply ingrained that there is no way to submerge them. The child who speaks the truth may be slapped down for it, yet might grow up to be a diplomat or a muckraking columnist. The parent's task is to help that child avoid making himself unwelcome due to displays of frankness that trample other's feelings.

On a daily basis the personality remains inside of you, except when you suffer torture, a painful accident, or other extreme circumstance. When it exits, it stays within thirty feet of your body as an observer. Accidents may cause your personality to jump out, causing you to faint, which obliterates fear and other emotions and also prevents muscles and bones from stiffening. Thereby a soft landing becomes the miracle ingredient in some escapes from injury or death in serious accidents. The personality's bodily home is in the heart chakra. During dream and trance states it also floats above the body.

The Creator-God's Breath　　　　　Your breath is your inner spark of the divine. This is the final component of the soul to enter an infant's body. It does so at the moment the emerged neonate takes its first breath. Care must be taken that people present at a birth do not suck in the life force (prana) meant for the infant. Pets and people attending a birth must keep their mouths shut so that the baby gets its full charge of God's breath.

Sudden Infant Death Syndrome is caused by this component of the soul leaving. Quite often an infant dies of SIDS because this part of the soul or the Source Self or the personality never really entered. When a child or an older person is sick, it is wise to have a healthy person present, keeping a hand on them, to prevent the divine spark from departing. It is also possible to sing for the person, or have someone who is capable do an absent healing or perform a recovery ritual. If you know how, you can summon your spirit guides to go to a sick relative or friend and keep the breath in their body.

In a comatose individual, the life force is consistent if the person is able to breathe unaided. Should breathing assistance be necessary, the life force may depart temporarily or permanently.

Although not indwelling in coma, the Source Self and the Witness watch closely over the body and use what influence they can to assist in recovery. The personality is assuredly absent in coma. When one is in a coma the Source Self may come and go; but the return of the personality, whether whole or fragmented, signals recovery. When injury is to the head, the personality doesn't always reassemble in quite the same pattern or with all its salient qualities intact. A person who's been knocked out for less than twenty-four hours still has the personality intact, and usually awakens much as before.

In examining your past lives, remember that the consistent parts of you are the Source Self and God's Breath. The Witness may or may not be identical, and your personality definitely changes.

Possession   You don't go hopping pell-mell into any old body. You must have a connection in order to trade places with the Source Self or the personality and possess the body legally.

Most cases of possession are caused by two separate beings (each a combination of Source Self and personality) trying to occupy the body at the same time, each fighting for control. This brings mental and physical anguish to the individual. Family and friends of the person may notice a change after the second soul enters the body. If the possessing soul causes no trouble and acts more responsibly and carefully than the original, family and friends are saddened by what they feel is diminished affection for them. Usually the relatives have no idea what is the matter and won't aid their struggling family member.

Real difficulty arises when the possessing soul and the original Source Soul or personality of the disputed body fight for control. If the rival personality is a co-being (a past-life of the person), then the same Source Self is in control of the body it shaped. When the Source Self and the Witness remain the same, the transition, whether temporary or permanent, is usually a compatible arrangement. A personality is often happier during a segment of life when their co-being is borrowing the body. Invaded by another Source Self and a new personality, without the balance of the Witness, terrible emotional states, irrational behavior, and physical illness are possible. If the body is occupied by another soul totally, the Source Self will be working to restore itself and all the levels of its incarnation to autonomy over the physical/mental/emotional bodies.

An exorcism may be essential. It should be physically nonviolent and firmly carried out by someone who is able to communicate effectively with spirits. Exorcism is not a job for amateurs. If you expel the invading soul and aren't able to restore the true Source Self and personality, you're likely to have a human vegetable on your hands.

Although a home remedy did a most credible job in one case, I don't endorse it as totally reliable. A man in his mid-fifties had surgery. Afterward, his wife and intimate friends found themselves speaking with a near stranger. His facial expressions did not match up with those of the man they knew. A couple of months went by and the wife caught sight of her husband combing hair above his bald pate. Comb in mid-air, he carefully styled an imaginary mane. Her rage was immediate and visceral. She screamed as loud as she could, "You're not Louie! Get out and let him back in." With that the imposter vanished. Her husband, personality restored, stared at the spray can and the comb in his hand. Plaintively he asked when his surgery was scheduled to take place.

Alcoholism and drug use, whether chronically excessive or binge consumption, open a person to temporary possession. During these times illegal, immoral, violent, and destructive acts may occur. The individual does not remember their own body committed the act. A word to the wise ought to suffice. Curtail your drinking and drugging or you may wind up in court while sober. The possessing entity will be free to occupy the body of another unsuspecting individual who is out of their body on a bender, while you pay the price for your lack of vigilance.

OVERSOUL

Powerful beings are in central charge of all types of forces in the Universe, guiding everything in the physical realm. Your spirit guides, Oversoul, Advisors, Master guides, and others are able to be in instantaneous contact with one another. Together they form your cosmic support network. All quotes in this section about the Oversoul come from *Companions in Spirit* by Laeh Maggie Garfield and Jack Grant.

An Oversoul is the advisor and guardian to a group of Source Selves. These Source Selves are usually members of the same Clan, but they seldom share every interest of the Oversoul who helps supervise their incarnations. Oversouls who do not help sentient beings (whether embodied or not) undertake other services such as planetary structure, chemical and alchemical functions, and overseeing the development of species.

"The Oversoul is the Source Self's Source Self. Each Oversoul also has an Oversoul. Your Oversoul is comparable to your grandmother, your Oversoul's Oversoul similar to a great-grandparent."

Your Source Self is much more interested in the details of your life than your Oversoul is. Your Advisors are relatively remote from your day to day events. Your Oversoul instructs your Source Self to prod your growth and refine your character as well as its own.

Whenever a Source Self desires to set up a lifetime or series of lives, they must take it up with their Clan's Advisors and their own Oversoul. Selection of an appropriate birth family, society, and the actual tasks for the physical being are part of the Oversoul's counseling capacity. The Oversoul frequently helps the Source Self traverse difficult and dangerous situations that their lifetime personality gets into. The Oversoul aids the Source Self to guide or challenge the incarnate through dreams, flashes of information, illnesses or accidents, spiritual pursuits, career changes, social upheaval, friendships, and marriages.

A Source Self may engage any Oversoul for a specific incarnation. Rules for governing souls are not as strict as they are in earthbound hierarchies. If a Source Self decides to invoke the talents or qualities of another Oversoul, even one from another Clan, it has the right to do so.

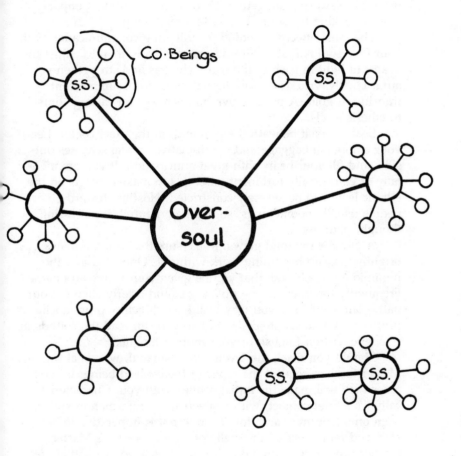

You have the ability to contact your Oversoul when in dire straits, and at other times if the Oversoul grants you permission to do so. Calling upon your Oversoul for insignificant things, for aid your spirit guide can supply, or in situations you could resolve using your intuition, may cause the Oversoul to chide you or avoid answering altogether. Discretion is of utmost importance in asking for your Oversoul's intervention.

The most effective method for initiating communication with your Oversoul is first to ground and meditate, then to adjust the beams of light in each of the trunk chakras and strengthen your aura. Finally, visualize a vibrational pyramid of luminescent, translucent gold. A psychic pyramid is a tool for raising yourself to etheric levels.

Seat yourself beneath the pyramid, in the exact center. Leave your emotional baggage and manipulative mental schemes outside, and fill your heart with great anticipation. If you are mentally or emotionally turbulent, attempts to make contacts on the etheric level will be severely constricted. Hostility toward other people usually boomerangs, so maintain neutral, if not loving, thought patterns.

A psychic pyramid glows. Make sure that yours radiates brightly prior to beginning work within it. Once you and the pyramid are ready, ask that you be given your Oversoul's name. Frequently the name is one utilizing sound utterly alien to your native language, and you may well have difficulty pronouncing it precisely. Ask to see it spelled out so you can read the sounds in phonetic written English or your mother tongue.

Should you reach the Oversoul's Oversoul, who is always a Master teacher, request the name of the evolved being. In most cases they will make the initial contact with you. Characteristically it's a brief contact, with a spectrum of information you've been on a lengthy search for. Therefore it is imperative to be alert and remember all they tell you. The Oversoul's Master teacher can tap into any vision or experience you've had at any point in your lifetime.

Spirit Guides　　　　　Each of us has one or more spirit guides to help us through the acquisition of skills and major shifts of focus that occur in a lifetime. Everyone has a life guide and may attract a healing guide, a single-purpose guide, an animal totem, a guide for their talents (music, art, sports, cooking) or be born into a family with a guide of its own.*

Although spirit allies can be your own soul or Source Self in another guise, the majority of spirit allies for everyone are from other Source Selves. Younger souls always get spirit helpers outside themselves.

Old souls have scores of accomplished past lives to reconnect with whenever they need aid and comfort. There are no hard and fast rules for the soul level at which one of your co-beings might become your main guide. It is an infrequent phenomenon.* Old souls are unequivocally in touch with the Source Self.

The variation of who Master guides and Oversouls allow to serve as a guide for specific needs you have is unlimited. Your insurance broker, recently deceased, may help with a business problem. A co-being who was a frustrated carpenter might help you build a house. An Oversoul related to your Clan, who knows the energies of the area you are moving to, may assist you for a brief period.

In May of 1986 a guide came to me solely to help me write books. He'd been a famous, sought-after writer of the early twentieth century. In the late Sixties, a friend of mine had lived communally in this writer's former Oakland home. He said he'd been "me," though since we're not a member of the same Clan and we don't share the same Source Self his remark seemed strange. He explained that he'd had my Oversoul supervise his lifetime, making us cosmic cousins.

Master Guides   Master guides are spiritual beings who strive to plant seeds of cosmic knowledge on the earth plane. They rarely channel for the sake of one individual, choosing those who will go on to teach others. Master guides act out of unconditional love and impart it to those they instruct.

One of their tasks is to debrief the newly dead, and reveal forgotten knowledge to them. They act as coaches helping the soul with self-analysis and evaluation of the life just lived.

I have a friendly relationship with White Eagle, who served as my master guide for many years. Early on I was in awe of

---

For a complete analysis of Spirit Guides read Companions in Spirit *by Laeh Maggie Garfield and Jack Grant.*

him; however it would not have been possible to work closely and receive instruction from him had I remained so. Respectful questioning is how I would describe the manner in which I interact with him.

Months sometimes go by without further instructions from my Master Guide, and then he'll begin a conversation with me as if he just left off ten minutes ago.

Rootman and Rootwoman Rootman and Rootwoman are internal guides and partial co-beings for a particular lifetime. Chapter 6 is devoted to this special and very private relationship.

Advisors Advisors are from the star level. They are not assigned or attached to a single solar system. Series of Advisors undertake guardianship for a galaxy and work in consort with other Advisors who oversee other galaxies. A pair of Advisors who have no other duties oversees each Clan. (See illustration, page 40).

Ordinarily your Clan's Advisors do not maintain active contact with you after you reach the age of two, although they observe your progress from time to time. It is up to you to relearn a method for contacting them. The sole reason to contact your Advisors is to plead for changes in your masterplan, or to clarify parts of your Mission. Most people do not have voluntary communication with their Advisors, since they are no longer aware of their existence. One of the Advisors' main functions is to guide incarnating souls through the selection process that precedes birth.

The Advisors always communicate with you as an inseparable pair. One holds conditions constant (contact with the Creator and other Advisors), and the other interacts with the Physical and Formation Realms making changes. The consistent one keeps access to knowledge open, the other one oversees change and concentrates more on the human aspects of your lifetime. Both will prod you if you stray from your Mission once you've undertaken it.

My original contact with my Advisors was spontaneous rather than relearned. Once a person knows their guides and has reworked several character defects in their own personality, as part of the refinement of their being, they are ready to meet their

Advisors. Are there shortcuts? Can someone exercise their personality in violent and antisocial ways and still achieve contact with the instructions of their Advisors? Yes, if the Advisors feel their intervention will be constructive, they will interact openly with anyone. However, they will not permit the knowledge they transmit to be misused. Advisors can cut your life short without your express permission if they deem it best, but their motivation is always unconditional love.

A Conversation with My Advisors   The familiar voice of one of my Advisors spoke through my inner ear. I half-dread an unbidden visitation, although on occasion I call the two Advisors myself. Their instruction usually signals an abrupt departure from the plans carefully made for my ordinary reality. This afternoon the Advisor's message shattered my belief system with a single statement, "This lifetime has been sixth chakra," the voice ponderously intoned.

I tried to narrow down their announcement, and questions tumbled out one after another. "Is the reference to sixth Mansion or sixth story in another house? Am I an old soul after all?"

"You're skirting the seventh chakra work," he answered.

I finally saw that is the floor I am on. That knowledge clarifies many of my experiences for me.

The second Advisor watched in silent support as the first Advisor continued instructing me. They talked about my Master Guide offering me another option. My Mission to give service through teaching and healing is well underway. Since most of this lifetime is free choice, they were only asking me what I want to do, so that they could set up a support system to integrate my choices with the Universe's needs. The moment I saw it the Advisors vanished.

One of the decisions I made following that meeting was vetoed by the Advisors. They said nothing; subsequent events announced their decision. Time has shown them to be correct. The Advisors still have to guide me as I improvise my plans.

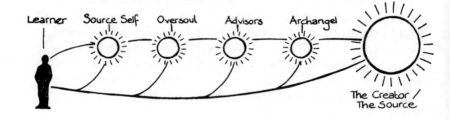

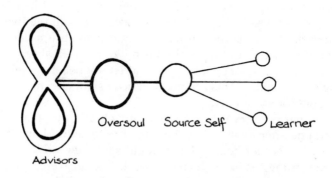

Archangels   Archangels afford unconditional love. They can be playful or serious. The common belief concerning Archangels is that they are all male and models of sobriety. Quite the contrary, Archangels have a sense of humor that borders on the absurd. They readily see through your human anguish. They giggle in great glee when one temptation or another is placed before you. As you pitch headlong into the forbidden event, they offer alternatives for extracting yourself. If you show temperance, maturity, and compassion in a perilous situation, they will match these gifts with greater ones which you can grow into over time.

Female Archangels scoff at the thought that they do not exist or that the Creator's feminine side would be cavalierly dismissed by a male chauvinist world so enamored of itself, that it believes its distortions are a mirror of the spiritual world.

Archangels deliver, and teach us, unconditional love. They are not cold and etheric. Each one is a distinct individual although a true angel. Like us, they have special Missions and areas of interest. Unlike us, they can enter the Realm of the Source and remain there.

Like every other developed soul, Archangels focus on love. They love us despite our personalities and ignore the fact that we aren't as developed as themselves. It cannot be stressed often enough, love is the strongest force in the Universe and it survives death.

The Clans   The Clan is a tribal family related spiritually rather than genetically. It is an affinity group like a family, but larger and more diversified.

Each Clan carries its own color or colors, mineral formations, molecular structure, sounds and tones, and energetic signature. Explicit knowledge of the function of the Clan system is open to those who are working on the Star spiral of enlightenment. People concentrating on the Moon or Solar level have glimpses into their own or allied Clans mainly through dreams, momentary intuitive flashes, and meditational states.

Various Clans work on making alterations in human society as a way of teaching themselves to be better instructors and cocreators. Other Clans center their earthly Missions around the development of phyla, flora, climatic conditions, or artistic endeavors. Successful Missions aid the evolutionary progress of the entire Clan membership. Entities belonging to a Clan may incarnate in any society, then leave to seek acceptance in another if it is beneficial to their sojourn in life.

You might assume that a Clan which oversees plant life would send farmers, herbalists, doctors, and others interested in the alterations of herbaceous plants in their growing cycle and overall development. That assumption may be only partially correct. Clan members can also have lifetime tasks in food preparation and storage, or urban planning, or having an abundant family to better augment their experiments in the Realm of Creation. Living on a planet, the physiological development becomes a reality as opposed to existence beyond the gate where everything is thought and theory. All corrections to make a specific life form survive are done in the Realms of Formation and Creation.

This is what White Eagle said about his Clan: "Our Clan coordinates the growth of divine consciousness in constellar formations. Not only your planet benefits as gentle strength builds, and understanding of every plant, mineral, chemical, and molecule throughout the cosmos is effectively altered as people grasp mystical concepts. Discord breeds discord. The more harmony each person has with Universal Consciousness, the more harmony there is everywhere."

There are presently eighty-four Clans operating in the Universe with deep attachments to our Earth. The number can fluctuate as Clans assign or withdraw their members from terrestrial lives during different eras. Souls that do not belong to Clans centered on our planet may incarnate for one lifetime or several under the auspices of a Clan that is.

After you fulfill the mandatory incarnations for ascension through the Mansions, you are allowed to leave the Clan you're part of to join with another set of beings.

4

Forty-nine Steps:
The Source Self's Journey

In my Father's house there are many Mansions
New Testament

There are seven Mansions of growth, each seven stories high. Achieving the blueprint of each story, you move upward from one floor to the next in successive lifetimes. A swift learner could theoretically take a minimum of forty-nine lives to go from the ground floor of the first Mansion to the top floor of the last one. Seldom is this the case, however. Most of us inhabit a single story at least several times, examining all the rooms, the nooks and crannies, sun porches and so on, until we are fully satisfied with our performance. Only then, with the encouragement of our teachers, do we move up to the next story.

You can spend more than a hundred incarnations on a single floor if you are willful, stubborn, or confused. "You" meaning your Source Soul and the co-beings it has spawned.

In an individual incarnation you work on a specific chakra or a linked set of chakras as long as you live. If you are learning about power, self-control, anger, manipulation, or respect, then the lessons of that lifetime revolve around the third chakra. If you are working on communication, assertiveness, music, singing, speaking clearly, being truthful, or clairaudience, the nucleus of your learning is the fifth chakra.* It can be perplexing to distinguish which chakra is the dominant one, because the issues of one chakra often cloud your perspective of another. A blockage may be due to the linkage formed by the first, fourth, and sixth chakras, although the obstacles around this triad are more likely to be between the root and heart rather than the third eye and the root or the heart. The other common dyads are second or third, with the fifth or the fifth and seventh chakras.

Should your fifth chakra be blocked you may fail to notice that it is keeping you from progressing with your real work: that of the seventh or crown chakra. Opening the seventh chakra can lead to insanity or death if you aren't centered and in control of your life. Many so-called madmen are those who opened the crown chakra widely without proper protection. Privy to instant information, they are bombarded with emotions, thoughts, and knowledge from everyone, everywhere. Tranquilizers are only a stopgap measure; what is really required is the wisdom and ability to open and close the crown chakra at will. Only then can one sort out all the data received. Fear of dying often keeps the top chakra permanently locked. The majority of human beings seldom open it except at the moment of death.

Every soul works in a curative manner on a stipulated chakra until its function is perfected. The chakra you are given to work on in your current body is an indication of the level of development you have attained. Whether concentrating on the first chakra for the twentieth or ten-thousandth time only signifies how much progress you are able to make. For some, only absolute perfection is acceptable. For others, good enough is good enough.

This information is presented to enhance your understanding of the developmental process a soul undergoes as it transmigrates the levels of development. It is not absolute and infallible, nor does a person who in your eyes falls clearly into one of the

---

For a full scale explanation of the chakra system please refer to Chapter 2 of Companions in Spirit *by Laeh Maggie Garfield and Jack Grant.*

categories necessarily belong there. It is only a guideline for your understanding of the concept, not a ratings system by which to judge your contemporaries.

The Mansions The Mansions, or houses of growth, number seven in the dimension known as physical life. They match up with the chakras as follows:

Chakra	Soul Nature	Purpose
crown	Volunteer soul	to enlighten other human beings
third eye	Old soul	telepathic skills, intention, control through thoughts
throat	Mature soul	communication
heart	Adult soul	to love, have compassion
solar	Teenage soul	power, control
sacral	Toddler soul	emotional balance, self-reliance
root	Infant soul	to learn survival and other aspects of physical life.

Your Mansion is your main residence irrespective of whether you are in the Realm of Creation or the Physical Realm. The Infant stage of life is analogous to the first chakra in any Mansion, and the period when you are an Infant soul, relatively immature, learning to adequately care for yourself. First your efforts are focused upon the root chakra. When you satisfy the requirements you and your Advisors have set with that chakra, you move on to conquering the emotional field by setting goals and meeting them for the second chakra. You progress from chakra to chakra until you work on the crown chakra. This may take you many lifetimes and great effort.

When a soul has attained competency on all the stories of a particular Mansion it moves to the next one: e.g. from the seventh floor of the Teenaged or Power Mansion, to the first story of the Adult Mansion. As a rule, the higher your soul level the fewer mistakes you make in the learning process and therefore the number of lifetimes per story decreases. Four lives per story seems to be the minimum required by most aspiring incarnate souls to fulfill the necessary tasks to move on to the next floor. In general, the toughest position to work on within a Mansion is the one associated with its overall focus. Therefore in the Adult Mansion, the heart chakra or fourth floor is the most difficult. For the soul residing in the Teenaged Mansion, the third story as the Power or Solar grade proves to be the hardest. The more stressful assignments demand more lifetimes to complete. What is stressful varies for each Source Self based upon the weaknesses and strengths they possess.

The Mansions and Lifetime Chakra   From Mansion to Mansion you do more refined forms of learning about a particular chakra. A Toddler soul might exercise power by having tantrums and battering all those who disagree with him, while a Teenage soul might blackmail all around him into behaving as he wishes. J. Edgar Hoover, who ran the FBI as a total dictator from his appointment until his death, threatened presidents, congressmen, and businessmen with exposure if they violated his will. Mature souls handle power by knowing what they want, holding firm without intimidation. They wait until the time is right, and desired conditions have been met.

An Adult soul, traversing the sacral floor of the fourth Mansion, examines and reappraises its emotional state repeatedly throughout its lifetime to gain more and more mastery of its emotional responses. One pitfall that Adult souls and younger souls must master is to preserve private time. When life becomes too busy with things one must do, there is too little time for introspection.

Working on a specific chakra doesn't necessarily indicate the Mansion that a soul is assigned to. The entire time someone is undergoing a passage through a Mansion, they work with the chakra governed by that Mansion. A Mature Soul would exhibit evidence of fine tuning the fifth chakra, whether they were actually third or seventh story. If they were third story, their behavior would echo many of the characteristics Teenaged souls are known for. A person doing the second step, as an Adult soul, may display many qualities of a Toddler soul due to the kind of emotions they are grappling with. Naturally there are slip-ups. Sometimes even the Old soul may display irrational behavior. However, Old souls have permission to break with tradition and societal norms in order to accomplish their Mission in life. Seldom, if ever, do they injure anyone besides themselves.

What happens if one of the incarnates completes all the tasks for a particular floor of the Mansion while other co-beings are still alive? The people still living have the choice to go on with their lifetime and do anything they like with it. It becomes a life of total choice lived virtually karma free, but they are usually cautious not to incur demerits on what has already been accomplished.

THE MANSION OF SURVIVAL
(Root Chakra)

You might assume that Infant souls have an exceedingly arduous time since their relative experience is so limited. However, the Clan Advisors are wise and, if the soul listens, it will be sent to Mature or Old soul parents. Infant souls need to be told what to do and how to do it. In spite of normal intelligence, numerous earthly concepts evade them. Infant souls may seem to be innocent and too much of the spirit world. Unlike Old souls, whom they resemble in this respect, they seem naive rather than wise. The western world contains far fewer Infant souls than Oriental nations like Bangladesh or Pakistan.

INFANT SOULS

Loving, uninhibited, defenseless, helpless, self-centered, temperamental, surrendered, innocent, placid, demanding, changeable, unpredictable, unduly open to or fearful of people, guileless, makes eye contact and tells blunt truth but needs to be told what to do.

Professions: *take boring jobs for financial reasons or apprenticeship positions that lead to acquisition of skills valuable for future lifetimes.*

Religions: *Fundamentalist Muslim, Hindu, or Christian with no real understanding of their religion. They secretly practice Animism with or without religious sanction.*

THE MANSION OF EMOTION
(Sacral Chakra)

Once the Infant soul stage is mastered, the Toddler/Child or second chakra is the focus. This stage can take a multitude of lifetimes. The soul progresses from chakra one to chakra seven as seen through the emotional veil. Often pedantic, demanding, obstinate, or overly sweet, this series of lifetimes deals with acceptance and rejection or outright abandonment.

Inhabitants of the Toddler/Child Mansion are frequently individuals who have walked out on their entire family, never to see or speak to them again. Sometimes they are abandoned in childhood, or let go of by successive partners. Typically, they overreact in situations and lend themselves to mass violence or individual deeds that spring forth from untamed emotional states. They're often followers of super patriots or religious zealots. They require supervised employment situations and constant monitoring to make sure they are performing their tasks promptly and correctly.

TODDLER/CHILD SOULS
Uncontainable, alternately cooperative and uncooperative, tiring, energetic, fun, oppressive, envious, greedy, curious, affectionate, selfish, selectively loyal and/or loving, perceptive, possessive, honest, charming, exploring, needs boundaries, not leaders, narrow-minded, intolerant, wants-to-be-helpful, work best as followers.
Professions: *carpenter, accountant, mechanized farmer, sailor, computer worker, logger, electronics repair, laboratory technician, Marine, laborer, non-commissioned lifer in the military, bookkeeper, clerk, guard and warden, voluntarily choosing careers that give close supervision.*
Religions: *Hindu, Fundamentalist Christian, Mormon, Satanist, Fundamentalist Muslim, Jehovah's Witness, fanatics of all kinds. Here, they assume secondary leadership positions and are true believers.*

THE MANSION OF POWER
(Solar Chakra)

Having acquired the skills and experience necessary to advance to the next Mansion, the soul becomes a Teenager seeing everything through the glass of power and control. No matter what chakra the individual is working on, the lifetime is perceived through the route to power and influence. They make plans and carry out their goals. Authority is something to be sought or disparaged. At present in America, Australia, India, and many other countries, the Teenage soul is the principal human expression. Greed is the motivating factor, the most deadly of the deadly sins because it is the one transgression which can cause you to commit all the others.

A Teenaged soul sees everything in terms of right or wrong. Their perceptions are in black and white and they choose sides passionately. They change strong feelings often, dropping the very beliefs they identified with at all costs for a new set they embrace just as fervently. The wrong ones must be vanquished.

The Teenaged Mansion is analogous to the teenage years of an individual. The ladder below shows the chronological age of a human being compared to the floor a soul resides on while developing. The first floor is analogous to the first chakra and equals age thirteen for an adolescent. The second story is equal to age fourteen and so on. A seventh chakra Teenage soul is the same as a nineteen-year-old, ready to become an adult.

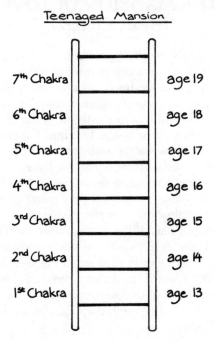

Teenaged Mansion

7th Chakra — age 19
6th Chakra — age 18
5th Chakra — age 17
4th Chakra — age 16
3rd Chakra — age 15
2nd Chakra — age 14
1st Chakra — age 13

TEENAGE SOULS

Challenging, idealistic, inconsiderate, maturing, ambitious, insightful, jealous, freedom-loving, ambivalent, rebellious, loving, fearful of differences, sexually preoccupied, con-artists, overly active or repressed, power hungry, seducible, inventive, helpful, dreamers, easily taken in by material world, obnoxious, wide emotional swings, cruel, humorous, supportive, conformists, iconoclasts.

Professions: *police work, schoolteacher, priest, traditional M.D., bureaucrat, writer, manager, technicians of all kinds, scientist, powerbroker, politician, songwriter, pop philosopher, sports figure, realtor, banker, salesperson, entrepreneur, corporate executive, contractor, city planner, middle management, commissioned officer in military, religious leader, actor, coach, singer, merchant, newscaster.*

Religions: *Catholic, Yoga, Sectarian Protestant, Russian Orthodox, Lutheran, Baptist, Jewish, Mormon, Greek Orthodox. Life is centered around religious practices more as social ideals than true faith. Church leaders interact with Teenage soul members on committees and governing boards.*

THE MANSION OF LOVE
(Heart Chakra)

Adult souls begin to view their life not just in terms of comforts and power but in terms of more important values such as compassion, love, grief, and kindness. At this stage, many people opt to redo work which was considered complete in earlier incarnations. They refine and redefine it through the filter of the heart chakra. How it feels in their hearts becomes the criterion. This is the crossover point between the ordinary self and the higher self. Adult souls stick to the work at hand and follow the majority of rules, if the rules make sense to them, but will circumvent the law or unwritten cultural customs if they aren't philosophically wedded to them. Philosophy and the development of personal ethics are an integral part of the soul's journey while residing in the Mansion of Love. Adult souls are status-conscious, with accompanying pretensions until they reach the sixth story of the Mansion. The entire world must move through this Mansion to gather the higher levels of development that will emerge over the next two centuries. Many countries in Europe are heavily populated with Adult souls.

ADULT SOULS

Seekers, adventurers, accepting, envious, generous, diplomatic, hides true self, caring, judgmental, controlling, conforming, explorers inwardly and outwardly, creative, competent, infrequent strivers, self-sufficient, hard working.
Professions: *nurse, healer, counselor, psychologist, translator, college teacher, linguist, consultant, computer nerd, lawyer, actor, arbitrator, physicist, astrologer, explorer, scientist, merchant, musician, data analyst, journalist, dedicated schoolteacher, mathematician, crusader, physician, caretakers of all types.*
Religions: *Buddhist, Jewish, Episcopalian, Methodist, Catholic, Brethren, Yoga, Amish, Taoist, Russian Orthodox, Quaker, Sufi. Individual opinions of members are considered carefully as are the human needs of the fellowship. Adult souls in churches do a great deal of secular social service and education.*

THE MANSION OF SOUND
(Throat Chakra)

Mature souls work on projects associated with the fifth chakra. Therefore, the lens through which they view the world is colored by inner learning and outer sharing. They will not be drawn into fights not of their own making. Seldom religious or members of any discernible group, they are nevertheless self-disciplined, principled, and committed. They are concerned for the common good, often pacifists, with a look-the-other-way attitude toward activities they don't care to participate in and don't quite approve of. People in this Mansion stay married irrespective of circumstances. Whether the first chakra or the sixth is spotlighted, the soul's operating values are those the fifth chakra is known for—honesty and communication. If any disease develops it will most likely be in the thyroid or throat.

MATURE SOULS

Reliable, serene, likes rules, sincere, honest, faithful, compassionate, doesn't impose their will on your life, adore good things in life (won't obtain them by killing or manipulation), adaptable, flexible, can fight constructively, openminded, sense of proportion, listens to others, helpful, has integrity, backbone of society, sensitive, insightful, rational.

Professions: *teacher, therapist, fine specialty shopkeeper, craftsperson, musician, healer, composer, translator, writer, innovative photographer, designer, semi-professional athlete, scientific genius, maverick social science philosopher.*
Religions: *Buddhist, Gnostic, Taoist, Quaker, Sufi, Yoga, Native American. Traditional mystical religious pathways including aboriginal ones attract the Mature soul.*

THE MANSION OF KNOWLEDGE
(Brow Chakra)

Old souls live by their own rules, desires, and principles regardless of the society they enter. These are the world's successful mavericks. They listen clearly to their own intuition. They are tolerant, do little violence, and give more than they receive. They know life is to frolic in and enjoy, even in the midst of serious and important Missions. Fortunately they are as wise in childhood as an ordinary person is in old age. Most teach only those who seek them out. Although they may have a mandate to instigate a new consciousness or set of values (along with others sent for the same Mission), they do it by convincement.* Old souls by and large have respect for other people's positions and beliefs, and keep silent when in the presence of fools.

The Old souls are usually accepting about their lot in life. They do not live in the grand villas nor stately homes as do Teenaged or Adult Souls. Their dwellings are modest, or they may have no permanent residence at all. They have a kindness emanating from their demeanor. If you meet an Old soul you will be struck by her deep understanding and knowledge of human nature.

OLD SOULS
Mellow, non-judgmental, accepting, caring, not status-conscious, giving and generous, wise, tolerant, strong, enduring, spiritual rather than religious, compassionate, self-knowledgeable, farsighted visionaries, break all rules without infringing on others.

Convincement: friendly persuasion, the Quaker way to change hearts and minds.

Professions: *artist, gardener, carpenter, craftsperson, musician, composer, organic farmer, teacher, wanderer, serene innovative spiritual leader, philosopher.*
Religions: *Avoid formalized religions, following their own contact with the Creator.*

THE MANSION OF WISDOM
(Crown Chakra)

Volunteer souls have attained full status as graduates of ordinary life. They relate to life chiefly through the seventh chakra. When they take a body, they come with access to all memory everywhere in the universe. These are the master builders. The Karmapa, Dalai Lama, and other Tibetan *savants* are among the most familiar Volunteer souls. Contrary to the Tibetan belief that the same Source Self reincarnates time after time as a specific lama, it is actually a series of different Volunteer souls who come to experiment for their own growth as well as to keep alive the essential mystical traditions.

Volunteers are keepers of the flame. They do not move through the Mansion in quite the same laborious and cumbersome fashion as other soul levels do. With all that knowledge intact they can move from first to seventh chakra competence, as an enlightened being does, in one single lifetime. These Volunteer souls are experimenting with breaking down the limits of the physical body by retaining consciousness and all-seeing powers while alive.

However, Volunteer souls are human too, and they may become caught up in the dramas of life. Lust, overindulgence, and loss of the bigger picture can subvert their Missions. No one is born without a fatal flaw to overcome. Advisers plant a profusion of seeds for success, and several for failure. How often do human beings ignore their abundance of good seedlings and crumble as a result?

The Volunteer soul is someone like the Karmapa who comes here with total recall of the experiences acquired by other Volunteer souls in the role of Karmapa. Contrast that with the papacies, a Teenaged soul position won in the same way as other corporate prizes. One is born a Dalai Lama or Karmapa, whereas popes are elected for life once the old pope expires. A faction of cardinals might poison a pope to gain more power for themselves, but killing the Karmapa only means that another of his lineage will go on representing him.

Volunteer souls have achieved wisdom, and as they climb the floors of the volunteer Mansion they make few mistakes, consequently spending only a single lifetime per story. This may be the sole Mansion where it is permitted to ascend more than one floor per incarnation.

YOUR MANSION

Discovering your own Mansion and story within it can be a challenge. It is easier to figure out the floor you are on than the house you dwell in. The less you know who you are, the more likely you are to be influenced by and to adopt the beliefs and values of the dominant Mansion in your particular society. American politics are conducted with the operatic-drama, continual-crisis mentality prevalent in Teenaged Souls. This appeals to the majority of Americans, who dwell in the Mansion of Power.

If you are a Mature Soul, on the fifth or sixth story, you may be uncomfortable while engaged in special transactions and activities, trying to fit yourself into the mold. Should you be a third-story individual of Adult, Mature, or Old soul status, you will be fairly comfortable, albeit wanting to make social and business interchanges more honest and truthful. As you mature, removing the trappings of childhood and family, you'll be less and less inclined to fall into the provincial patterns of behavior your culture esteems.

By noting the chakra through which you have the greatest trouble expressing yourself (usually the one that is vulnerable to almost all your physical ailments), you can accurately determine the one you assigned yourself to work with. Do this in an honest manner by examining the problems you have had during each decade of your life. Stomach, adrenal, and gall bladder troubles originate in the third chakra. Skin problems begin in the kidneys, ruled by the sacral chakra. Headaches habitually form in the area governed by the third eye, but they can also be due to constipation riding up along the triad from the root to heart to the sixth chakra. If you continually feel insecure in addition to having regular headaches, your root chakra is out of balance.

If during a given lifetime you fail to achieve the goals you set for yourself, you and your Advisors-in-spirit will set up another incarnation in which similar conditions prevail. You will then renew your attempt to complete them. Let's say you have chosen to work with health, luck, romance, and relatives all within the context of marriage. How would you know?

Without delving wide-eyed into the world of mediums and channels, you can ascertain what your goals are for this lifetime. All you will need are two decks of ordinary playing cards. Take out the jokers. Shuffle the deck thoroughly.

Deal out a seven-pack solitaire game (see illustration on page 56). Play the game by yourself, no cheating and no outside help. Begin with seven cards, of which only the first is face-up (open). Next time you go along the row, pass by the first position and place a face-up card over the second position, then put one card face down over all other positions. Next lay a face-up card on top of the third card position, and a card face down over every position in the remaining pile. Continue in this manner until there is one face-up card over every pile. The seventh packet will have six cards facing down and one facing up.

To play, go through the portion of the deck in your hand, two cards at a time. Stock is the portion of a pack of playing cards not dealt out. In solitaire, cards left in your hand are to be drawn from. As they are opened they are renamed Talons.

With the cards left over (called the stock), turn two at a time and place them, if you have an opportunity, in descending order, alternating red and black suits on the tableau or open cards.

Place the cards on each other in reverse numerical sequence alternating red and black. A red king is balanced with a black queen, a black king by a red queen. If you have a red six face up on top of a pile and a black seven on another pile, you may move the six onto the seven, and turn up the card that was beneath the six. A red five isn't a match for the red six, only a black six. Kings are foundation cards and may be moved into another position if one of the seven packets has been completely reassigned. Aces can be moved above and outside the seven stacks or directly from the stock as a card appears which will fit in sequence onto its suit. The two of spades goes over the ace of spades, then the three, the four, and so on. The same process is followed with the other suits. If the three of hearts is hidden or

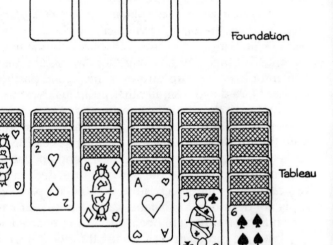

Foundation

Tableau

Stock   Talon

blocked, you cannot remove it from its place to put it on the pile. The object is to come out with no leftover cards.

Go through the stock twice only. When you can no longer make any moves, count the cards that have not been uncovered in the stacks and lay them aside. Whatever is in the stock doesn't count.

The norm is to have between seven and thirteen cards remaining. If you have played out all your cards and uncovered all the hidden cards, it may be that all aspects of your Mission are either completed or are progressing well.

Take another deck and lay out a second seven-card solitaire game (see illustration on page 58). Place the leftover cards from the first game face up above the second game matching them to the open cards of the second game. Check illustration to see if you have done it correctly.

Whatever appears in your layout is work your family, peer group, or education helped you to begin. (See page 59 for the Keys to the meanings of the cards.) Whatever remains is work you must initiate. To be successful, all cards in the second deck must be opened and moved to another line. As the entire pile of cards is moved and replaced by a king, remove the cards from the first game that were placed above that line. These symbolize tasks you either have or will successfully complete in this lifetime.

Pay attention to the cards that you open on the table. If one of the cards you need from the first game is open in a stack, place the one from the other deck crosswise above the row you find it in. This is work you brought up due to your self awareness. Cards from the first game that remain on top when the second game is over represent unfinished work that still has to be done for your current incarnation to fulfill its Mission. Cards from the first hand of solitaire unrevealed at game's end epitomize work that you haven't yet begun. If it is a jack of spades, you need to learn to control your thoughts. An unexposed two of clubs means you lack self-examination, while a six of diamonds tells you to appreciate life more and treat yourself better.

The object is to wind up with all the cards exposed and in order. Whichever ones are still covered when you can no longer make further progress without cheating, represent those things you must accomplish to successfully ascend from the section of the Mansion in which you now reside. These are your assignments. If

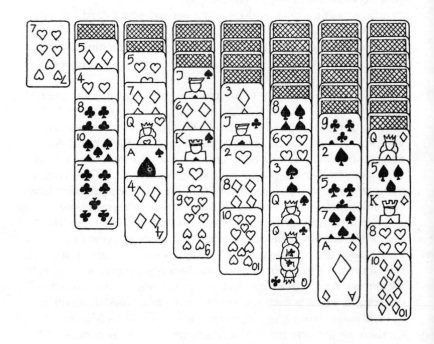

you win the game square and fair you have found your correct path in this lifetime and are well on your way.

Winning the second game means you have already successfully completed your Mission and are on free time. Enjoy yourself and do no harm. You are ready to move up one floor in your Mansion, or graduate to another soul level upon dying.

THE KEYS

	Diamonds	Hearts	Clubs	Spades
Ace	new ventures	the home	gifts	death
2	change	personal love	self-examination	peace
3	hard work	abundance	virtue	sorrow
4	power	marriage	completion	truce
5	torment	disillusion	craving/desire	defeat
6	pleasure	rationality	victory	caution
7	success	happiness	messages	health
8	inheritance	universal love	achievement	troubles
9	dreams/visions	wishes granted	luck	disappointment
10	money	family life	journey	creativity
J	letters	popularity	principles/ideal	mental clarity
Q	intuition	friendship	yourself	gratitude or selfishness
K	decorum	enjoyment	career/calling	surprises; systems and the unanticipated

Overview This game may help you obtain an overview of your life's purpose and the direction you require to do your Mission well. A director, a general, a football player, all have to be aware at every moment where everything and everyone is positioned. Being vigilant toward details eliminates confusion, makes for accuracy, and determines your future employability. Most football players only have to play well and be pleasant to the coach. A director can be very surly or congenial, she can take many roles. However, a general must be a consummate politician before he can prove or disprove his competency in the field. Generals who become too arrogant frequently go down in defeat, or cause thousands to die needlessly. Corporate executives also must have these skills, which are ways to operate in the Teenaged Mansion or within the third chakra stories of other soul levels. The overview is very important to anyone who is grappling with learning leadership or the uses of power.

Whether you are an Infant soul or a Mature one, getting an overview of your own lifetime is a great advantage in successfully completing your Mission.

5

The Path

*To feel there is something greater than we are that en-
compasses us, and that there is a master plan, is more
than comforting, it confirms what we know in our
heart of hearts.*

Anon.

You are born and you die, and what happens in between is a
measure of your skill at maintaining a harmonic balance between
fate and choice. The activities and relationships you pursue stimulate your mental, emotional, physical, and spiritual selves. To
keep your life in perspective, you must learn the vast difference
between fate, in the sense of doom, and the kind of fate involved
in selecting your assignments for an incarnation. Fate in the
form of your Mission and personality is sealed before you are
conceived. Specific circumstances can be renegotiated during
gestation, and later at crossroads in your life. This is choice in
action. You continue to make conscious and unconscious selec-
tions throughout your life, choices which contribute to the success, retardation, or irredeemable failure of your Mission.

61

Fate and Choice Fate is comprised of aspects of your life that are predetermined; choice is the promise of free will within these predetermined parameters. Life is a cooperative effort between fate and choice. Sometimes the choices you make seal your fate. At other times your fate closes off your choices. Your race, ethnicity, sex, religious heritage, genetic code, constitution, and natural talents are all set in advance of your birth. Whether you use your good health to become an athletic wonder or squander it on drugs, sex, and alcohol is a matter of choice. Whether your birth family's life was pleasant or miserable you may, by fate or choice, have the opposite in your adult family. You may abandon your home town due to toxic pollutants (fate), or to pursue a different lifestyle (choice).

The Path What is your path? How do you know it when you find it? Why is the bulk of the population distracted from the work they contracted to do prior to being born? Some people always seem to be aware of the blueprint for their lives. Regardless of how eccentric they are, or conventionally successful they may be, their blueprint is always functional for them. Others have no obvious plan nor are they willing to adopt one. They go floating through life as if their youth and unexplored talents will forever be available to them. Others stagger through life thirsting for an answer they cannot accept. The majority forfeit their birthright for the standard dream espoused by most of their contemporaries.

During the selection process, prior to conception, your Advisors and teachers in the spiritual arena speak with you about your prospects for incarnating. You are given a choice of parents,* nationality, planet, race, sex, relative circumstances (economic and social) in life, and desired goals. With their advice and consent you choose the tasks for the lifetime to come. The characteristics you wish to develop and the preconditions that must be set in order for you to follow through are represented by the roots of the tree.

You actually choose three or four potential sets of parents and do not know until the cosmic spiral stops spinning whose child you shall be. The Advisors are permitted to veto your first, second, and third choices.

Tree Trunk   The tree has three sections. (See illustration on page 64.) The roots are your tasks, the qualities you promised yourself to master and perfect in this lifetime. The roots, hidden while you are standing on the earth, are essential to your life the same as your life's plan. The tree trunk represents your life. The trunk, thick and hard to scale like physical and emotional reality, stands waiting for you to get a grip on your life by beginning your assignment. If you're lucky your tree has a low hanging branch you can grasp to start your climb. The branches you see as you gaze skyward represent the tasks you've rediscovered. Some trees are lush and full, while others have been topped off. Dead limbs or large broken branches on your tree stand for qualities you chose to abandon this lifetime. Abundant healthy twigs and leaves on another branch show how well you've fulfilled that portion of your Mission. Trees can also be diseased and gnarled. Illness is a good way to avoid your work on earth. A tree that is beautiful from every angle is like an inspired lifetime with an ongoing blueprint.

Characteristics you're developing are illustrated by a line running from the roots to the branches. An arrow on a line denotes the age at which you begin to work on your assignment. Other arrows show when you resumed working on a trait again after a dormant period. Squares indicate when you ceased exploring that trait. A star on the line running from the roots to the branches shows mastery of some aspect of the trait. Although the illustration here shows a fairly accomplished individual, a line can go astray, moving to the wrong branch and intercepting the exploration of another quality.

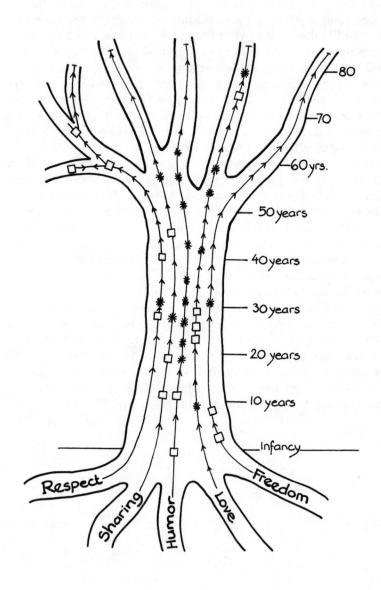

The qualities listed below may be ones you have selected to work on during this lifetime. It is only a representative sample; others too numerous to list are available to the incarnate.

Ambition	Handsomeness	Obstinacy
Amiability	Handicrafts	Occult
Brotherhood	Happiness	Passion
Charm	Hardiness	Persuasiveness
Clarity	Harmony	Power
Compassion	Health	Principles
Competence	Healing	Prudence
Daring	Heart	Radiance
Diligence	Hope	Respect
Discretion	Integrity	Secrecy
Empathy	Intelligence	Security
Enthusiasm	Intuition	Self-esteem
Fluency	Irreproachability	Sensibility
Foresight	Jest	Sensitivity
Generosity	Joviality	Sexuality
Glamor	Joy	Sharing
Graciousness	Justice	Temperance
Gratitude	Kindness	Thankfulness
Grounded	Likability	Truth
Growth	Manual Skills	Wealth
Hallucinations	Nurturance	Wisdom

LOVE

In addition to the three to five characteristics that wiser souls select to work on during a given lifetime, there is always LOVE, so intrinsically tied to life that one cannot live without it. Studies have established that infants and older children denied love fail to thrive. The elderly, neglected by society, often die from emotional deprivation.

Love can be expressed as love for the Creator; love of a geographical location; love for your fellow beings (agape); love for your family (parents, children, relatives); or romantic love. You can emphasize a single type of love, or a combination of two or more forms. High drama occurs when you face a choice between expressing one kind of love or another. Overzealous love of country gets in the way of loving others on earth. It can even make you leave your family at a time when they critically need you. Romantic love versus love for family is a classic theme lived out every day. Serving any form of love teaches you how to live more in harmony than in dissonance.

Maternal love for a new baby is one of the most powerful and compelling loves there is. That initial openhearted, all-embracing love lasts as your children grow, changing so you don't smother them overprotectively. It also stays alive as your children go through interesting role changes and challenging behavior patterns as teenagers and emerging adults.

Your feeling of unity with every living person, animal, tree, herb, and mineral formation is Universal love. Love in its sacramental form is compassion. Love is a feeling of belonging, an alchemical process that defies words. If you've never known a sacred moment wherein you experienced the wonder of it all, you can barely understand the quality of being in love.

People who carry a heavy symbol (generals in wartime or other heroic figures) are often cut off from others and starved for love. They must turn to the Creator for sustenance. The Creator becomes their delight and wellspring. Via service to All That Is, they become appealing to others and overcome obstacles.

Before you are born, your Advisors apprise you of your developmental needs. From among the available Missions, you choose the qualities you are ready to tackle and cultivate. During the socialization process (which is represented by the lower part of the tree trunk), you are often diverted from segments of your path. Fortunate youngsters are encouraged to investigate a number of their tasks in their youth while unlucky ones feel trapped, damaged, and out of place, realizing that something is not as it ought to be.

Members of your family help launch you onto your path, but they can also crush your efforts and delay your life work until you shake off their influence. Adulthood brings opportunities to explore various qualities, but by then a large percentage of the population is so maladjusted that they forsake their inner longing to pursue hedonistic pleasures or live miserably in states of addiction and psychological traps. Throughout life everyone has many propitious times for abandoning their escapism and progressing with a successful incarnation. This necessitates learning about both the negative and positive sides of the qualities chosen to scrutinize and develop.

Karmically, there are two ways to work off past wrongs: hard work or illness. Sickness is chosen to make amends for lifetimes of negativity and for failing to work hard to relieve it. Instead of sticking with the karmic payment of hard work, a man plays around work hours, drinks evenings and weekends. In old age he finally decides to pay off the life debts he owes by taking on afflictions. That's why so many elderly are ill. They didn't do the personal work they were supposed to do and are atoning with a variety of debilitating, painful ailments.

Your attitudes have a great deal to do with whether or not you remain healthy or develop an ailment. "One illness," the Chinese say, "long life; no illness short life." A disease awakens the immune system and teaches it to fight back. Once it learns something, your body continues to hold that knowledge.

Infirmities taken on prior to birth are karmic, even if they are fatal. Sickness in childhood assists the working out of the family's socio-emotional blockages. In adult life, illnesses occur to make you speak your truth and pay off debts you cannot defray otherwise. Many personal weaknesses and infirmities are indicated in the birth horoscope. By studying astrological charts, you may be able to discover what crosses people have volunteered to shoulder. Don't sit in judgement of anyone's fate. Do help alleviate their difficult choices to whatever degree you can.

People die when they have decided, unconsciously or consciously, that they have done the best they could. Either they are satisfied with the results or they are so displeased that it's hopeless to continue. The decision to die has many variables. After the age of two, a child must have permission from its Advisors. Before then, it is completely up to the young incarnate to decide whether it would be better to continue, or be more advantageous to fulfill their work in another body.

Circumstances initiated by your parents, your older siblings, the manner of your birth, your doctors, other family members, and friends set in motion the wheel of fortune or misfortune, thus assisting or disturbing your self-image and self-esteem. Those with a good sense of self are more likely to succeed at the only worthy game in life, fulfilling their contract with the Universe and themselves.

If given the choice while here on the earth, everyone would want to be born to elevated economic and social status, as it appears to be the easiest route. Luckily, you are on the other side while deciding. Prior to incarnating, your goals for character development and spiritual growth are usually foremost in your consciousness. Your Advisors continue to pump you full of information and give you insights. You are permitted to disregard what they tell you and make what is often a foolish or regrettable decision. Then again, your own judgement may happily surprise the Advisors.

You and your co-beings grow in dissimilar ways from one lifetime to another. It is, therefore, forbidden for a Bach or a Mozart to return to life as a composer again. What your co-beings have perfected is no longer an acceptable pathway for you to attain higher consciousness. For this reason, many children who exhibit great musical or artistic potential do not pursue it during their teen and adult years, although exceptions to every rule do occur. Knowing that your co-being was an excellent artist, who lived in unremitting misery, your Advisors might permit you to be reborn in another era with a new cosmology to an acclaimed, lucrative artistic career in a new medium. You might also be allowed to exercise previously developed talents as a way of providing for yourself materially, so that other conditions you chose to work on can take priority.

Within every path there are many kinds of work. A path may lead you to round out a characteristic or trait left unfinished from other lifetimes. A soul who already understands marital relationships may choose to enter marriage, because it provides a comfortable context in which to explore other weaknesses or strengths. By selecting a mate who is easy to get along with, one sets the stage for a nontraumatic home life, although one may be beset by illness, social unrest, or economic travail. The happy home may lay the foundation for a triumphant life. Souls who decide to take all their pain in poverty of spirit, unhappy family life, personal injury, and catastrophes will have these conditions show up in their natal horoscope or numerology chart. Success can also be forecast by a person's astrology and numerology.

Judging from the blockages manifested by the current world population, unfinished projects from past lives continue to significantly impede earthly peace, prosperity, and spiritual growth. Normally, a look into the previous incarnations will resolve any anxiety or mental agitation for an individual. But many deny contact with former lifetimes due to things their religion teaches. Christians, Jews, and Muslims do not officially believe in reincarnation. This is due to the way in which the Torah is written. Since it is holy it cannot be destroyed if sacred words are written fully. As a result letters were left out of words and the information given from master to student. Adam means one incarnation and Adom many lifetimes. Through the ages the knowledge was taught different ways by learned rabbis. The discrepancy was settled about the time of Christ by a board of rabbis who decided upon the first meaning: Adam. Despite the religious tenets millions of people do believe in past lives and do use them to resolve conflicts in their current lifetime.

A young woman hoping to become a chiropractor came to me for counseling. Although she was twenty-eight years old, unmarried, a partner in a popular local restaurant, and the recipient of a sizable inheritance, she was afraid to go pursue her dream. I suggested she try a past-life journey.

Once in the trance, her initial past-life seemed pleasant enough. I could see it coming, the terror of her most recent life, before she went into the second lifetime. At first she spoke easily about her life, growing up as the eldest son in a loving Jewish family. But her horror grew and her emotional state became quite agitated as she discovered him to be a twenty-three-year-old medical student confined to the Warsaw Ghetto, where he eventually died in the sewers as a freedom fighter.

Small wonder she was afraid to apply to chiropractic school. Medical training preceded death in her mind. We talked it over, and she determined that this was truly a new life in another country and she wasn't Jewish this time. A year later she entered a program at a highly respected school. Three more years went by and we unexpectedly met in Santa Fe. She explained that she'd switched to the best acupuncture college in the United States, having found that method of doctoring more compatible with her inner nature.

The circumstances of her past life that ended in 1943 were attributable to the fate of being born Jewish, which negated the soul's power of choice regarding survival and pursuing a chosen career. As a woman alive today, she could take up the medical calling with a new twist.

Past Life Exploration   The majority of your incarnations resemble those that you see in the present world's society. You have starved, feasted, died young, died old. You have taken your turn, as has each of us, as a predatory warrior, a war victim, a criminal, a priest, a drunk, a leader, a follower, a protector, a traitor. You have been rich, poor, free, subjugated, wise, foolish, tragic, comic, repulsive, and loveable. In short you have been all things imaginable from matriarch to prostitute, from pauper to magnate, from multitalented virtuoso to an incapable dolt. Your prejudice and intolerance are as much a reflection of your distaste for circumstances of previous incarnations as they are acquisitions from your parents and the society you are now part of.

Currently you may be repulsed by mental retardation, yet have an affinity for the deaf and hard of hearing. Examining a former lifetime you note a hearing impairment at that time forced you into the same social classification as idiots. Your normal intelligence attracted attention when you began weaving intricate patterns and cooking fine meals by observation and taste. After a past-life session, you have infinite compassion for those who are mentally deficient.

A young woman who had been a black female in a fairly recent lifetime found herself very attracted to and fascinated by black people in this lifetime. Though her skin is rather light and her ash brown hair straight, she has often been asked if she is black. She couldn't understand why white people fear and hate blacks, yet she had an aversion to Latinos. Her family has always been the opposite, mingling freely with Hispanics but indifferent to blacks. During a past-life session she saw herself as black in several incarnations. This brought her a great deal of joy and comfort. In one lifetime, she experienced tremendous difficulty with people who looked Spanish-American. After coming to terms with this problem during her session, she is no longer averse to friendships with Latinos and continues to socialize with blacks.

Should you fail to achieve the goals you set for yourself during a given lifetime, you and your Advisors in spirit will design another life in which similar conditions prevail. You will then attempt to complete your Mission. Not everyone is born to win; some are here to teach others, some to learn by example. Others are born to be the hard-working founders of a new world order (e.g. democratic principles of the United States founding fathers) that brings them a modest amount of recognition while alive and posthumous fame of far reaching proportions.

Let's say you have chosen to work with health, luck, romance, and relatives all within the context of marriage. A woman who came to me for a past-life journey had these same working premises to resolve over a multitude of lifetimes. She had remained on the same story, in the same Mansion, for centuries. Time after time she had refused to marry or left her marriage because she couldn't bear to be told what to do. In this life, in keeping with the same old pattern, she was on the verge of dumping her live-in lover of five years despite the fact that she knew this man treated her as an equal. After reviewing four prior lives wherein she abandoned all of her marriages (though completing many other tasks successfully), she understood that her present life had little further purpose unless she undertook the plans she'd made before incarnating. She married her lover and they went off to buy a farm in New Zealand.

No accomplishment is without some struggle. The strife within must be dealt with for the lifetime to be successful. It is better that no one else tell you your past lives, for so much of it can be made up in the imagination of the reader or channel. Plenty of past-life readers do not understand the labyrinth of the soul network, or the information they are receiving. How much better to see your past lifetimes yourself, and to interpret them to your own satisfaction. Past lives are best explored with a helper who knows the route into the Akashic records. However, you can travel on your own if you so desire.

Unassisted Exploration of Past Lives

Dream sequences during sleep are the most common past-life voyages. Some see portions of one or more past lives during ecstatic experiences like orgasm or unintentionally induced trance states. Under unique conditions, people may spontaneously slip into a past-life reverie. You will be on two or three levels of consciousness at the same time, aware in some respects of your current circumstances yet in a familiar and distant place.

This is an intimate account of one woman's journey:

My boyfriend was attached to a Hindu guru. He wanted me to attend darshan [the Hindu liturgy] with him. Originally I loathed it, but I went along to please him. I learned to accept the format, but detested the obligatory chanting before the swami gave his sermon.

One evening I thought I'd fool everyone by going off into an ecstatic trance to avoid chanting. Men and women sat on the floor on separate sides of the hall. The monitors and the women sitting around me were the ones I wanted to throw off-track, as my boyfriend was out of sight.

I began chanting with the group. At chant #19 I began my act. I dropped my book and rocked back and forth mimicking the ecstatic responses that I had witnessed. Suddenly in my mind's eye, I saw a woman hanging. I felt as if I were in a cangue in two separate scenes. Then a weight was lifted from my shoulders and my neck snapped into place.

I opened my eyes, disappointed at being plunked back into the scene I'd planned to exit. Looking down, I lifted my book which was open to chant #118—exactly what everyone else was singing. Not until then did I realize I'd been catapulted through two past lives and I had cleared them from my body. I'd fooled myself right into a deep state of meditation.

Previous lifetimes are available to you only if they have some effect upon the one you're now living. If you are finished with past-life karma, as is the case with many senior citizens, you may not see anything. Here is what it takes:

Requirements for past-life work:

1–An ability or willingness to meditate.

2–A couple of hours of free, uninterrupted time.

3–Clean, uncluttered surroundings.

4–A friend who will check on you after three hours to make certain you have returned to the time frame and reality you started from.

5–Curiosity and the ability to observe yourself without guilt or attachment to a previously elevated or depraved state.

Some people do excellent trance work in a rocking chair—the gentle swaying lulls them on their way. Others are at their best warmly covered, lying on their backs, knees up, feet on the floor. Another comfortable position is to sit, legs crossed, back against a supporting wall. Whatever you find most relaxing is the way to approach meditation. Regular meditators already know what position is best for them. If you begin in one pose and are not at ease, feel free to change at any time. If your foot hurts don't ignore it. Move.

Dress warmly even if you are indoors. Prolonged trances tend to cool the body. Better to be overly warm than too chilly.

Open a window: the fresh air will bring in prana (life force), an important component in altering your state of consciousness.

Breathe in deeply, filling your abdomen, your lungs, and your whole body all the way to your toes with fresh clean air. Exhale, letting go of tension, anxiety, and other unpleasantness. Inhale and exhale fully for thirty breaths. (This may make you a bit light-headed.)

Tell yourself that you are immune to being disturbed by sounds outside the room. Take a few more full breaths. Then summon your highest ability to visualize. Treat what you see as if watching a video tape.* Instruct your superconscious to allow you complete access to a past life that is meaningful for your present existence. If it is scary, run your video backwards or forwards to a portion of the life that was fruitful or merely provocative. You can be slow or fast in your review. It's your experience and your show.

As painful moments arise causing tears to flow over the loss of loved ones, ask yourself if these folks are in your present life and identify them. Usually you'll find that someone you loved and lost is with you now. Also be sure to ascertain the lessons of that lifetime.

Once you have been able to inspect one lifetime, you can proceed to investigate another. If a lifetime seems vague or disturbing, just change the "video tape" to see another.

Survey a maximum of two lifetimes per sitting. At the close of the session, return to the day before you were conceived in your present form. Review the tree trunk you constructed for yourself. See which tasks were selected. Note each carefully, if necessary repeating them out loud one by one. Tell yourself that you will immediately write them down upon awakening. Breathe deeply and instruct yourself to return to today's date in good health, ready to resume your life in the light of your new knowledge. After opening your eyes, sit quietly for a few minutes. You have been in another level of reality. To hasten the transition to normal reality eat a small snack. The illustration on page 74 shows which pressure points will re-energize you following a past life trance. Hold each one thirty seconds.

A tape cassette to go with this exercise can be ordered from the address in the back of the book.

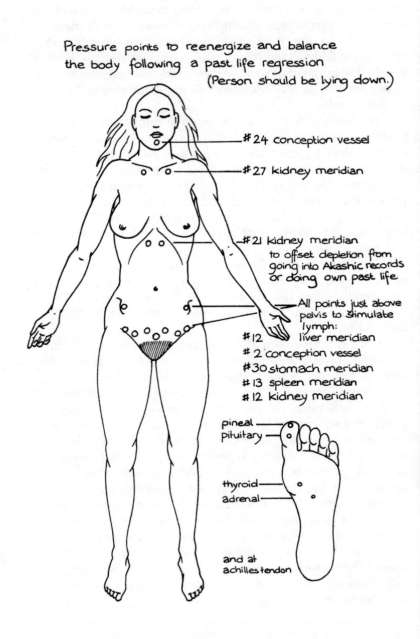

Pressure points to reenergize and balance the body following a past life regression (Person should be lying down.)

#24 conception vessel

#27 kidney meridian

#21 kidney meridian to offset depletion from going into Akashic records or doing own past life

All points just above pelvis to stimulate lymph:
#12 liver meridian
#2 conception vessel
#30 stomach meridian
#13 spleen meridian
#12 kidney meridian

pineal
pituitary

thyroid
adrenal

and at achilles tendon

Mastering the Game of Life   To fulfill your soul's commitments requires diligence, fortitude, a willingness to change direction, and mindfulness of the outcome at every turn. It is to your advantage to be ever conscious, always seeking knowledge, wisdom, and beauty; to avoid becoming stuck in ideas and ways of living; maintain joy in life, a sense of wonder, and a sense of humor.

Trendy people rarely know themselves. They are always caught up in things that hardly matter five years later. Pace-setters like the late Andy Warhol are following their inner guidance. Fashion-conscious people are imitating others, but since they're ahead of the pack they feel they are original. Being attached to a current image of yourself, or of life, may not lead to self-mastery but it's good for the economy. Shopping endlessly or letting plastic surgery be your hedge against ageing just emphasizes the emptiness of your life.

Propitious periods to take up your path coincide with the patterns of Saturn and Uranus as they transit your natal horoscope. Uranus's solar revolution takes eighty-four years, which equals seven years per sign or house. The seven years aren't exact; there is some variation. Saturn (giver of form and setter of limits) moves in approximately seven-year cycles. The underlined years indicate the ages at which Saturn has returned to the position it was in at the time of your birth. Saturn takes about twenty-nine years to revolve around the sun, nearly two-and-a-half years to transit each horoscope house or 'zodiacal sign. To find out your exact degree of Saturn consult an ephemeris. The chances to regain equilibrium and do parts of the obligatory work occur at ages: 18–21; <u>27–30;</u> 33; 39–43; 49; <u>55–58;</u> 63–65; 70; 77; <u>82–85;</u> In case an entire lifetime has been wasted and longevity has been in one's favor, both Saturn and Uranus move across a person's life between the ages of 82 and 85 to let individuals have one last try at fulfilling their Mission.

Occasionally someone comes to me who knows they have a big Mission in life and either cannot find it or are hesitant to make the necessary sacrifices. They feel tremendous conflict and sense of confusion. Insomnia, brainstorms, constant activity with no real purpose, or depression so severe they are disabled, are signs of the psyche pushing a person toward her path. If depressed, exercise until you are able to function. Brainstorms, even half-baked ideas, should be written down. They'll make sense a few years later. Hyperactivity is balanced by meditation, painting, sculpture, and other creative endeavors. Insomniacs should use the time for activities, thinking, and deep breathing until sleep overtakes them.

On his days off, a professional man, age thirty-nine, who deplored his work, took long walks that lasted a whole day, or cleaned every nook and cranny in his house. To relax, he took up beadwork to fill his overactive mind and keep himself somewhat still. A born artist, his creative beadwork was shown at a gallery. He took retraining courses in another area of his profession. This made him more comfortable, but he still sought his Mission. Unfortunately, he was more attached to his grandiose lifestyle than to finding his path and is somewhat relieved by having attained a measure of comfort.

Another man, age forty-nine, born in Mexico and raised in the United States, felt the tug of his Mission seeking him. Finally prosperous and too young for retirement, he was also reluctant to change his lifestyle at a time which might prove critical for his family. Risking all, he rented his house, arranged a family adventure, took a sabbatical from his job, and went to Central America to do a year of service under the auspices of an international organization. The pay was minimal, but in a year he returned knowing his Mission and what he would do once his children were on their own.

Chapter Test A chapter test is like a final exam in school. Once you have examined your behavior whenever a specific issue arises, or seen how you have created your own reality and have successfully demonstrated your ability to function in a new manner, an equivalent situation comes back on you as a final exam that you either pass or fail.

Looking back over your life you'll notice chapter tests that you've sailed through, and others that came around again and again until you either gave up or learned your lesson.

An illness can be a chapter test, structured so that you'll nurture yourself more diligently. You may find that you need more sleep or must surround yourself with only the most supportive friends, weeding out the rest. You might need to indulge in less competition or fewer stressful interactions, or change your dietary and exercise patterns.

Suppose your chapter test is about money. You've learned how to earn it in sufficient amounts to satisfy your wants and needs, or you've adjusted your lifestyle to suit your income. In addition, you have successfully budgeted for enough leisure time—you don't feel deprived living within your means. Now you decide to take a trip, for which you have already saved the money. The vacation is all booked and paid for, and you will lose a large percentage of your investment if you cancel your ticket. The test begins in the form of your car which requires a major, unexpected repair.

You assess your choices: (a) borrow money; (b) cancel the trip, lose money and the vacation; (c) abandon the car by the side of the road and claim it was stolen, in order to collect the insurance money and get a new one; (d) take the bus to work until you can afford the repair; (e) work overtime or get a part-time temporary job; (f) sell something you aren't so fond of to cover the repair costs; (g) attend to the inequity between your income and your actual lifestyle.

Remember, this is a chapter test. If you fail it, all the other valuable lessons that you have learned in connection with money may evaporate like mist in the morning sun. Tension and fear might bring on a mind set so stressful that you fragment your whole economic superstructure and you flunk the test. With this in mind, approach each twist and challenge with an open and trusting heart.

How to begin to tackle this problem from your current vantage point? Request help from your spirit guides and from Root-man and Rootwoman. Ask them to help you check out your options. It may be that the financial snare caused by the emergency car repair is solely a way to get your attention. Perhaps what is called for here is "a leap of the absurd" as Kierkegaard called off-balance and impractical decisions that succeed in raising you from one stage of development to another. The "absurd" decision would be to go on the vacation with the faith that somehow the money will be found. As a result of this twist of fate, you may notice the portions of your life you have been neglecting while mastering the monetary game. There is also the possibility for you to learn more about working on cars so you can repair the damage yourself.

One client of mine, a woman in her mid-eighties whose age-mates had died, had only her family for company. Her chapter test was proof of her ability not to be too dependent upon her children and grandchildren. She pushed herself out into the community, where she was discovered by a couple of young psychologists who spent time with her as friends. Her humor and insight provided great help to them as they established their practices. She suddenly found herself in the active role of teacher, making her last years much more joyful. This led to a remission of the stiffness in her joints, the condition she had come to me for.

LIVING FOREVER

If reincarnating is such a challenge, would it be better to live longer to undo negative patterns or have more years in which to complete your Mission? Exceptionally long lives do exist, but for most people the assignment is a travail. The only way to live forever is to always be a stranger, forming no attachments. It could be a gift for an old soul, being spared having to undergo countless incarnations marked with childhood. After all, most of us are forty before we're over the ordeal of our upbringing. Not until then are we able to really carry out our Mission.

At whatever point in the life cycle you split completely from your biological family, that is the age you will be for many centuries before you begin to age. Ageing, in this type of assignment, goes very slowly. You can also learn to redo the body—lengthening, shortening, widening, and thinning it, altering face structure with your mind so as not to be recognizable fifty years later by people you circulated among when they were *young*.

Imagine looking middle-aged for two centuries, or youthful for three. After a normal life-span you'd have no family, no lineage to fall back on. For a man in more patriarchal times this would have worked. For a woman it would have been nearly impossible due to societal restrictions, although cases do exist.

There are numerous legends of nine-hundred-year lifetimes for ascended masters, or those working on the ascended path. These sagas are widespread because many Hindu Babajis, Oriental Buddhist incarnates, Christian mystics, The Wandering Jew, and a present day European, St. Germain, are said to be exemplars of these existences. Not all are without human faults or frailties. They just keep adding to their mastery of new tasks as their lifetime progresses.

According to believers these nine-hundred-year lifetimes are totally shielded from disease. In order to die you'd have to perish in a car wreck, drown, or die some other sudden violent way. It won't be easy to get out of the Mission once you undertake it. You may be protected from death, even by accident or a war you decided to die in.

Whether or not you believe in these extraordinary lifetimes, it isn't advisable to try to become one, or falsely say you are, unless it is your Mission. It's a difficult path, at best, that demands selfless service as well as a wisdom beyond ordinary mortals. If you live to a healthy and ripe old age, become wise, and fulfill your Mission you will have done well indeed.

SECTION TWO
SPIRIT IN OUR WORLD

6

Rootman/Rootwoman

Male/female is the key to the source of the force.
Paul Williams, Nation of Lawyers

THE ROOTBEINGS

Everyone has a male and female self: Rootman and Rootwoman. Women commonly notice that there are male aspects of themselves they have never understood. Achieving insight into the functioning of their own maleness can be difficult. Men have an equally trying time reaching their inner female. Incomplete contact with their inner female will produce discordance in men's lives when they interact with women and girls.

Rootman and Rootwoman are partial co-beings assigned to you as a three-in-one package. You are mutually entrusted to one another. Rootwoman, you (the Learner), and Rootman. This is the human analogue to the spiritual trinity.

The Rootbeings voluntarily cooperate with you, the incarnate Learner, in exchange for skills and knowledge you already possess. They lend you whatever wisdom and capabilities they have. In addition, they both are missing characteristics and abilities you are seeking. You do the earth plane work, and the Rootman and Rootwoman feed you with advice and give consent or dissent to your decisions.

Each Rootbeing reveals to you solely a male or female face. Rootman's feminine facets remain inactive throughout your lifetime; Rootwoman presents nothing of her male self. Rootman is able, at will, to merge with and use your male capacities, competencies, limitations, and emotional repertoire. Rootwoman finds all your female patterns, strengths, and characteristics equally available to her. Both of them are open to your needs. Together you and your Rootbeings exchange insight and know-how, and try out different strategies and behaviors in order to fulfill your Mission.

A student asked me, "Does this mean that Rootman and Rootwoman are only partial incarnations, while I am a full incarnation?"

Precisely. They have no Witness, breath, or body of their own. The attention of a Source Self isn't focused as strongly on a Rootbeing as it is on a fully embodied soul. Although Rootman or Rootwoman can bring multiple images of their womanly or masculine selves into each of your interactions, their function is to learn from your experience while serving as co-creators of your reality. Usually they are members of the same Clan as you come from. The illustration shows a common way of linking you together.

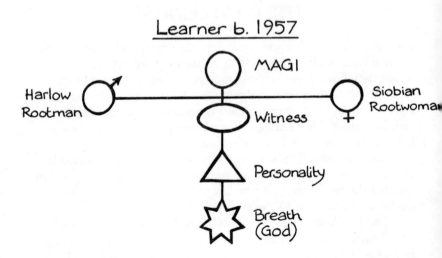

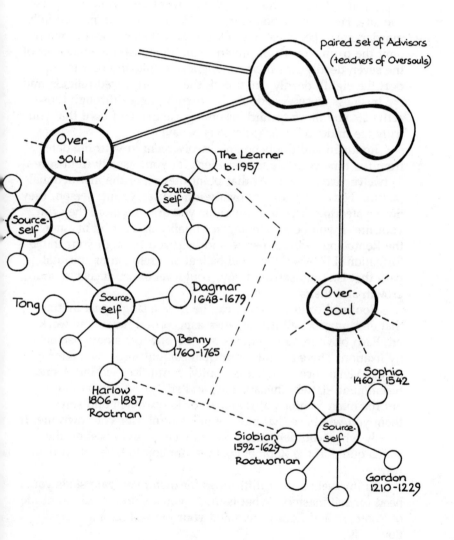

A Rootbeing attempts to force the hand of the Learner to act out the negative characteristics that they share in common. If you are terribly decent out of a repressive sense of righteousness, you will never challenge the limits of your collective personality. People have boundaries so the majority do not willfully murder, steal, lie, cheat, and otherwise wreak havoc. But many omit the truth, cover-up, pretend, and demonstrate whichever of the seven deadly sins their conscience permits in order to support the eighth deadly sin, greed, the one organized religion and big business always overlook. By learning to see through those activities you move toward becoming the being of light that you truly are under all your ridiculous behavior.

Rootman and Rootwoman's involvement in your life dates from the time your life material jells for you, usually from seven to twelve years of age. At that point they enter the instructional picture. For a rebellious or overly introverted young person, they do the steering. The less conscious you are, the more they run your life. If you begin seeking spirituality in a caring manner, the Rootbeings will cooperate and help you through your transformation. Likewise, they will balk at any religion or spiritual path that isn't indicative of your soul level or conducive to your growth and theirs.

Rootman or Rootwoman can be from a single past lifetime that encompasses all the negative aspects you must now work on. Each of your shortcomings may be due to a single personality fixation. There are nine principal compulsions, each a form of denial: vengeance, indolence, vanity, cowardice, self-indulgence, resentment, flattery, melancholy, and stinginess. If you figure out the main fixations of Rootman or Rootwoman and solve them you will have that much more control over your own life. It is only when you deny the need for change and insist on the status quo that the Rootbeings pressure you to take action their way.

In unraveling their difficulties for them, you gain skills you need for self mastery. What is more, you'll gain the full gratitude of Rootman and Rootwoman and your life will have a special flow to it.

If your Rootman is vengeful and you come up against an unpleasant situation, he may press you to be nasty and try to get even. Rootwoman, on the other hand, may be compassionate and want you to see that you have been a victim of a victim.

Retaliation, she will tell you, is unproductive. As Learner, you deliberate over how most effectively to react to somebody who has caused you pain, wanting to push them into seeing themselves as they truly are, and into realizing what they have done to you.

Take another example. Say your Rootman is a rascal and stingy as well. When you ferret out these traits, you may find that there is something hidden underneath, qualities like freeloader and spendthrift.

Rootwoman may present a similar set of hard to solve conditions as a controller easily able to overpower Rootman who is shrunken and immobilized. Once Rootwoman is more balanced and easier to communicate with, Rootman may be attended to and may even express himself more freely. Working with them helps your partnerships, friendships, and love relations, as you too may have been overpowering others or inappropriately acquiescent.

Provided you effectively tame the harsher sides of your Rootwoman or Rootman, a chain reaction will occur in your life. Your whole viewpoint and way of expressing yourself may alter rapidly, affecting the matter and manner of your job, your friendships, and your family dealings.

Many people who sense the presence of their Rootbeings are afraid to communicate with them, fearing death, and so muddle painfully along through life. Very few realize Rootman and Rootwoman are internal and external at the same time. They are you, and they are separate. You will not be assigned another Rootman or Rootwoman regardless of how ill-suited you imagine they are for you. Death seldom occurs when you enlist cooperation from one or the other of your Rootbeings, for part of your Mission is to harmonize your Rootman, Rootwoman, and yourself. But fear of death is why the great majority of Learners leave unresolved, until the very end, a sliver or ribbon of their Mission.

The Opposite Sex   For a woman, every man in her life embodies one or more aspects of her Rootman. For a man, parts of his Rootwoman become accessible to him through getting to know various women as friends. Each friendship seems lacking to one degree or another as it satisfies only a fragment of your total Rootbeing picture. A woman may have only a few men friends who feed her intellectual side, but all of her relationships can contribute to her quest, bringing out the best in her.

Laurie, a successful artist in her late thirties, described her experience in nonsexual friendships with men as reflections of her own Rootman.

"One younger male friend's love body is missing. He is a man whose repressed loveability and lovingness are mirrors of my Rootman's same deprivation. An older male friend of mine has sunk into a lifestyle that limits joyousness. He is an artist hiding his talent. Except for an occasional publication, he restricts his money supply. This I also find in my Rootman. I used to have an artist friend who was rather similar, except he was also a binge alcoholic. The alcoholism did not match my Rootman's sobriety, so the friendship did not last."

If you are a heterosexual woman, your male partner represents prominent traits of your Rootman. When you dialogue with Rootman and modify some of his characteristics, your mate, the outward expression of your Rootman, also changes. Once you work out something your man doesn't want to let go of, he can turn away from you, sometimes ignoring you completely or forgetting anything you say to him. He may even leave you to protect that part of himself. As soon as you refuse to play with, or get caught by, the behaviors and fixations your lover treasures, he won't be able to exercise those aspects of his personality in a relationship with you.

It could be that your mate is willing to work out a defect in his character, but you do not want to face the adjustments that this will require of you. Consequently, you take on the role of the distancing partner. Sometimes you embark upon the role of devil's advocate, pointing out his incongruent speech and behavior that shows he doesn't want to find truth.

Rootman and Rootwoman are forbidden to intervene in the relationship between an established human couple, although they frequently do so at the initial meeting. Because anything can change at any time, a sort of tantric process develops between the partners that can cause one or both to grow rapidly.

When you have mastered the function that an opposite sex Rootbeing is supposed to teach you, your partner of the moment may become superfluous. If there is nothing more to learn together yet you choose to remain coupled, you may abandon each other due to an addiction to alcohol, drugs, work, sexploits, constant fighting and bickering, or by indifference, chronic illness, or death. In a bad relationship, people hinder each other's growth. But no matter how verbally and emotionally snarled the relationship, if the couple is growing the Cosmos views their relationship as lively and positive. Such a duo will eventually live in harmony. Around the twenty-fifth year of marriage, husband and wife often fall completely in love again and proceed to remain felicitous partners throughout the years ahead. From the outside it's difficult to judge whether a relationship is sour due to healthy fermentation or disintegrating in a way that will ultimately destroy one or both individuals.

What are the hurdles in a same sex Rootbeing relationship? In the choice of same sex friends you may find a mirror for something you do not express. One may be a weaver, like your Rootwoman, though your art form is to sing in a choir. Another friend may have a gentle voice, one you wish you had and know you could cultivate, but don't. Oftentimes you sort of merge with a friend and do not firmly keep your own identity. Commonly a friend is living out a value your Rootbeing holds dear, but you don't. For instance, you may have a Rootwoman who lived a simple life caring for her large extended family. You also have a family, but it's much smaller and you have a job outside the home. Your friend with the large family fulfills this desire for you. Are your longings to be at home, living an uncomplicated life, Rootwoman's or yours?

Rootman or Rootwoman have aspects that were triggered by people during your childhood, or occasionally later on. A person who is indelibly stamped in your memory may have served as an illustration of some positive or negative manifestation of your Rootbeing. A client told me her Rootwoman always felt like Billie Holiday, as she portrayed a character in a film. None of Holiday's other roles stimulated this same rapport in mannerisms and approach to life.

Multifaceted Rootbeings

A few rare individuals are bound up with a same sex multifaceted Rootbeing, and it's most unusual for a multifaceted Rootbeing to be the opposite sex of the Learner. A woman's are usually to be found in her Rootwoman and a man's in his Rootman. Seldom are there any exceptions. A multipersonality Rootbeing is much more complex to work with, as it represents three or more lifetimes of a single soul. The unfinished work of each lifetime vies for prominence and expression through the Learner, who may feel overwhelmed until he or she recognizes the many archetypes the Rootbeing is presenting.

A man whose main energy is funnelled through a multiple personality Rootwoman can have tremendous confusion in his life. Until he is able to make sufficient contact with her, he may feel he needs to have several lovers at once to compensate for his inability to play out everything he is with one woman.

The Learner, Rootwoman, and Rootman have sub-parts. Two sub-parts always present to one degree or another are:

Narcissus—the part that is vain and self-praising.

Wormmouth—the part that is destructively critical.

If you find your Rootbeings are either overly praising or denigrating toward you and your life, be aware they may not have full control over these tendencies. Paradoxically, if they do not, it's because you don't either. It is up to you to take the initiative to communicate with Rootman and Rootwoman more frequently to work on those parts of yourself. As these sub-parts are better understood by you, they'll be less unruly in your Rootbeings as well.

Recognizing Your Rootbeings   The costume or clothing your Rootman and Rootwoman appear in can be indicative of their previous life connection to you, or the main lifetime essence they are working on while attached to you. Normally the style of dress is a mirror. If you find yourself drawn to deep cut waistlines with bustles and floor-length dresses of the 1890s, and objects of that era also excite you, it may well be that your Rootwoman is from that period.

A jaunty hat set to one side might be one of your sartorial trademarks. When you see your Rootman attired in a similar manner, you discount it as your imagination. The hat may have magnetically called to you, due to the firm connection Rootman has to that head covering.

A specific hue may also belong to one of your Rootbeings. If it is one that is commonly out of vogue, like bronze or brilliant orange, you'll find yourself drawn to it nevertheless. When you habitually see your Rootwoman in mauve and silver, colors you mix readily when most of society ignores the combination, you can appreciate the subtle yet powerful influence she has in your life.

Consequently it would be better to be in active conscious communication with her, rather than feel propelled along or suffer internal conflicts. Blockages to your own success may be Rootman resisting when you are ready to forge ahead.

Rules for Meeting Your Rootbeings

A few rules for meeting your Rootbeings. Be polite. State your case simply. Make every attempt to get to know them.

Sit or lie in a comfortable position, covering yourself with a blanket if the temperature warrants. Breathe in and out, letting go of your daily cares. Announce your intention to contact the Rootbeing of the same gender. You may feel, see, smell, sense, or hear your Rootbeing, or you may have a combination of these phenomena. Talk to them as you would anyone you know but haven't seen in a long time. Remember, they're on your side, yet may not be pleased that you've been operating without their assistance. Negotiate without rancor.

Their assignment calls for communication once you initiate it. If they refuse to speak to you, it is permissible to chase them all over hill and dale until they do.

If you cannot elicit cooperation, send for the opposite sex Rootbeing and lay your request for concord on the table.

Usually it is best to allow Rootwoman and Rootman to mediate between themselves and receive or renegotiate the terms of their compromise and pledge of support. Remember to live up to any agreements you make with them to ensure continued rapport and unity. You are permitted to rework the terms of your contract at any time.

Students' Meetings and Dialogues with Their Rootbeings.

Some of the people who've participated in my workshops agreed to share the stories of their contacts with Rootbeings.

Here is the first meeting between Susan Fisher of Kern County, California, and her Rootman.

> *During our group meditation, Laeh guided us as to how to approach our Rootman. She said some of us may have denied our Rootman and banished him and his influence early in*

our lives. If this were the case, we might have trouble contacting him and we would need to apologize to him. She also told us he might appear as a young boy.

I called to Rootman and told him I was sorry if I had denied him in the past. I told him I wanted to see him and talk with him, and that I would like to work with him in the future. In a few minutes of calling to him, I felt an adult male presence (I never "saw" him).

I asked his name and he told me "Arthur." I asked if he had any information to tell me and he asked me why I had denied him his power. I apologized and said I had not meant to deny him (and in turn myself) of power or any other attribute he had to offer. He said he had been communicating with me all along and that I only rejected his power. I told him I would keep dialogue open to him, and hoped we could work together on developing our power.

Since that time I have made contact with Arthur several times and have also met my Rootwoman, Monique, with whom I was very familiar. We seem to be working harmoniously together and she seems aware of Arthur. I have told both of them and my life guide Roddy, that I would need all their help if I am to embark on the path of healer.

They were very supportive, but told me it's up to me to make the commitment.

Report of Gabrielle Gern, artist, illustrator and performer, Mösli, Switzerland:

I was looking out for Rootman and I called him: "Okay, where are you? Yoohoo!" No sign of Rootman anywhere. I saw Rootwoman instead. She was an Oriental woman and looked very much like a wife of mine from a past life. She was kneeling, afraid of disagreement, and always subservient, always yielding.

I cajoled: "Come on, Rootwoman, you've got other sides to yourself! Remember, in your time and culture, the grandmothers were the big bosses. And you have access to that old knowledge of power, so please express it. I could use it."

Rootwoman was really scared. Standing up for yourself and stating your opposition were taboo where she came from. You could be stoned to death for such behavior.

"Look," I said, "let's do this together. This is my lifetime—you won't get into trouble. It's going to be me and I

can handle it. Besides, this is a different time now and women have more to say. So will you please come out?"

Boy did she grow! She got to be really tall and straight, about twice my own size. She was almost a bit too big for my taste, but there was no way I could get her to be small again. Once the spring has come out of the watch, you can't put it back in again.

Now it was time to find Rootman. He was a pixie with pointed ears sliding at high speed up and down between fire and ice. He wore invisible boots that left no tracks. There was no way I could have caught him. Somehow he reminded me of Mickey Mouse as the sorcerer's apprentice.

It took Rootwoman's help to get him to stop and stand still. She was standing next to me radiating a lot of love and patience for Rootman. I had to think about what I really wanted from him. He was standing there, nervously shifting his weight from one foot to the other, saying: "Can I go now?"

"No, certainly not," I declared. "Look, I do like your playfulness, spontaneity, color, and shape, but I need your help in my life. I can't have you zooming around and being nowhere. So would you please grow up and put on shoes that leave footprints? Please take responsibility for your actions!" "Responsibility? Arghhh!" Rootman was just about to run away again. "Stop, don't go running off, Rootman, I need your help. Rootwoman can give insight and depth in my work and you can help me express it and give it shape. You can still play, you know—work playfully! And you could help me do theater. Wouldn't that be fun, to really play on a stage?"

That got him. Together with the loving support Rootwoman was giving while I was getting quite impatient, he came around. Rootman agreed to grow up. He grew until he was about twenty-five. He had a beautiful body. He was athletic, energetic, barefooted, dark haired, and very handsome.

I asked him to still keep the fire and ice experiences and not forget them, and I asked him for help in doing art and expressing myself. That seemed okay by him. There was a good feeling among the three of us, Rootwoman, Rootman, and me.

"Thank you for showing up. See you again sometime," I called after them as we parted.

Edwin R. Knight, of Ashland, Oregon, tells how he made contact with his Rootwoman.

My first encounter with my Rootwoman was not as easy as meeting my Rootman, although they occurred in the same meditation. When I asked her to appear to me visually, nothing happened. I began to apologize to Rootwoman for ignoring her all these years and asked her forgiveness. After about half an hour, I began to see a very vague form of a young teenager. I thanked her and continued to coax her to appear in a more solid form. I saw a teenager, just past puberty, with light hair. I asked her name, but she did not reply despite my entreaties. I thanked her for her efforts and told her I'd contact her soon.

Three months later my second attempt to communicate with Rootwoman became quite an adventure for me. I got no response, even with repeated cajoling. My reaction really surprised me. A kind of negative feeling overcame me. I tried to dismiss it as inconsequential, but in further attempts to contact Rootwoman this feeling blossomed into overwhelming anger. I finally gave up.

That night I had a very symbolic dream. In it I was deeply in love with a woman whom I ultimately got up the nerve to ask for a date. On the day of the date I got drunk with some guys who were really macho types. I failed to show up for the date, by choice, knowing the woman totally disapproved of this type of behavior. My date came to my house and told me she never wanted to see me again. I was distraught and started weeping uncontrollably. Then, in the dream, my mother and female dog died. These were all the significant females in my life who'd left me.

The next day I contemplated what the dream meant. It symbolized the time in my life when my Rootwoman left me because I refused to listen to her wise counsel. Next time I tried to contact Rootwoman I apologized for what I had done and with a little coaxing she came. She showed me her profile; her age seemed to be in the late twenties and she had dark hair. Her name is Shirnee.

People who resonate with the idea of having Rootbeings often ask similar questions. I've assembled some of the most frequent or thought provoking ones, some of which you may have formed as you read the material in this chapter.

A mature woman in a long-suffering relationship with her Rootman, finally asked him, "Rootman what is your main function in my life?"

He answered, "In your case, Rootman represents the will to live. As you may have noticed, it can be extremely shaky. I am from the same Source Self as you. This is unusual. That's how they link us up, not to have more than four bodies alive at once. Rootwoman is from our Oversoul. Many are attracted to our Rootwoman."

Another Learner asked whether affirmations take the place of these Rootbeing exercises? Her Rootwoman patiently answered, "All the finest affirmations, done endlessly, won't work if your underlying belief systems do not agree with the goals. Affirmations do not work well for souls who are in Mature, Old, or Volunteer mansions. They work best with Adult, Teenaged, Toddler, and Infant souls."

A thirty-year-old woman wondered why so many of her beliefs seemed to come from the family she grew up in. Her Rootman responded, "Families are only to reinforce what you already have to work on. That is why so often psychologists find different scripts for same sex siblings within the same family. A family can successfully impart four or five different scripts to various offspring. The Rootwoman and the Rootman each espouse portions of the parental cosmology."

Identifying Your
Rootbeings' Characteristics

Assessing the qualities your Rootbeings possess is an important part of having stable, healthy interchanges with them. If you find out something you've assumed about Rootman or Rootwoman is untrue, instead of bending the truth to fit your fiction update the list and see if you have a better concept of your own mode of operation.

Once you know your Rootman and Rootwoman fairly well, you can figure out their characteristics by listing them. Take care not to assign only negative traits to your Rootman if you are female, and to the Rootwoman if you are a male. This is a frequent misconception in the early stages of relating to the Rootbeings. Negative traits are easier to spot than positive ones.

The list below is offered solely as an example. You may have different information about your Rootbeings, and your inventory may contain many phrases and characteristics that do not appear on this one.

ATTRIBUTES OF THE ROOTBEINGS

Detriments		**Strong Points**	
	Rootman		
1	Fear of being in the spotlight	1	Good-hearted, adventurous
2	Spending, not saving for the future	2	Helpful
3	A staccato pattern of working	3	Doesn't eat when upset
4	Sloppy non-existent record keeping	4	Lies back and savors life
5	Cuts off sexual pleasure and excitement	5	Gentle and sensitive
6	Vengeful when wronged	6	Analytical
7	Judgmental and overly emotional	7	Enthusiastic about projects, energetic tireless worker
	Rootwoman		
1	Overworks herself, pushes unrelentingly	1	Well loved and appreciated
2	Eats when upset	2	Warm and caring. Earthy, insightful, magnanimous
3	Never has time to enjoy life	3	Lays down a good foundation for every project
4	Finished product often has loose ends to it	4	Willing to look at all sides of any situation Fairness, tolerance
5	Overly sensitive, solicitous of others, ignores own needs	5	Interested in everything. Zest for living.
		6	Tidy, orderly.

The Rootman of a close friend of mine appears to him as a full bodied and muscular woodsman with an axe. My friend says, "He looks like more than he is, not too worldly wise, yet good-natured. Knows the woods and his job. Rootwoman looks like a Chinese porcelain blonde. Fragile, but when she falls, doesn't break. Stands with both feet on the ground. Into everything, wise, knowledgeable. She's a woman who takes care of the man."

His wife, who is the very image of his Rootwoman, has been giving him more opportunities to stand on his own two feet by providing less wifely or motherly care. Originally he was angry at his wife and wanted to separate, since his Rootman felt inadequate to the task. As he comes to see himself as fully capable, he accepts his wife's new role.

Frequently I work with the Rootman and/or Rootwoman of clients to aid them in resolving long-standing issues. Certain compulsions show up clearly in image and behavior of the same sex Rootbeings.

Marissa, a lovely looking thirty-eight-year-old woman, had been the live-in lover to a series of older men since shortly after she left home as a college freshman. She had dropped out to live with her first partner, an actor's agent with a splendid house in Malibu. She had met famous people and traveled extensively with this man. Their union lasted for seven years.

Her next liaison was with a highly successful playwright who owned a beautiful home on the North Coast. She entertained an assortment of Hollywood and New York elite, and was a charming companion to her lover. Her life revolved around his need for quiet and privacy, so she amused the endless trail of visitors he invited. She was not aware that these people were not her friends until she and her lover ended their eight-year relationship.

Marissa's next live-in, a jazz musician of some renown, fell into a cesspool of drug abuse forcing her to leave him after only three years. At that time they were living on a charming island off the coast of Canada. Unfortunately for Marissa, she'd been in dreamland, living well, without making provisions for the day she might be alone, no longer a beautiful, naive young thing a man could mold in his own image. She was ageing, which frightened her. She was devastated, unable to care for herself. Other women on the island insisted that she see me.

The woman I met was fragile, nervous about her future. Marissa had no education, no work history, no children, and no money. She had been the perfect mate, without any benefits an ex-wife might be entitled to.

I saw that her belief in her own weakness was firmly ingrained. I carefully explained the principles behind Rootman and Rootwoman and had her go into a mild trance to contact her Rootman. She screamed in agony when she saw that her Rootman was "a jive-turkey, in a powder blue suit." Her rejection of that image was so strong that I immediately had her send for her Rootwoman. Up came not a child, not a pubescent girl, not a woman, but Tinkerbell, the fairy from the story of Peter Pan.

She was astonished. I was horrified. Her magical, yet infantile Rootwoman's Disneyesque personality didn't allow Marissa to take decisive, productive action. Tinkerbell illustrated her estrangement from womanhood and her unrealistic dependencies. Slowly and patiently we worked together until her Rootwoman's more human characteristics surfaced. The figure evolved as a teenaged girl, and then as a young woman, while Marissa was communicating her emotional turmoil and desire to center herself. The Rootwoman became more forceful as she emerged. In the introductory interview, Marissa's Rootwoman urged her to attend the local junior college to learn a trade.

She took the advice of her Rootwoman, but during the year that followed Marissa, accustomed to a grand lifestyle, was suffering. She was broke. Near her goal, grappling with what it would mean to work for a woman's salary in industry, she thought about living with yet another man.

To this day when I meet women in their late thirties to midforties who've lived a similar lifestyle, I remember Tinkerbell.

Some people have no strength in either their male or female selves. They function without balance, frequently ill or addicted to substances. Willis, a binge drinker, who had numerous life-threatening health problems, achieved some measure of maturity through contact with his Rootman and Rootwoman. A multi-talented twenty-six-year-old diabetic male, with a seriously enlarged heart, Willis had been seeing me irregularly for his chronic health condition. Oftentimes he came for a quick fix, only to return to his self-destructive lifestyle as soon as possible. He disliked having to take care of his health, and resented being burdened by his ailments.

He greedily absorbed the healings, but refused to look for insight into the underlying nature of his illnesses. One evening all seemed hopeless. Unless he could reintegrate his beliefs about himself, he would languish. I suggested the Rootwoman/ Rootman technique. He halfway decided to go along with it.

Willis' resistance was strong, his breath labored and erratic. He required some relaxation and breathing exercises to enable him to visualize his Rootwoman. He must have known her in the layers of his subconscious, for he was quite fearful of encountering her. Despite his resistance, he visualized a black haired vampire, attired in a slinky floor length black dress and wearing violent red polish on her excessively long fingernails. Even in a relatively deep trance, his terror of her was obvious. He sweated and made short jerking movements with his hands and feet.

By my consistently encouraging him to speak, he found his voice which came in short raspy gasps, unlike his normal resonant tones. He said, "Rootwoman is in the shadows, a darker place. She has a charming smile and a gleam in her exotic eyes. She is wearing large silver earrings." He further described her as "fiery, energetic, mysterious, strong inside, creative, and temperamental. She loves deeply, has a capacity for hard work." As soon as he said this, Willis' fear vanished and his voice became more stable. "Her eyes are gold, she sees very far. She comes from the stars." Rootwoman confirmed his description of her. She wants a place to surround herself with her things, and a base of power—a dwelling with a hearth, lots of pillows, cushions, and quiet. Willis spoke in his own voice saying, "She can be very cruel, becoming a woman who draws blood with her fingernails while making love. She's sorry about it and doesn't want to do that anymore. She is afraid of getting old."

At that instant, he realized that all his diseases might cause his death at an early age and then Rootwoman would never have to grow old. He thanked her for coming and sharing her knowledge with him. Then, he began to renegotiate the terms of his life with her.

His Rootwoman informed him that he was suffering from shame. His task was to get over it by hard work, helping people. He had to learn to love, and to teach others to love one another. He also had to write and talk. My client disclosed his secret hope to become a writer. He'd done little to progress along those lines, although he had considerable talent. The healing ended with my instructions for him to write his feelings and thoughts down until we could meet the following week.

By the next week he had recovered remarkably. His heart had shrunk in size by a third. He'd also had an office visit with his doctor who, seeing his unexpected improvement, recommended an experimental reduction in his insulin.

Enthusiastically, Willis called for his Rootwoman. She no longer seemed threatening. Still dressed in black, her appearance was softer, stronger, firmer, and friendlier towards him. She told Willis it was his job to pave the way for other people, as his Mission in life. He accepted that quite readily, and thanked her for her help during the previous week.

At that point, without request, Rootman surfaced. "My Rootman is in the light, strangely boney, frail, fragile, with partially contorted muscles. He seems to feel a great deal of pain, but has courage. He likes to drink beer. Rootman is lonesome; there aren't many interesting people where he is, yet he's got some work, drawing things in patterns, to do there. Rootman is comforted because he knows there are other souls and beings elsewhere who are comrades. The work he does has its own hazards. He gets his thumbs smashed sometimes (a reference to the spiritual digit on the hand).

"He likes Rootwoman and they get along, but they don't meet often to see how they can cooperate better. He likes the sun and the ocean. He's got a sense of what it is to be human, and given a chance he'll snivel up a storm. Talking to me is enjoyable and he says we should do it more often. It gives him a chance to come in and warm his cold, sore hands on Rootwoman's hearth. My Rootman is afraid of women and doesn't know how to go about getting close. He feels good about himself, but he doesn't feel debonair around women."

As he came out of the encounter, Willis asked if his difficulties with women were due in part to his Rootman's unpolished manner and lack of confidence. We explored that possibility. Over the next few months Willis began to participate in classes, join in community events, and abstain from drinking. The women he met liked talking to him. He became better at being real with his opinions and feelings. All the while his insulin intake for diabetes shrank and his heart returned to a normal size. He's still working on himself, dialoguing with his Rootbeings, slowly changing into the person he'd rather be.

Barbara, a client in her late thirties, had learned to work on her own with her Rootbeings. She reported her self-inspired communication with her Rootman and its reflection in her current boyfriend. "My Rootwoman is enraged at my Rootman for withholding on us. She throws Rootman out, shuts the door, and he works like a dog to appease her. He even brings home more money to please her. James (Barbara's lover) has become more cooperative and financially generous as I've worked on this process the past few months.

"Since Rootwoman is so angry, I called up my Rootman. 'Have I found how to work in tandem,' I asked my Rootman, 'or just a way to avoid arguments? Is my lover's monetary imbalance a reflection of your/our low expectations, or is it his own?' I confronted him with a more serious accusation. 'Rootman, do you allow me to make headway on the ladder of success, as we are now, and then in terror jump off leaving me stranded?'

"James came over as Rootman and I were still examining these concepts. He actually came to show me how my changing male beliefs reflect in him and how adaptable he's willing to be, to stay with me. He wanted to meditate together, something I'd done with a former sweetheart and had long desired we do.

"James then offered to take me out to dinner, but stood around eating up a half bowl of fruit I'd bought for my sons. This irritated me. To assuage me, he took me out for dessert, buying himself one twice as large as he bought for me. I saw his lack of generosity. He'd given me one thing I wanted, but he wouldn't give me an equal share when it came to spending money. The money is my self-worth issue. Am I worth it? His behavior is his own, yet I've still got to negotiate with that part of Rootman. If Rootman weren't miserly and stingy I would not attract selfish men.

"I really like James, aside from some of these issues. I'm also afraid to be alone," Barbara truthfully related. "Therefore, I do not go in deep enough with my Rootman to resolve the monetary imbalance in my life, and in that way I am stingy with myself. If Rootman and I come to a solution, it may destroy James' attraction to me. In other words, I am using my conflicts in this relationship to keep myself from integrating my own deep needs as expressed by Rootman and Rootwoman's opposition."

A major part of Barbara's continued progress lodged in her ability to solve her own paradox. I mainly listened. Then I suggested that she call upon her Rootman while I served as her witness. She could relate their interchange without any interference from me.

Readily, Rootman arrived. "I am prepared for your success at this time," he offered. "My objection to making money is that Rootwoman wants us to keep it for ourselves. If she agrees to share it and live on less than the full amount you earn, I am fully prepared to allow you unlimited earnings. It's the selfish personal aggrandizement and consumerism I object to."

Barbara called for her Rootwoman, asking Rootman to step aside and permit her to do all the negotiating. Rootwoman claimed she'd never known Rootman's opposition was based on her own feelings about shared community resources and helping others. She'd been pushing Barbara to get ahead precisely to implement these values. Barbara let out a grunt of relief and asked Rootman and Rootwoman to talk it over with each other to insure their underlying beliefs and values were actually clear. "I am not up for another false start," she announced.

After some five minutes, Rootwoman and Rootman announced they were in agreement. Barbara seemed pleased and then remarked that it would most likely end her alliance with James. She knew she'd have to sacrifice it in order to stay true to herself.

7

Birth

A baby is God's opinion that life should go on. Never will come a time when the most marvelous recent invention is as marvelous as an newborn baby.
Carl Sandburg

One of the most magical transformations that occurs in human life has happened to every one of you. Very likely you will be a major player in a few of these transformations during your lifetime. The miracle of birth is still a mystery, in spite of all the scientific inquiry that has probed into the most minute details of sperm and egg maturation, fertilization, cell division, in utero development, and birth.

Doctors are unsure of the emotional, intuitive, and intellectual capacity of the unborn. Yet many a mother will tell you she heard her baby crying in her womb, patted her belly to comfort her child, and the fetus was calmed. Women also claim their babies like one special song, or can be felt moving in rhythm with the beat of what she's listening to. Babies have inadvertently been heard to cry in utero by health professionals listening for the fetal heartbeat.

Adults under hypnosis recall things that happened in their families before they were born. Afterward, they seek confirmation and their folks are shocked that they know. "How could you know that? It was before you were born," was the response of one mother to her daughter's exact description of the house her grandparents moved out of seven weeks before she was born.

Fetal memory is active from the fifth month of gestation to birth. We can be fairly sure that once the mother has felt life, the little one's emotional, psychic, and intellectual faculties are active. The unborn have telepathic skills far more advanced than an adult.

Once in a great while a mother-to-be will not feel life for a few days, and then feel that the fetus isn't the baby she's been carrying. She is convinced the personality or the vibration aren't the same. That is true. The healthy body that is developing must be offered to any soul who wants it before the Source Self who created it can abandon it. Usually another soul who planned to be a future child of these parents takes over the body, and in doing so forfeits the right to choose their gender, physical dimensions, and other features that could be crucial to their earthly Mission. Sometimes the mother goes through a mourning period, missing the soul that has been with her since conception. Her baby will be born inhabiting the same physical body she's been carrying all along. Hopefully she will love it as much as she loved the soul who had a change of heart.

CHOOSING A LIFETIME

Being born is a type of death. It is an absence for a set number of years from full activity within the spirit realm. The process of selecting a lifetime is covered in several earlier chapters of this book. If you are unclear return to "Forty-nine Steps: the Source Self's Journey," "Realms of Existence," and "The Path."

There are some circumstances of birth that might insure you will be appreciated and well cared for: being born as the much wanted daughter after two or more sons have already arrived, or being born to a couple who've tried for many years to conceive a child. Choose at least one parent whose soul attachment to you is so firm that whatever you do in life you have their unwavering loyalty. Consign yourself to a family that has a karmic tie with your life's work, who will train you and point you in the right direction.

Death, birth, and conception are different manifestations of the same energetic force. Without conscious death there cannot be conscious conception. What really is consciousness in these moments? It cannot be all the trappings that innovative people claim. All too often a home birth or death is held as part of the illusion of a spiritual passage, while all around the scene chaos and emotionalism transpire. Home births have been known to occur with Dad watching the big football game on TV until the show in the other room really gets going. To have a truly conscious birth, you must have faith in the guardians of birth. It means you are cognizant of the birth occurring on many levels of consciousness, and in several realms at once. As you are greeting your newborn, their old friends are bidding them farewell and wishing them well.

The circumstances of birth almost always originate in the memories or injuries contained in previous incarnations. Breech babies may have had severe head injuries, or undergone surgical brain procedures in another lifetime and therefore are reticent to present their vulnerable head to the molding pressure of a vertex (head down) birth. This is especially true for the offspring of a primipara mother.

Physicians, unsure of their skills or lacking knowledge in vaginal delivery of breech babies altogether, perform Caesarean sections wantonly, depriving the infant of a normal entry into the world. Far too many doctors perform C-sections on the slightest provocation to increase their income. Although some say babies choose to be Caesarean born, more likely they just acquiesce, as it is a condition of the times to have the birth process as unnatural as possible. Due to the laws against midwifery and the vise-grip of fear and legal restrictions the medical authorities have put on childbirth, a soul wanting to be born in our society usually takes it as a package deal. This is not so in other Western countries where babies with healthy mothers are born at home with a midwife in attendance.

Exceptionally helpful folk wisdom from the Pomo Indians concerning childbearing goes as follows:

- If a mother is diagnosed as carrying a breech baby she should switch sides of the bed for sleeping. Sleep on the opposite side to disturb the in utero pattern, and your baby will roll from bottom down to head down to continue sleeping in the same position. The vast majority of unborn infants subjected to this treatment will, within three weeks, automatically turn themselves to the head down position. Do not change your pillow from head to foot, just left to right or vice versa.

  For nearly twenty years women who are in this predicament have called me. If they're between six and two weeks away from delivery, the Pomo method works almost every single time.

- A woman who cannot make a basket, cannot make a baby. The western equivalent is the old adage, "If a woman can't bake a cake from scratch, she can't carry a child to term." A pregnant woman is not permitted to make a basket, either, because she might, in the process of completing the circle, trap the baby inside herself. Or if she doesn't finish it, the child won't be born. This last statement mirrors an old English superstition about unbraiding the mother's hair when she's in labor so that the baby will be free to come out.

Katsi Cook, an Akwesasne, the granddaughter and niece of traditional Native American midwives, wrote of her clan's wisdom in *Daybreak*, a periodical, Autumn 1988: "Margaret Cook Narcissian, my grandmother's niece, claims that my grandmother knew that when there's a birthing going on the spirits come to give the baby gifts. All of traditional Indian ways, whether Iroquois, Pomo, or Sioux, recognize that these spirits are not always human spirits of our relatives, but that they may also be animal spirits, or the spirits of the place where you are, of where the birthing is taking place."

Let this be a word of cautionary advice. The spirits around hospitals may be horribly unhappy, since so many die lingering, tortured deaths in those buildings. Women and their families ought to have separate lying-in hospices as there once were in this country. Birth rooms adjacent to, but not in, hospitals are a good alternative. Better yet would be more capable, certified midwives, for safe home deliveries.

Shortly after birth, within the first five days, the newborn is an open book. You can instantly see whether a child is an enlightened being or a factor for chaos in the world. Parents who see the latter in their offspring must be extra careful in guiding their child, setting realistic limits and helping the child with the development of compassion. Parents whose babies fall within more ordinary potential often have an inkling at this point that tiny Sophia will be a wise woman, or baby Joseph will work with the land. By the end of the first week, babies mask themselves. The original look they wore won't be available again for five or six months, when it briefly reappears to let you know, if you already didn't, what is in store for you.

Savants have claimed that the time of year a person dies is the season or month that they will be reborn. I have witnessed this, and none the less, do not subscribe to it as an inviolate rule.

Labor and Birthtime   Having chosen a family, the soul has to decide upon the correct time to be born. Timing is crucial to the success or failure of the lifetime.

If a child is induced and is thereby born on the wrong day or at the wrong time, it will have an incompatible birth horoscope. The child will have the impetus to do the tasks and follow her path, yet lack the right astrological construction that would aid and compel her.

The ones who know their Mission is of the utmost importance will seek it anyway. The rest will choose to live the easier life, sacrificing the work of this lifetime to the unplanned for ascendant, moon, or planet their pre-planned Caesarean birth or hurried up labor caused them to bear. They join the vast majority, relinquishing their life's Mission for the material world and a few of the Moon spiral's rewards. Those who do the work to the best of their ability have a much harder lifetime and must call forth whatever natural skills they may have acquired during prior incarnations.

As an illustration, let's examine the trait of diplomacy as if it were your assignment. Whatever you have gained in the way of mastering the principles of diplomacy while working your way through previous rungs of the ladder, through the Mansions you've ascended, stays with you. Unfortunately, this mastery is not as available to you as it would be had you been born under the ascendant that would produce the quality either by sign or polarity. The further along you are in your journey through the Mansions, the easier it is for your soul, regardless of the unintended natal horoscope, to recognize the crucial issues and adjustments that must be made.

Each of the the astrological signs has a hallmark. Librans tend to be natural diplomats, highly skilled at convincing you that their ideas and desires are yours. Aries, the polar opposite, can be blunt and cutting, yet when operating out of phase have access to Libra's ability with soft-spoken ways and words. Taurus has a honey-dipped voice with mellow beautiful speaking tones. A baby who is supposed to be born with Libra rising can be delayed several hours if the drugs the mother was given during labor retard its progress by putting her to sleep or relaxing the uterine muscles. Instead the infant is born with Sagittarius rising, which is quick of speech, like Libra, but has no natural aptitude for discretion. So that child has an additional task, learning to think before he speaks, which will slow down his response time until measuring his words wisely becomes natural to him. If this was a condition of your birth, you will have to exercise caution in situations where none is demanded, so that the skill is intact, available when you need it.

Being born under an incompatible or incorrect sign, whether it's your ascendant, Mercury, Venus, moon, Sun, or Mars, lets you in for personal setbacks that aren't part of your master plan. Birth at an earlier or later degree of the sun, or any other planet, will interfere less with your pre-planned developmental projects than to have a sign that is the antithesis of your work.

Sometimes a child will begin labor before the planned C-section date. It is likely to have chosen the date, and perhaps even the exact hour for its birth, as more compatible for its path than the one the doctor has decided upon. Far too many C-sections are done by appointment at the doctor's convenience. An emergency C-section can be done without harm to the infant's Mission, but only real emergencies qualify, like audible fetal distress. Monitoring equipment, used indiscriminately in hospital births, interferes with the natural birthing rhythms. In and of itself, the machinery with its unfamiliar vibrations causes the baby to go into stress reactions. These tools are hypnotic for the attendant, and useful for a doctor who wants to make big bucks from obstetrics. The safest and cosmically most accurate delivery is still a natural home birth with a well trained midwife. Birth is a normal process, not an illness.

When you are born under the wrong rising sign there is a tendency to get the weaknesses rather than the strengths of the out-of-synch astrological sign. Birth at the wrong time frequently means one is a strong contender at best, never quite a winner in life. The ones who know this, and cannot face the uphill struggle, settle upon worldly success and have a fun life rather than swim against the tide. Hindu and Buddhist astrologers, and court astrologers in many ancient cultures, ascertained the most auspicious birth time for heirs to the throne and other important personages. The monks, swamis, or priests would then pray for the birth to go well, and for the child to be born at the correct time.

What about midwives in villages and other places where babies are born at home? If they give the mother an herb to speed her birth isn't that an interference? Herbs are natural substances and their commands can easily be overridden. The mother will feel sickened by substances taken orally that she and her baby ought not to have. If she has an unusually strong reaction to the herbal mixture, a wise midwife will back off and allow her the space necessary for the baby to come at its own best time.

If the midwife is one who breaks the bag of waters to accelerate labor, it still allows the baby to come in its own time. Some mothers will deliver rapidly once the waters break. Others will take a few hours irrespective of the fact that the labor is progressing more rapidly than before. In some cases there will be little change.

How does a baby knows when it should be born?

Each of us has a body clock that is regulated on a 24 hour basis by the pineal gland. Chinese medicine assigns a different two hour stretch per day to the functioning of every one of the glands and organs. These glands and organs are the focus of the body during that timespan. Pituitary hormone is released at 5 AM, the pineal gland secretes its hormones at 6 AM, and thyroxin is emitted from the thyroid at 8 AM. The large intestine is stimulated from 5–7 AM and the kidneys from 5–7 PM. If you travel by jet, you upset your body's inner clock. The light entering the body will be altered and, depending upon how quickly you adapt, you'll have jet lag for a day or more. A full illustration appears in Chapter 14.

The fetus, in utero, gets its organs stimulated at the same rate. He or she already knows that it will be born at 11:34 AM and calculates the onset of labor so that birth can occur then. Every baby knows from its mother's patterns whether it will have to begin labor far in advance, or close to the time it needs to be born. If for some reason in a natural labor the time is missed, the contractions may stop or the mother may be in labor for an additional twenty-four hours before delivery.

Expectant parents should know that regardless of whether the waters have burst twenty-four hours or more prior, as long as no one inserts a hand, gloved or otherwise, into the mother's vagina before labor begins there is no danger of infection. The birth attendant just has to check for the heart tones, and to hear that the umbilical cord is still feeding the baby vital nutrients. Disturbances in the heartbeat and placental secol can indicate genuine fetal distress.

Infertility There are indications in a woman's astrological chart that inhibit conception. Women with relative infertility will conceive during certain astrologically favorable times. Transits of Pluto by opposition, conjunction or square to your natal Mars are far too dangerous a time to conceive. The resulting infant is likely to be defective.

Endocrine disorders, like hypothyroidism, can cause successive miscarriages or obstruct conception altogether. If you know these diseases run in your family it is wise to bear children early in life, before twenty-five years of age. Natural fertility is highest in those years, and your glandular function is more likely to permit a pregnancy to go to term.

A sure-fire indication for thyroid disorders is to have a prominent planet in Taurus in your natal chart. If your moon or ascendant are in Taurus, make babies while youth is on your side. Another factor for hormonal problems occurs when your moon is opposite or square to Saturn in your horoscope. Venus square to Uranus or Saturn is another combination that might potentially lead to hormonal imbalances. Venus in Capricorn frequently is a factor for sterility.

The fifth house in your natal chart gives a good indication of your potential childbearing and childrearing difficulties. Your fifth house cusp and your fifth house reveal a great deal about your childbearing opportunities. It is the house of children and lovers. A barren sign on the cusp shows difficulty conceiving, although planets in that house, especially if in another constellation, can offset that factor. Neptune in that house indicates ease adopting children or that you will be a step-parent. Jupiter shows good fertility. The offspring born to a woman with Venus in the fifth house are usually all girls. It also means you're exceptionally fertile.

Saturn in the fifth house often denies you children, or the children may be lost (as in a custody battle) to the father, or through illness. Uranus in the same house can equal loss of the first child by separation or an extraordinary, sudden event. Uranus retrograde in the mother's chart can bring about a dangerous delivery; however if it is well aspected by another planet or by a transiting planet at the time of the baby's birth, problems are unlikely. A fifth house moon means you can bear many, many children, but the sun in this location shows your family will be either small or extremely large. Mars in the fifth house means that all your children will be healthy. It also portends a difficult and dangerous childbirth. Yet, if your child is conceived under a good set of transits, all danger will be minimal.

Mars in whatever house it occurs is the indicator for the delivery of children. Generally if your Mars is in a fire or air sign you will have quick childbirths. The Martian fire signs Sagittarius, Aries, and Leo are known for uncomplicated deliveries. Mars is the father's energy for the birth; it indicates the type of man you have attracted to father your child. Will he be out playing golf or there in a loving supportive way? Is he going to be filled with fears or allaying yours?

Transiting Pluto square natal Pluto usually seals shut a woman's fertility at approximately forty-three years of age. It's a premenopausal condition for healthy well-fed women, more cosmic in origin than physiological.

The solution to your infertility or problems in pregnancy can be astrological. Your best option is to consult an experienced astrologer well versed in medical astrology.

An infertile woman may conceive in group sex because the volume of sperm can better wear down the thick shell of her egg. A heavy mucousy shell needs a high sperm count for fertility. That is why some infertile women conceive after leaving their lower sperm count spouse. The man with a low sperm count may successfully father children with a woman whose ovaries manufacture a thinner egg wall.

A woman who ovulates infrequently will conceive with a man whose sperm count is high and whose sperm are active.

Fertility drugs release more eggs, and the ones that come out are thinner shelled because the body cannot produce the thicker mucous around so many eggs.

You may be one of those women who is so afraid of the commitment a new child places in your life that your vaginal environment is very acidic, making it impossible for the sperm to survive. Your body fluids are regulated by your mind. It's important that the regulation be consciously redone to make it favorable for fertilization, if you want to become pregnant. In other words, whether the vaginal fluid is overly alkaline or acidic, the woman has an effective natural spermacide.

Bringing Down a Soul You may have trouble becoming pregnant because you have no soul who specifically wants to be with you. You may appear inhospitable to a being who would otherwise choose you for a mother.

Envision a soul descending from outside of your body, along a shaft of golden light. Picture it coming through your aura, and direct its entry into your body just five centimeters below your belly button. Lift your left arm up to guide the descending being toward your second chakra, where it can successfully pierce your auric field and enter (see illustration on page 113).

If your lover is willing, he can stand with you and together you can invite an incarnating soul to become your child. Whenever more than one person's energy is dedicated to achieving something, more power is focused. A couple have more than the two of them backing up a pregnancy, they also have help from the guardian of their relationship. The soul is only looking for a way into the world. Since millions of beings are waiting to be born, ask for one whose life plans will be compatible with yours. Genetic lineage does not guarantee that the child will be of your own spiritual bent. After you call down a soul, make love slowly and tenderly. The energy with which you call your child sets the stage for your relationship. The lovemaking is part of that same ceremonial attitude. Consciously creating a child together is a sacrament.

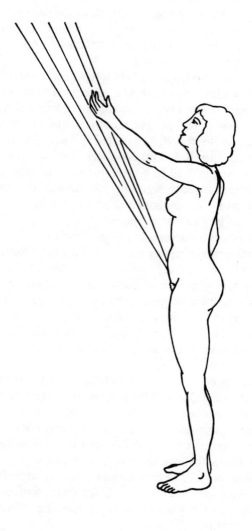

You might require an experienced assistant if you aren't used to operating in total trust and faith in the beneficence and miracles of the Universe. Anxiety is a real killer of energy. The frustration of waiting for a pregnancy that doesn't occur sets up its own barriers to success. The younger you are, the greater your chances for becoming pregnant. Many women have had a first baby, yet aren't able to conceive another viable infant. This is called secondary infertility. It is just as painful, except that you are already a parent.

If you have read this section to overcome infertility, my heart goes out to you. I wish you success. I write this section from long experience both personal and professional. I spent my nineteenth year pregnant, but no other child could make it to term except my firstborn. My horoscope has every single planet and aspect for infertility and consistent miscarriage. A long-planned pregnancy had to be terminated due to excessive X-rays following a serious auto accident. Neptune in the fifth house (adoption) gave me the chance to parent again.

It cannot be said often enough:
The best ally for a successful pregnancy is youth.

No matter your age or financial condition, there is no perfect time to have a baby. Have one when the opportunity arises. Every baby brings their own luck. Age in parenting is not necessarily wisdom, it's a job you learn by doing. The wisdom older parents are credited with is from their hands-on expertise. Subsequent children are generally easier to rear than the firstborn. First time parents of any age are only learners.

Gender Selection   The Talmud states "If the man emits seed first, the offspring will be a girl; if the woman emits first, the offspring will be a boy." This dovetails with an old wives tale about infertility that posits that if an infertile woman achieves an orgasm conception is assured, but if she doesn't she will remain barren.

The Chinese believe the conception of male offspring is associated with the Chi of the woman being greater than that of the man when sons are conceived. A female birth results from the father's vital force being stronger than the mother's at the time of conception.

In Vitro Fertilizations   The reason in vitro fertilizations seldom work (most clinics have a only 3–14 live births per

100 procedures), is that the mother or father has to call down a soul while the fertilized eggs are being inserted. This is a rather natural skill that occurs without your conscious mind being aware of it during, or immediately following, love making. Either parent can draw down a soul looking for a family to be born into.

In vitro fertilized eggs are inserted into the uterus through a tube placed in the mother's surgically opened navel area. The procedure itself causes pain to the subconscious, and the surgery is far too uncomfortable for most souls to brave the barrier the mother sets up to further intrusion around her navel. Unless a soul desires the early experience in a test-tube as part of its destiny, it will not voluntarily brave the pain in the auric field.

Artificial Insemination   Artificial insemination is a solution that has brought fertility to many families. The long sought after baby is born to the biological mother. Since the genetic code that contains the section of the unbreakable gene chain is passed by mother to child, the family lineage is intact.

Farm animals, artificially inseminated, have shown many difficulties in gestation, delivery, and the energy of the offspring. The first generation is normal, although it's posited that they may have a slightly reduced vitality over animals impregnated via intercourse. The second generation fertilized via the same method has difficulty delivering, and the third often "will not breed up."

What this means for the continued vital force of a human family line isn't possible to determine at this time. The fault may be that the sperm is frozen, losing some of its vital force. Another factor is that the father's excitement and spiritual transmission are missing at conception.

Unwanted Pregnancy   In an unwanted pregnancy someone unwittingly called a soul and didn't know how to send it back. The mother-to-be seldom knows how to ask an Essence Being (Source Self) to depart. You can reverse the process by moving the soul from the uterus upward along the shaft of light. If this makes you feel weakened or dizzy, pull the energy back in as shown in the illustration on page 116. Crouch down or assume a squatting position. Using your right hand, remove the Source Self guiding it along the beam of light surging through your body. Pull it downward into the earth. This is a miniature birth experience for the implanted Essence Being. Aid in doing so can be obtained by communicating with your own Higher Self for permission to dismiss the unwanted fetus. The method described here works in the first eleven to twelve weeks of pregnancy when the Witness has not yet entered the conceptus.

CAUTION: Only the mother can do this. The father, relatives and friends, however well meaning, can do irreparable harm to the pregnant woman and to themselves. Anyone besides the mother could replace their own Source Self with the one she is carrying and never be the same person again. They might also discharge their personality in the process.

Souls have been coming to the earth through unwed mothers forever. There's no reason why they should respect a rule common to most earthly societies, when its violation most often allows them to live. Up until the second half of this century, these infants were given away by their mothers. Single motherhood is no longer an issue. Due to the rise in the divorce rate, one-parent families are accepted. Souls know they stand a good chance of being raised by their biological mother.

If you are the mom and truly believe you will be able to have children at a later date, promise the soul that it can come back when your life is better prepared for good parenting. Promise nothing you cannot fullfil. The soul will understand your predicament, although it doesn't quite see it from an earthbound point of view.

Dr. Gladys T. McGarey, a holistic physician who specializes in home births, tells this story in her book *Born to Live*. Dr. McGarey was "torn between the two warring factions," concerning abortions until one of her patients told her the following story.

"This mother had a four-year-old daughter whom she would take out to lunch occasionally. They were talking about this thing and that and the child would shift from one subject to another when Dorothy (the child) suddenly said, 'Last time when I was four inches long and in your tummy, Daddy wasn't ready to marry you yet, so I went away. But then, I came back.' Her eyes lost that faraway look and she was chatting again about four-year-old matters.

"Mother was silent. No one but her husband, the doctor, and she knew this, but she had become pregnant about two years before she and her husband were ready to get married. When she was four months pregnant, she decided to have an abortion."

Abortion   Beliefs about abortion vary from culture to culture. Religion in the western countries no longer holds an iron grip over morality, foibles, and human frailties. Muslim women routinely have abortions. The Chinese government supports and encourages abortion. The Bible is singularly silent on the question of abortion. Always it's been the province of wise women who knew what plants induced miscarriages to aid other women in their community. Ecbolics, herbs which produce abortion, have been in use since antiquity. These herbs are also known as abortifacients. You can find many listed in herbal books and botanicals.

Hanna Kroeger, a nationally famous herbalist from Boulder, Colorado, lists specific herbs, used for centuries, to remedy late menses, in her 1979 edition of *Instant Herbal Locator*. "To promote menstrual flow, Mugwort tea; scanty period, Thyme tea; menstrual trouble, no flow, Yarrow tea two cups per day." Peyote, in any form, is well-known to cause uterine contractions forceful enough to expel a fetus. Pregnant women are customarily forbidden to take part in peyote rituals, no matter what trimester they are in.

At the time of an early abortion, prior to fourteen weeks gestation, only one part of the soul's quadrinity is present, the Essence or Source Self. When it's rejected by the impregnated woman, it either finds another body or waits until a more opportune time for the woman who rejected it. She can agree to undertake this Essence Being in another lifetime, or later on in this life. A woman may refuse to continue carrying a fetus, embedded in her womb, for a multitude of reasons. Aborting the conceptus is done without incurring karma if it occurs before the fourteenth week of gestation.

Adoption vs Abortion   Adoption is a very significant part of creating families. You become a parent when you care for and fall in love with a child. One out of nine children in America is adopted. In group homes and residential treatment programs the ratio of adopted to birth children mirrors society exactly. One out of nine minors in those programs was adopted. Sad but true, not all adoptions are ultimately in the best interest of the child.

Adoption agencies do not truly understand what augurs well for a child they place. The important thing is that the child be freely borne and given by its mother to people she knows will raise her baby well. It is vital for the infant's Source Self to have agreed to the placement. Without the Essence Being's consent, the adoption cannot be completely successful.

Unwanted babies are crucial to infertile couples who are willing to adopt a child rather than be childless. Much as the plight of the childless is a harsh sentence, so is the one given a mother who gives up her child without hope of ever seeing it again. It is not a simple act to give up your child. The act of having borne another human being stays with you forever. For some women, it ruins their capacity to mother. Others suffer guilt over what they've done, and many wish to their dying day they hadn't done it. If adoption is such a fine solution, why are so many adults adopted in infancy looking for their birth mothers? And why are the mothers hoping they'll be found?

Open adoption is a better solution, but it still contains many pitfalls. It requires the ability to love your adopted child enough that you're not threatened by the love the birth parents have for that child. Almost all people who have been adopted suffer unreasonable fears about abandonment. Adoptees claim they feel a terrible sense of loss, even when friends leave to go on vacation.

Adoption is a good thing for families, especially when all parties freely participate together. According to the Talmud: *He who raises an orphan in his house is considered as having brought the child into the world.*

Parturition   At the time of delivery the father, a good friend, or the mother herself can talk the baby into an easy birth. In the early stages of labor the mother can accept another's touch, but as the contractions get swifter and harder she becomes extremely sensitive. Coax her to touch her own belly between contractions and talk softly to the baby. Reassure the infant that this eight-inch journey will be safe, and that its struggle will be rewarded. Tell your baby you welcome it with loving arms. It can hear you, and also receive telepathic messages. Whatever energy is in the birth room the infant will absorb. A frantic or fear-filled room doesn't reassure the baby.

The most important person is the mother. Her emotional state is the one the little one reads most clearly. Create the right conditions for her, not only on the day of the delivery but in the weeks before, and the baby will have an easier birth. The mother goes into a state of bliss during childbirth. In that state she is united with all the guardian spirits of birth and souls on the other side.

A spiritually attuned birth attendant can see the past lives of the infant within a couple of hours of its birth. Some mothers and fathers are so attached to their new baby that they witness or dream about their other incarnations together, or the life the child will have. Mothers often have a dream or two a few weeks before the birth that shows the sex of the child and its destiny.

One winter I was asleep and I had a memorable, lucid dream of the birth of a baby girl, 8 lbs. 0 oz., named Rose. The guardian spirits took me up inside the mother's birth canal to show me there was enough room for the baby to have a safe passage. At 8 AM the phone rang. It was a friend calling to tell me a mutual friend had become a grandmother just minutes before. I gave her the information about the birth, and with some surprise she asked how I knew. It was exactly as the guides had told me.

Within ten days a couple of midwives I knew called me about a birth I was going to photograph. "Don't come just yet, we think the baby is breech," they warned. I sat stunned for a few minutes and then remembered the technique given to me in the dream. Visualizing myself inside the uterus I saw the baby, a male, wasn't breech. I showed up and talked Joshua Montgomery out by twilight. He'd foreseen his lifetime and was afraid to appear. Once assured that he'd be raised by his Dad (as he has been since his parents divorced), he allowed himself to be born.

Birthdays   The anniversary of your birth is a significant time in your yearly cycle. You are usually in a kind of limbo for the three weeks before your birthday. Decisions, especially binding, long-term ones, ought to be postponed until the day after your birthday, by which time you'll have restored and renewed your mental and emotional harmony. Your better judgement and common sense will have returned.

The emotional and physical letdown are a true anniversary as well: a precise reenactment of your fetal self, near term preparing for the eight-inch journey down the birth canal, out of limbo as a lungless water creature, to become one who lives in the air. It's also the preparation time for the life that lies before you.

8

Parenting:
The Sacred Trust

A person is never a himself but always a mask; a person is never his own person, but always represents another, by whom he is possessed. And the other that one is, is always ancestors . . . .

Norman O. Brown

The Choice   Half the families in industrialized nations have a baby as the culmination of a well planned event. The rest of us bear blessed "accidents." Having a child is a sacred duty. Once you have accepted a pregnancy and decide to raise the child yourself, you are obliged to give the person coming to you the greatest devotion and most conscious upbringing you possibly can. Second best, or a lick and a promise, won't do. Cruelty to a child, whether mental or physical, carries with it karma you will have to deal with either later in this lifetime or in a future incarnation.

If you fail your children out of indolence, indecision, or by being violent or overly strict you will have failed all of society and thwarted the Universe's plans for a peaceable world.

Many parents-to-be ask themselves, "How can I bring a child into the world when I'm hardly worthy or able?" If only those who'd achieved sainthood became parents, very few children would be born. Parenting is a learning experience, you just have to be open to the process. Even the youngest of children will teach you, if you are able to attune yourself to their nonverbal communications.

It is very convenient to say, "They came to me for that experience," in excusing your behavior during the childrearing years. Yet selfishness and obstinacy are not rewarded on the other side. It is for your own growth that a particular soul chooses to become your child. Most people react to their children by reliving their own childhood experiences. Invariably, adults express dissatisfaction with their own parents' methods of discipline and the education they received. Seeking other ways, they read *au courant* psychological ideas or fall back on ideas used a couple of generations ago that seem to work until implemented.

Making Space Each child responds differently and each has a separate rhythm of life. My younger daughter always talked to me in the car when traveling to and from school, or on long journeys. My older daughter also used the car as a place for private talks in her teenaged years. Until she was eleven years old, bedtime was when she unwound her day before me. Then I could suggest ways for her to handle a classroom problem, or hear her out and let her fall asleep at peace. I'd have to think of what support each one needed, and supply it if I could. The younger one had many behavioral problems that I was called upon to cope with until she became secure.

A child is born with some past life programming, or very challenging tasks they must undertake in this life. It is up to the parents to channel each child's energies in a direction which allows the children to pick up their path, living it willingly and gracefully. All children are a challenge, but to fail them is dereliction of your duties as a parent and abrogates your own path.

The soul connection you feel with each pregnancy is an indication of how close your attachment to your new baby will be. A father may feel nothing toward his son until the boy talks and he can make intellectual contact. A mother may look at the new-born and fall head over heels in love, while the other parent feels as if an alien has been dumped on them. An adoptive father's heartbeat quickens when the agency calls him to say they have a child for him, but the mother takes months to warm up to the little one. The mother connected by aeons of positive contact with the soul incarnating as her baby is thrilled, whereas the parent who barely knows or has had distasteful experiences with the child's soul warily establishes contact.

If the bonding doesn't take the family can suffer. Seething problems that may lead to child abuse, neglect, and rejection of the child result when the parents do not make a conscious effort to overcome their initial hesitancy and reservations.

As children we often think we were switched at the hospital and got the wrong family. This is true especially of creative peo-ple who don't have kinfolk with artistic, imaginatative lives or those who are mechanically inclined born into erudite intellec-tual families. A Mature Soul whose parents are Teenaged Souls will also secretly believe that he was adopted and they'll tell him when he's older.

If you believe shaping a baby is solely in the hands of the people raising it, you're missing the point. You only have to re-read this book to realize that parents are merely caretakers who'll hopefully do a better job this time than they did when the same souls were entrusted to them as children or comrades in previous lifetimes.

Children will do more for you out of love and rewards than all the fear and punishment you can manufacture. Touching, moderate teasing, playing, and above all talking with, not at, them are ingredients for successful parenting. Unfortunately, over-indulgence does as much harm as beatings, scoldings, parental alcoholism, or drug addiction. Send your child warm glowing love directly from your heart and you'll make few mistakes.

During a session, a client made this astute observation about her own life: "My mother has loved Paris at least as much as I've hated it, without either of us ever seeing the place. I must have opposed her in every way, even down to reviling what she liked, especially her romantic dreams. She had a whole secret in-ner fantasy life she shared with no one. I remember it from the days when a child reads minds with such clarity that nothing need ever be said before they know it."

From parent's mind to child's mind there is no barrier. No wonder so many children suffer trauma even when the parents hold it all in. They already know, and keep silent to protect their parents.

Ages of Childhood
Man is a conglomerate of three partners: God, his father, and his mother.
The Talmud

From birth to seven years a child's worldview is shaped by the parents, siblings and others who are within their sphere. In the first years of a child's life when things are often confusing and mysterious, the youngsters look to their parents to explain the world. Every child has a wellspring of former experiences and their own soul nature to cope with; however, it is society and cause and effect that are most bewildering. Frequently children do not comprehend accepted ideas about reality and physical limitations, such as heights. Adults must intervene and teach children what is and is not dangerous. Until children comprehend poisons, heating devices, traffic, and other potential hazards, they require constant surveillance. And yet they require freedom to wander and wonder in the physical world and to have a fantasy life. You must remember that they are also receiving dreams, speaking with their spirit guides, and contacting human beings who remind them of their Mission. Many pre-schoolers call their spirit guide "my imaginary friend."

Between eight and fourteen years, they explore the world independently and then return to the parents for support. The child must learn self-discipline, critical faculties emerge, and he begins to reason for himself. Respect for the self and others is a painstaking developmental process for most children. A middle-aged child, not ready to rely on herself but also not able to be totally under the parental wing, is influenced by school, peer groups, and the media which affect the child's view of herself and the world.

Between seven and nine years of age, a child is fully able to rationalize and understand the motives behind other people's actions and reactions. They often begin to have sporadic conscious contact with their Witness. What we call the conscience is now in place.

During the first and second segments of a child's life their life cord, which holds them here on earth, is attached to the parents or parent figure. At fourteen years of age the child picks up their own cord. Teenagers run their own educational or sports programs, experiment with social scenes or economic endeavors. If successful, the parents are gratified and relax, letting the child hold her own life cord more and more of the time. If the offspring do poorly, the parents are chagrined and attempt to install more overt control. The best course of action is to visualize the child safe and sound, making certain that the teenager is holding firmly to his life cord, and if not, taking over while the teenager assumes he has control of it. Usually their beliefs are most passionately held at this time in life. Adults interacting with young folks can instill wisdom by helping them temper the exercise of their beliefs with moderate action and level headed detachment.

Between fifteen and twenty-one, young people try out all the adult stances that might fullfil their Personality's desire and that of their Source Self. Some of this behavior can be terrifying to adults who have experimented extensively in their own youth, or those who obeyed the norms set by their elders.

One of the most fearsome things for an uninitiated parent is the child's communication with the spirit world. Young children have dreams and visions that reintroduce them to their Path. Even infants have contact with spirit guides.* If these experiences have been nurtured and appreciated by the parents, children will not be secretive about them, nor terrified of spirit interaction.

Pubescents and adolescents whose Path is fated to be great have visitations from Master Guides, their Advisors, Archangels, and even The Creator. If they have a vision of their future and instructions in how the world really functions, they will never be the same. From that point forward they will see the three planes of reality that cause every act, speech, and thought of anyone they are dealing with. A young person who has undergone that type of transformation will have the gifts of prophesy, healing, teaching, creativity, and wisdom. But these do not come free. They will be ever learning from their inner guidance and the Realm of Creation. They will be asked to harm no one, keep growing, and follow their own principles.

---

*See Companions in Spirit *by Laeh Maggie Garfield and Jack Grant.*

Visions like this often accompany symptoms mimicking the flu, including fever. In the most serious cases, the youngster may be delirious or unconscious. Even if it is a spiritual illness, treat the ailment. Bring down the fever. It won't interfere with the vision, which will continue once the patient is alone again or apparently dozing. Be careful not to intrude by keeping your own energy and agenda in check. Being overbearing or too solicitous can subvert a life vision the child is receiving.

A woman whose eleven-year-old daughter was having a life vision with flu symtoms stayed home from work, held her daughter, massaged her, talked to her, and reassured her. The girl did get psychological relief and self-confidence, but her spiritual messengers will have to wait until she is older and goes seeking for herself before delivering her life vision. The mother, also hungering for a spiritual journey, literally stole her daughter's chance. Sometimes the missed opportunity cannot be rekindled.

Teenagers receiving messages may be frightened until reassured that they can write down what they receive and digest it over time. If your daughter is particularly agitated, have her lie down, face up, and put a low pillow under her head. Gently place your hands over her temples and along the sides of her cheeks. Rest them there lightly for about half an hour. Then move your left hand and your right over the corresponding bones of the occipital ridge on either side of the juncture of her head and neck. Do not under any circumstances allow her panic to trigger yours. Remain calm and take appropriate reassuring common sense action. Feed her root crops to help her grounding, allow her to take cat naps when tired, and encourage her to do physical exercise every day.

The majority of these visitations last from one night to ten days. If the spirits bother her at school she should tell them not to speak to her there unless she is endangered. Spirit helpers will not interfere with normal life when it is made clear to them that there are other times they can communicate.

Within a few days your daughter should have her bearings. All this also applies to male children who have spiritual breakthroughs.

No one who hasn't received this gift at an early age will understand what a Western teenager goes through trying to be normal and keep their gift intact. Most abandon the gift. Life without it seems easier, yet there remains the feeling of loss. That is why, as adults, many try to recapture their lost birthright. Yet such a child having received a covenant from the Universe is under special protection. I can attest to that.

Inborn Personality Traits and Fixations   Nine personality variations exist in the world order. These personality types are generally known by the name Enneagram. Gurdjieff brought the concept out of the monasteries of Asia, and Claudio Naranjo taught the personality fixations to people interested in the spiritual aspects of psychology.

Parents shape how a child handles her or his fixations and obsessions. However, no amount of discipline, cajoling, or bribery will alter the basic thrust children are born with. Once you know the fixations of your children you will be equipped to help them access the positive aspects of their personality type to beneficially modify their behavioral responses.

The list of personality types below is a rudimentary one. In depth studies with helpful suggestions can be found in Margaret Frings Keyes, *Emotions and the Enneagram: Working through Your Shadow Life Script* (Molydater Publications), and Helen Palmer's *The Enneagram: The Definitive Guide to the Ancient System for Understanding Yourself and the Others in Your Life* (Harper and Row).

ONE—Anger Type: *Resentment*, Perfectionist, Self-Righteous, Judgmental, Hysterical, Compulsive, Jealous, Firm, Wants Approval, Buries Emotions, High Internal Standards, Seeks: To Do Good, Rejects: Dealing Directly with Anger, Needs: Self-Control, Serenity, In Stress Acts Like: Four, When Centered Acts Like: Seven

TWO—Image Type: *The Helper/Giver*, Ambitious for Others, Manipulative, Seductive/Aggressive with Opposite Sex, Flatterer, Covets Approval for Self, Proud, Dependent Personality, People Pleaser, Seeks: Freedom, Rejects: Own Needs, Needs: Self-Esteem, In Stress Acts Like: Eight, When Centered Acts Like: Four

THREE—Image Type: *Status Seeker*, Workaholic, Cynical Pessimist, Deceitful, Vain, Efficient, Classic Type A Personality,

Manipulative, Demanding, Wants Publicity, No Time for Private or Personal Life, Covets Approval, Is a Performer, Seeks: Success, Rejects: Failure, Needs: Hope, In Stress Acts Like: Nine, When Centered Acts Like: Six

FOUR—Image Type: *Tragic Romantic*, Ultra-Thin/Gaining Weight Is Tragic, Vindictive, Prone to Depression, Wants The Unattainable, Envious, Manic-Depressive, Believes They Have Forever Lost the True Love or Main Opportunity, Artistic, Temperamental, Competitive, Dramatic, Self-Loathing, Sabotages Success, Wants Intensity, Seeks: Uniqueness and Excellence, Rejects: The Ordinary, Needs: Contentment, In Stress Acts Like: Two, When Centered Acts Like: One

FIVE—Fear Type: *Stingy and Greedy,* Withholds, Isolates to Prevent Closeness, Avoids Involvement, Competition and Success; Hoards Time, Money and Knowledge, Pursues Privacy, Witnesses Life Instead of Experiencing It, Ultra-Thin body, Seeks: Infinite Knowledge, Rejects: Purposelessness, Needs: Commitment, In Stress Acts Like: Seven, When Centered Acts Like: Eight

SIX—Fear Type: *Coward or Recklessly Courageous,* Loyal, Conscientious, Blames Self or has Paranoid Projection, Careful, Warm and Affectionate, Seeks: Security, Rejects: Originality, Needs: To Develop Inner Warrior, In Stress Acts Like: Three, When Centered Acts Like: Nine

SEVEN-Fear Type: *Planner,* Easy Optimism, Uneasy at Taking Action. Usually keeps busy to camouflage goal of staying upbeat or high, Wants Pleasure and Creature Comforts, Can be Corpulent, Seeks: Work, Rejects: Pain, Needs: Levelheaded Moderation, In Stress Acts Like: One, When Centered Acts Like: Five

EIGHT—Anger type: *Revenge,* Defines self as Powerful, "Can do" type, Own sense of Justice coupled with Arrogance, Lust for Life, Highly Controlling, Puritan/Libertine Split in Behavior and Standards Expected From Others, Seeks: Truth, Rejects: Weakness; Needs: To Develop Trust, In Stress Acts Like: Five, When Centered Acts Like: Two

NINE—Anger Type: *Denied Anger,* Sees Self as Easy-Going; Obsessive, Lazy, Indolent, Indecisive, Dreamer, Passive/ Aggressive, Non-Judgmental, Can be rotund or very lean. Good Mediator and Negotiator, Seeks: Love, Rejects: Conflict, Needs: Action, In Stress Acts Like: Six, When Centered Acts Like: Three

Parental Dilemmas of the Twentieth Century It is especially important that you point out to your children that this has been an unusually violent and vulgar century. This is not always how humanity acts. Many other centuries have been less violent and proceeded without widespread war. As of 1989 we entered a new era of practicality and realistic human perspective, after 680 years of death and destruction. If your children are young now, the world will be better by the time they are adults. If your children are teenagers in the 1990s they will raise their children under the values western society says it has and live in more compassionate times.

Teach your children to be principled in and of themselves, and not to follow their peers and others who advocate things they do not believe in. Show by example the highest ideals you have by *living* them. Be your brother's keeper and a steward of the earth. If you children see you do this and participate with you they will grow into their Mission with ease.

Acting on your beliefs demands courage. Most people do what is expedient.

You Will Live with This Forever (Karma) What you do to your children has a profound effect on their difficulties later in life. Cruelty, unthinking verbal barrages, all will take their toll on the child whom you believe you sacrifice everything for.

If you cannot see what is taking place in your children, you will lose the bid to help them find their rightful place in society.

Children raised by nannies often feel a great loss in adult life upon hearing of the death of the woman who served as their substitute mother. Therefore, it is very important to reorganize society so that a child's first year can be spent with parents and other relatives. Working parents who come home at night and devote several hours to their children and spend weekends with them are the ones the child will be corded to. If not, parents cannot expect to influence the child who bonds to peers in their absence. The less quality time spent with the child early in life, the thinner the psychic cord will be.

Take time with your children teaching them skills that will help them to get along in the world. Youngsters require a broad base of experiences to help them find activities and interests to serve them throughout life. Museums, county fairs, concerts, live plays, travel, and sports influence their development. If you work on cars, sew clothing, meditate, or play tennis, share the activity with your child but do not force it.

By six years of age most children have an interest in food preparation and how to cook. If you teach them they'll be making meals on their own that feed the family well. Many children are adept at preparing breakfast and lunch at an early age. At ten years of age boys and girls can do their own laundry if you've shown them how to sort clothes and select water temperature. Comparison shopping and how to be an astute shopper begins as soon as the child is old enough to make purchases. One schoolteacher I knew taught her two sons how to shop for the family's groceries. They were eight and ten years of age when I spied them at the supermarket smelling cantaloups to make certain they were ripe and figuring out which brand of tomato sauce was the cheapest. These lessons take effort on the part of the parents but the kids will feel a growing competence. A sense of responsibility is instilled by gaining skills that will make for independence. When a child knows their contribution to the family means something it gives them an extra sense of belonging.

I was about seven years of age when the summer's heat warped my parent's bedroom door. My Dad showed me how to take it down by knocking out the hinge pins. We carried it to the living room, placed it over two saw horses, and he planed it. All the while he showed me how to work with the grain of the wood. Twenty-three years later when my front door swelled in wet weather I did exactly as he had showed me, getting help from my ten-year-old daughter.

Spending time playing or sharing your interests and talents with your children creates lifelong memories and provide opportunities for rebonding with your kids. They are a bank of heartwarming experiences for your children to recall when the teenage years come and the going is tougher.

Hurts that just don't go away are the result of incidents that set your child up for the material they will have to process in more and more refined ways as they mature. What one child experiences or remembers as the significant factor in a family that is undergoing stressful times or tragedy may not be perceived by their siblings. For the brothers and sisters too young for conscious memories, there are shadows and seedlings that surface as unaccountable fears, pains, or ailments. The residue of buried family traumas or personal dramas causes them to avoid growing in directions that might bring up these subliminal memories.

Everyone avoids going into harsh memories for fear of what they'll find. Yet when led to remember, each person's childhood yields insight which frees them to expand their horizons and look at all the potential of life. They can then live life fully, once the past is integrated.

Of course seeing your own Truth is very difficult. Many have been unable to face the challenge and give up on life, adopting a defeatist outlook. You can hate yourself forever over what you've found, or you can correct each flaw as you understand its origin and examine the original hurt.

You may not notice your abusive way of dealing with your children, but they will. Children who are told they are stupid, incompetent, and immature will live up to these expectations. The lucky ones will become rebellious and do the opposite, just to show you. And, they may also have as little to do with you as possible as they grow older.

Life's so unfair. The man whose children place him in a rest home and never visit him is the one who played with them every weekend and took them camping. But he's also the one who beat them with a belt, abused their mother, and put coal in their stockings.

The elderly man who wears adult diapers is the one who humiliated his sons and beat them when they accidentally urinated in their beds. They were frightened of him, or forbidden to cry, and so they let it out through their urine in their sleep. Compassion wasn't his trait then, and now he can feel sorry for himself and recognize how little the children could control their bedwetting when they were small.

The mother whose lover abused her children physically, emotionally, psychically or sexually, may find herself on her own, abandoned in her later years. She did not defend her children or protect them at a critical time in their lives.

Take extreme care who you live with or marry while your children are growing up. The cruel or uncaring stepparent usually exits from the home just about the time the children are grown, leaving them scarred and you alone. Did you, and do you still, side with him or her instead of your children? Is your "adult" partner always demanding your full attention, jealous of your children? If your children do not like your intended partner, give the partner up. It wouldn't be "your happiness" to have such anger and misery as an unblendable family under one roof.

Incest   At all times a mother must remember that stepfather sexual molestation is tragically common. What kind of harvest will you reap if you fail to protect your crops? Listen to your child if she says she's been abused, and intercede on her behalf.

Children who were sexually abused by a trusted person (parent, family friend, close relation, teacher, priest) block their femininity (females) or masculinity (males) or become promiscuous. Forced sex destroys a person's self-image and trust.

The first woman who came to me with sexual dysfunction had had her marriage marred by the memory of her father coercing the little girls in the family to take turns catering to his sexual appetites. All I could do was help her to restore her self-image, her sense of power, and her self-respect. Fortunately, after thirty-three years of unsatisfying sex, her husband was loyal and loving. As she gained self esteem he began to shower with her, throw his arms around her exuberantly, and kiss her in front of their adult children. They resumed lovemaking. She was delighted.

Anyone who remembers being molested as a child should tell themselves the truth. What happened is not your fault. Even if incest is kept a secret, the entire family feels the vibration and all suffer because of it. There are no secrets in the Universe. Everyone knows everything at all times. We've just had our telepathic skills reined in to appease the churches and political entities. As a result society continues to function with destructive lies and ills from generation to generation.

Discipline   *One should not promise a child something and then not give it, as he thus teaches the child to lie.*

The Talmud

Before Christianity usurped Native American religion and culture, even tribes who went to battle frequently had this philosophy about rearing children: "If you hit a child, he will never learn to trust you." Maybe this is what is wrong with our entire culture. Inflicting pain is no way to inspire anything but fear, anxiety, anger, and other negative emotional states.

Humans, as ensouled beings, learn from being loved. They're more likely to do what you want out of love for you. Children will express gratitude for the way you raised them if you've been consistent, available, warm, loving, and compassionate, more readily than if you are cold, distant, judgmental, or abusive. Praise them for their accomplishments, console and educate them when they fail. Be truthful with them without being brutal. To instill trust keep your promises to your children and have them keep theirs to you.

No matter what some street-corner psychic tells you about the torture your child put you through in a previous lifetime, it is no excuse for emotionally or physically abusing, or overdisciplining your child now.

Children, no matter how you strive to protect them, face hard knocks that cannot be avoided. Deaths in the family and community, divorce, moving, economic swings, and abrasive kids at school all present them with significant challenges. They'll require your most loving support when undergoing these passages.

Nonviolent Childrearing   Teaching by example is the only way, since children follow more closely what they see than what is said to them. You should also talk to your children, sharing anecdotes from your childhood that are fitting for them to hear. If you fell out of a tree, or took a walk on the beach with your cousin getting into trouble for coming home after dark, these incidents will make you seem more like your child. If you struggled to learn to play the piano and felt great satisfaction once you could play well enough to entertain yourself, your children will have a good story to grow on.

Listen to your children, really hear them out. If you ignore what seems like childish prattle you might never hear that their homeroom teacher shakes children she doesn't like, or their boy scout leader showed them gory photos. You'll also miss their joy in discovering a secret garden in the neighborhood with a kindly lady who tells them plant stories. Children who know they'll get a good hearing at home are freer about sharing their adventures and misadventures away from home.

It can be difficult, if not impossible, to think of nonviolent ways you know will work to discipline your children, especially if your family did not appreciate and use such methods. If yours was a family that hit first and asked questions later, you may not have been impressed by shaming, or time out, or grounding as punishment. Whatever you do as a parent must fit the child you are interacting with, as well as be nonviolent.

A Native American veterinarian, living far from his plains tribal elders, still used coyote stories to train his three boys in proper behavior. These worked better than any physical beatings would have to teach his sons to act out of conscience rather than immediate desire.

One night he left a fifty-dollar bill on his dresser, along with the contents of his pockets. In the morning the money was gone. At the breakfast table he told the boys that Coyote had come during the night and stolen the money. He then proceeded to tell the children all the things he'd planned to do with the cash, including taking them to a movie. He asked them to find Coyote and tell him how his activities had hurt the family. That night when he returned home, the money was on his dresser. At dinner he informed them they were lucky, Coyote had come back with the fifty-dollar bill. He then did the things he said he had intended to do with the money.

The father did not try to assess blame or demand that each boy put up with a spot inspection of his room or other personal effects. The father simply told them there was a problem and led them to a solution. By blaming the bad behavior on Coyote's faulty judgement, he did not encourage tattling or competition among his boys, nor affix any negative character traits to the children. He also avoided getting caught in the middle as someone to fear.

To be able to use this method you will need a few books of coyote stories and the patience to create a story about Coyote interfering in your family life when something has gone wrong. You will have to tell and retell the coyote stories to your children until they believe in the power of the trickster, who knows all, sees all, and gets caught in his own traps.

Time out, cornering, and other forms of moderate isolation help. Less than half an hour is sufficient for children up to seven years of age. Before that the child's conscience isn't developed and more isolation will frighten or harden them.

Young children cannot be expected to have a sense of time. A long time can be an hour or two days to them without differentiation. Their attention span is actually only twenty minutes, so that longer periods of separation from parent or group cease to be effective. Common sense dictates that you would never put the child in a garage or storeroom where hazardous substances or situations could injure them. Bring the child back into the family room if they want to return once their time out is over. An angry or embarrassed child may want more time away to absorb their hurt feelings before facing others.

Placing a child in a corner of the room while others go on without them is another form of isolation. If they talk, no one is to answer them. If they are not silent, remove them from the room. Whatever time out you issue, place a timer with a bell where they can hear it, to signal the end of their time out.

> *One should not threaten a child with future punishment.*
> *Rather he should either punish the child immediately or control himself and say nothing.*
>
> **The Talmud**

Threaten only what you will follow through on. Threatening to throw away all the toys on the floor if you have to pick them up won't make an impression unless you actually throw them out. Alternately you can keep playthings hidden for several months and bring them back one at a time.

Threatening does not work with all children. My older daughter was tidy, never needing more than a reminder to put her toys away carefully in their rightful place as she finished playing. My younger daughter cried when faced with cleaning the massive messes she made. She was about five years of age when she refused to clean up a wild mixture of straws, wheels,

Tinkertoys, and Lincoln Logs she'd left helter skelter in the living room for two days. I threatened to burn them if they weren't off the floor by dinner time. She said, "Okay, burn them," and proceeded to help me gather them in paper sacks. I dropped the sacks into our woodstove, right in front of her. The following spring I bought her a huge Lego set. She took excellent care of it, so much so that she will have it for her children to play with.

Older children respond well when the punishment affects their free time. Loss of allowance, treats, movie and television restrictions, and grounding are efficacious means of reprimanding school-aged children. Teenagers become more responsible when they have to pay for lost items, or damage they've done in the house. No punishment should be excessive. Only one punishment for any single incident. Remember, anyone can have a bad day.

Delayed punishment does not work on youngsters until they have developed a conscience. It has a negative effect on a child's psychological development and builds resentment and fear.

A client read me a poignant true story she wrote to illustrate the difficulties she faces in adult life. Her father, who often worked late, would punish her for infractions her mother reported during the day by violently waking her by hitting her.

"While I was meditating this morning, Brandy, my dog, came up and unexpectedly kissed me on the lips. I moved to hit her, eyes closed, not knowing it was her. Upon seeing the mutt, my response changed. All the times my father pounced on me in bed as a form of discipline has made me wary of surprise contact. It's no wonder I stay up half the night worrying when there is nothing to worry about."

The client was unable to shake herself of endless anxiety, unable to form any kind of deep trusting bond with another human being. If someone who says they love you will do this to you, who can you trust?

Sons and Other Duties
A bad child in one's house is more unbearable than the most destructive war.
The Talmud

Why do so many powerful women raise nagging, uncentered, clinging, destructive sons? Many are out and out young rascals. Pesky, whiny children are a nuisance to have around. A son, unwanted by either parent once a custody fight or the demands for complete loyalty to each parent have been played out, becomes a discard at an early age. The mother overlooks her son's behavior, hoping you will be blinded by the charm that works so easily on her. Girls, with few exceptions, aren't this obnoxious and unbridled when over-indulged or neglected. They look around, find the socially permissible levels of behavior, and conform.

One couple, still together, have an unmanageable only son. Their discipline is unpredictable and inconsistent, and the child is the mirror of the family's problems. The wife mothers her husband, right down to commanding him, "Jerry eat your cereal." Why they have a dysfunctional sexual life is apparent in that very remark. How can an immature fellow, wishing to be seen as a man, make love to the woman who acts like his mother? Their son as a Thanksgiving weekend guest tore his hostess's house to shreds, broke a valuable piece of pottery, cried, screamed and disrupted every meal, conversation, and outing. His parents, both present, were at a loss to intervene. These overly loving parents had decided never to tell him "no," believing it would ruin his spirit. At this point this practice has ruined more than that. At six, he has no self-control, no concept of consequences, and no idea why people avoid him.

Are many parents unwilling or unable to set guidelines for their male children because they need the child's love so badly? Even a couple whose boys are quite sweet allow them to interrupt any visit. The boys, as guests in other people's homes, do not interrupt. There is no damage to property and the children are polite.

The common thread for spoiled or rejected sons in most cases is that the mothers and fathers separated, if not physically then emotionally, by the time each boy was four. The cases described below are the usual scenarios for overly adulated sons.

The older brother has a different father than his much younger sibling. He acted like a selfish, mouthy, intelligent, conceited brat. His mother, unable to alter his behavior, overlooked it bowing to his demands. In desperation she sent him to his father, whom she blamed for her son's anti-social actions. In another case, a family whose two younger children were models of balanced, creative, inquisitive, and pleasant behavior in childhood, have an older brother, an indulged, big mouthed, disrespectful person. In adult life he cannot take care of his finances although he's a devoted husband and father.

Therein lies the answer to some of the problems of male children whose intelligent able mothers and vague uncertain fathers indulged their whims for the fleeting peace of the moment. All the mothers I mentioned felt they owed something to this child of theirs. They gave in to their better judgement, or had no better judgement. As a result, the now adult terrors need their parents' constant intervention in their lives to function.

In late teenaged and early adult years these sons aren't self-directed, well-motivated, or mature. The more fortunate ones are at least compassionate. Others are abusive, abrasive young adults stealing from family and friends, taking drugs, and getting into fights and legal trouble. The parents' good name in the community can rescue such a misanthrope just so many times before he falls into difficulties outside the family's scope of contacts.

When parents refuse the job of really being parents and they fail to set limits and act in an overly permissive manner, the child must become a parent to himself. The lucky ones pick up the social cues outside the home by seven or ten years of age. Others latch onto the families of friends and learn acceptable behavior in their teen years.

Unfortunately, for the wildest boys, there are not many tolerant, patient parents of friends who will help. Without extended family, they are sunk: lost souls, destructive to themselves and society, or lonely misplaced individuals wandering and thirsting for human comfort as life's leftovers. They are the men no women want, nor will have, for any length of time. Untamable boys grow up to be unemployable men. The Talmud says: *If the father does not teach his son a profession it is as though he had taught him thievery.*

Divorce and Separation A child born of parents' love for each other is a real love child, conceived for the sole purpose of furthering the parent's bond. Once the love has died for one or both of the parties the child, as the symbol of that love, may receive the same rejection as the union. It is less apparent when the mother still loves the father, as she may shower that love upon the child. Until her ex-husband's utter rejection makes her finally loathe him, the child is fairly safe. The child will be most protected when the mother and father part mutually and amicably, for then the love they shared can easily become a treasured memory, free of bitterness. The child can then make the switch from love-child to being loved for himself.

As an adult you acknowledge that you are most bitter and angry at yourself for not having been what your partner wanted. You admit you're upset for having failed in an intimate relationship again. The parents must protect children in a divorce by allowing each parent as much access as the youngsters require to reorganize their relationship. The custodial parent and the visiting parent can arrange equal time. If you are on good terms with your ex-spouse, family picnics and other outings can be shared events. This becomes problematic if your former mate has a new flame and you don't, and it is even worse when the new relationship figured in your break-up. In all these trials and tests of modern family life, you must stick to your path and be respectful of yourself and the others.

Reparenting Yourself   Frequently you encounter people so damaged from events in their early childhood that their parenting skills are non-existent. Society is reaching out to resocialize people, but regrettably this usually happens when the adults have reached their mid-thirties or early forties. Not very many younger parents attend these self-help groups and workshops, so as they raise their children they tend to carry their parents' mistakes forward.

Reparenting themselves aids the current generation to be better caretakers of their children and the Earth. Older souls, exposed to whatever mistreatment, rise to be good stewards of the Earth, the environment, their children, and friends.

Having a guru can be a method for reparenting. People follow gurus to be reparented by an omnipotent, benevolent authority, in whom they place all their trust. They hope this new parent will grant them favor, and envy all who the great one gives his or her attention to. All too often the guru is despotic or manipulative.

The word guru probably conjures up a vision of an Eastern mystical sect, functioning by taking great amounts of money from Western followers. Televangelist's colleges and retreat centers, large congregations run by demagogues and preachers claiming to be ordained by some Christian body, Catholic seminaries and churches, mental hospitals, reform schools for juvenile offenders, and prisons are all run on the same principle.

Gurus, like parents, have rules that the devotee must follow. Most limit access to the inner sanctum. This is much like the adults in your birth family whose grown-up activities excluded children. Belonging to the new family requires that you give up your autonomy and obey the dictates of the guru. What you eat, when you sleep, who you may room with irrespective of marriage and family ties are determined by the rules of the sect you have cast your lot with. Where you are to work, how much of your own money you may keep, and who you can associate with are also prescribed. Instead of being loyal to your kin, you are loyal only to the devotees and members of your chosen group. Longtime friends that you cannot recruit for the guru are abandoned as more and more of your life becomes devoted to that journey presented to you as your own salvation.

The guru has all the power and you acquiesce. Toadies further up on the ladder than you enforce the rules with a vengeance. Someone, usually not the guru, is the tough guy to the devotees. If you have it soft while others have it hard, it's likely the guru has plans for himself using your money, your body, or your skills.

Gurus, entertainers, people the public adores, can sap energy from their followers by hooking into their third chakras. At concerts where many fall asleep, or when the guru's followers appear to be meditating in his presence, it is because the charismatic leader is taking too much energy from the fans. People feel tired, and sleep or doze to regain their energy. A smart entertainer only borrows the energy temporarily, flinging it back to the audience at the end of the show so that they are uplifted.

Enslaving the followers is an unpleasant form of bondage that eventually destroys the adored one as well as the devotee. This is true in families as well as religious organizations. Respect for each person's divinity and Mission here on earth is the rule of the Universe.

You can only be successfully reparented if you choose to be, and it must be on the basis of appreciating and supporting the skills you have already acquired. Skilled therapists, self-help groups like Al-Anon and Co-counselling, allow you the freedom to be your own person while gaining strength and ability to carry your share of responsibility in a non-despotic, non-manipulative manner.

9

Intimate Relationships

Love is an endless mystery for nothing else can explain it.

Tagore

Loving a well-loved lover is as spiritual an act as can occur on earth. It is the bridge, the gateway between heaven and earth.

The Source places all of us here to learn from each other. Whatever you call your Maker, remember we are all loved equally. As best as you can, work not to hurt others regardless of how pained you are. Self-respect means not leaving yourself open to continued abuse. Love yourself as much as the Creator loves you, and loving another comes easily. Inability to love yourself keeps you from bonding and committing to another in a healthy manner.

Associations that begin voluntarily, from the perspective of the Realm of Creation, are the reuniting of souls you've known from countless reincarnations, as well as beings formerly unknown to you, who need to undergo the same lessons. Your friends, your colleagues, your lovers and your marriage partners will be viewed from another level of wisdom. Naturally there is an intertwining of relationships between the Physical Realm and the Realm of Creation. From a reincarnational vantage point you have been, or will be, related to everyone on Earth at one time or another. That knowledge alone should make it easier to love your neighbor as yourself.

The Marriage Guardian   Marriage is an ordeal and a sacrifice. It is a mystical union of two separate souls made one in the flesh. A loving union is good for this lifetime and beyond, implying no further commitment to marry in subsequent lives. In a mythic marriage the parties know they belong together from the start. Not in the sensory, romantic ideal, but in a spiritual sense. Their love is strong, so strong they will remain together irrespective of political, social, or economic obstacles. They love and respect each other, remaining fiercely loyal to one another. No political or religious system, no number of interfering relatives, can part a couple whose partnership is derived from spirit. A union of this magnitude has a Marriage Guardian.

In a marriage there are three entities, each of the partners and the Guardian of their union. Marriage Guardians stay close to the couple to assist them through a variety of lessons they must seek to further their growth. If one of the partners refuses to cooperate in building the union, the Guardian may become disenchanted and go on to another couple who are willing to work out their patterns through the match. An entity interested in helping two people harmonize will go to great lengths to aid the Missions of the pairing.

The methods of the Marriage Guardian, who is always an emissary of the Creator, vary according to the type of union and the depth of the work the couple can achieve together. If any number of future relationships with other mates could teach the twosome about power and control, then there is no use in holding on to a bond where the degree of uproar is too intense for the spouse's issues to be resolved. However, when two strong people interface and their capacity for use or abuse of power is equal, the match can be too valuable to let squabbles obscure the potential growth for both parties. The Guardian will intercede on every level, spiritual, psychological, social, and familial to insure the pair's success. Whatever qualities the couple must explore together, these are usually the issues with which they individually experience difficulty.

The image the Guardian emits is elliptical, luminescent, colored light. Spirit guides are round glyphs of light in a variety of colors. A Source Self hoping to become your baby looks like a spirit guide. One foolish man sent away his Marriage Guardian because he thought it was a soul hoping to become one of his children. His once wonderful union was in bad shape before he realized his mistake.

Four Types of Unions   In categorizing marriages there are four main types. Their titles are: unconscious union, karmic union, companion relationships, and lifemates. A conscious person is unlikely to be happy with a less aware individual. The marriages wherein the partners tend to grow progressively unhappily locked together fall into the two major kinds: the unconscious, and karmic union. The fourth type, lifemates, lends itself readily to a joyous union. These marital bonds are predetermined in the Realm of Creation.

Unconscious Union   The script, with some variation, goes like this. I am a boy, you are a girl, let's get married and make a family. Let's get married and share expenses. Let's get married so I can live off of you. An unconscious union is formed by people who see marriage as a way out of their own inadequacies, or who want to limit their own search for truth. Limiting your prospects in favor of a quickie union deprives you of the option for a good choice first time out. It is a way to avoid taking your own path. The majority of these marriages fail within a few years. They collapse from lack of substance and an insolvent foundation, irrespective of the couple's attempts to stay together. If they do salvage their marriage it'll be an empty spiritual journey wherein little is accomplished.

Naturally if enough unconscious marriages take place some of the couples will, by reason of sheer numbers, after a span of years discover they are in the most compatible union they could possibly have made.

Karmic Union   The second form of mating is karmic union. Couples join together to work out past life damage, or in more traditional societies to create a union that will join two important family lineages. The duo have a particular task that they need to accomplish that will take a few months, or a set number of years, to complete. Once that has been fulfilled, whether it's the birth of children or to begin an organization, they stay together out of inertia. Karmic unions are categorized by a lot of fighting wherein the more aware member of the couple is completely frustrated by their lack of progress. Frequently that person has knowledge of their deeper bond and the commitment they made to share a portion of their current lifetime in order to rectify past injustices.

Companion Relationships   Companion relationships are based on work of a spiritual nature to travel closely allied or parallel paths together. Couples who unite with this in mind have already made a commitment to a single path that each can travel in tandem without setting aside their own life's work. As a matter of fact, they instinctively recognize that their Mission is a common one. These marriages, whether they last seven, twelve, twenty-eight years, or until one of the partners dies, feels to each of them as if it's on the cutting edge. This type of marriage offers high growth with big rewards reaped from ordeals faced and handled together.

Lifemate   The fourth type is rare in the west and often misunderstood. The lifemate is someone you contracted to be with prior to incarnating. You each chose your families and your circumstances in early life to foster the marriage to the person you knew you were born to be with. This kind of matrimonial condition means endless sacrifices which do not feel like deprivation. It also has much humor, or serious enjoyment of a single career or set of life goals. Children of these unions expect to find the same goodwill in their own relationship, and are often shocked that their marriages aren't as warm and single-minded as their parents.

Winnie and Nelson Mandela are a perfect example of the Lifemate marriage.

Marriage and Belief   What makes a marriage work? Beliefs. Belief systems can work against a permanent mating, or foster it. The belief that marriage is for creating children was so ingrained in society that women rarely remarried past menopause. Young widows were so plentiful that men were under a biblical directive to marry the childless widows of their brothers.

Otherwise, these women might never bear young and have no one to look after them in old age.

We are no longer surprised when people of any age find each other and want to marry. We believe it prolongs life and adds to individual happiness.

Core beliefs create obstacles to successful pairings. If you know in your heart of hearts you no longer wish to create children, then you will raise excuses to be unavailable for another partner. You will have to remain a perpetual single until death. Or you could take a spouse who wants no more offspring in their life. Your core belief must be dealt with before the alternate is viable.

You must also examine your potential mate's expectations for marriage. In large part, this can be done by noticing the language they use in describing their relationship. George Lakoff, a professor at the University of California at Berkeley, has done a great deal of research into the language of metaphor. This quote from an interview he gave to *The Express,* of January 27, 1989, entitled "Food For Thought" is an excellent example.

> *"You can imagine a couple where the wife viewed the marriage as a means for* growth *that must never be allowed to* stagnate. *Suppose the husband saw it as a durable structured object that they had to* work on *and* build *and* make strong and stable and secure *so it would* not *fall apart when* burdens were placed on it. *His idea of a successful marriage would be her idea of a failed one."*

English has many metaphors that indicate love as a journey: "on the rocks," "spinning our wheels," "reached a dead end," "at a crossroads," "we travel well together." Another set of metaphors describes love as madness: "crazy over you," "wild about her," or as an illness: "fever," "bewitched," "love sick," or magic: "spellbound," "he's magnetic," "under your spell," and loss of control: "to fall in love," "it's the chemistry between us," "head over heels." If you and your beloved do not use the same category of metaphors to describe your relationship, it may be a clue that you're not on the same path and your relationship isn't viable, because your core-beliefs do not match.

Our language tells us, in its inability to find words to describe conditions of commitment, whether the unions are really socially acceptable or just above the tolerance line. Are relationships so little treasured, so little thought of, that we as a culture of creative individuals cannot come up with words to describe the levels of commitment outside the bonds of marital law, which men and women and couples of the same sex have for one another? Is this good for permanence in bonded relationships?

Money is so important, that a term for economic remuneration given by a previous partner to the former live-in, "palimony," was immediately devised as a counterpart to alimony.

Sexual, nonmarital relationships have descriptions which are either derogatory or ambiguous. How, twenty years after it has become commonplace, do you describe the man or woman you are having a committed live-in union with, when clergy is unable, unwilling, or not required to sanctify your liaison? Do terms like "my old man," "my pal," "my roommate," "my girlfriend," "my mate," "my partner," cover the situation? They are disrespectful to the very nature of a union, whatever your sexual orientation. If it's not taboo any longer, where are the new words which symbolize the unmarried committed relationship? It takes a mouthful of explanations to convey what society considers an acceptable, but not entirely endorsable, pairing. How long will we allow the language to go on lacking what the culture permits?

Coupling unites the inward and the outward journey. Combining your inward journey and outward lives challenges the coupled relationship. Compromises take something from each partner. To keep the balance of your outer lives, neither has to give up their autonomy, personal freedom, or rightful path. Successful marriages harmonize the personal, practical, public, and private needs of both parties.

The early part of marriage most often experienced early in life is through the marriages of your parents, close family friends, and relatives. The second stage of marriage is at best misunderstood. Joseph Campbell summed it up fairly well in this interview with Bill Moyers.

> **Bill Moyers:** *So marriage is utterly incompatible with the idea of doing one's own thing.*
> **Joseph Campbell:** *It's not simply one's own thing, you see. It is, in a sense, doing one's own thing, but the one isn't just you, it's the two together as one. And that's a purely mythological image signifying the sacrifice of the visible entity for a transcendent good.*

This is something that becomes beautifully realized in the second stage of marriage, what I call the alchemical stage, of the two experiencing that they are one. If they are still living as they were in the primary stage of marriage, they will go apart when their children leave.

The years of childrearing, especially the first nine years, require exacting cooperation. Otherwise one person, usually the woman, sacrifices her focus. Interrupting your process can make for resentment and is the underlying cause of most marital break-ups during the childbearing years.

It is possible you have married, even several times, without making a marriage. The union is usually unsatisfying, often brief. If the fated set-up is not to your liking, apply to your spirit helpers for a change in your script. It is possible your request will be granted. Should it be rejected you'll have lost nothing by asking.

Your constellation of discordant belief systems may serve you in good stead, especially if you discover you had agreed to be single before incarnating. You might even learn what lessons of single life you are to master. At least then you'll feel more at ease being one of the unpartnered, instead of driven to find Mr. or Ms. Inappropriate to fill your time.

In the days before mass divorce, there was a general consensus among women that the real marriage didn't start until the silver anniversary. It was only then the couple had been through so much together that compassion and true acceptance entered the relationship. At that point each of them had toned down their personal passions and dissatisfactions sufficiently so that they could view their spouse with love. Tragically, unconditional love and a union of the spirit was not the lot of every couple. Many went on hating and disrespecting one another, suffering the spouse's presence, ignoring the partner as a way of holding a guarded truce, unable to separate or divorce due to religious and social scruples.

More often than not you are disappointed by your relationship falling far short of your expectations. As a civilization in flux, there are not many universally held standards by which to measure the choice of a well suited life partner, or even a temporary one. Seldom does anyone state that they are looking for a violent, abusive person to be oppressed by or to conquer.

Yet your own lack of knowledge about the nature of intimate relationships may leave you wide open.

My aunt used to tell me, "A man is what he makes himself and a woman is who she marries," and, "It's just as easy to love a rich man as a poor one." She also gave me advice about how a good woman can encourage a man and help him to grow so that he becomes more than he could have been without her. A poor woman, one without wisdom, could make a man worse than he was naturally, or be unable to improve her lot in life through influencing her man to change. In all cases it was up to the woman to make the man better. She was responsible for the state of the marriage. If he was cruel to her it was because she didn't have any sense. Her goodness, wisdom, and purity could change all that. However, it was important to pick a man wisely for "You can't make a silk purse out of a sow's ear," she'd say.

Comparable attitudes underscore most marriages. Redemption is the burden of the woman. Her constancy and her ethical practices keep the man on his course. His failures are hers and her failures are hers.

Women who've endured a lengthy marriage are often bitter that they didn't receive the benefits such service originally promised. However, the unfulfilled material and social recognition they complain of has a deeper basis. Theoretically a couple exists to cross-fertilize one another for more than producing progeny. Her inspiration is required to turn him into a *mensch*. And he in turn is to supply her with fertile ideas, act as a sounding board, and provide encouragement to hasten her on her spiritual journey. Women know that in an affirmative relationship their intuition, healing powers, and connection with the divine are amplified.

Great sex is a channel to the divine that the lovers take together. In the moment of ecstasy, when your bodies have merged to the extent that you don't know whose is whose, you achieve oneness with each other and the realms of Creation and/or the Source. In an invective or indifferent pairing ecstasy seldom, if ever, occurs.

Some tribal cultures know how difficult it is to achieve cross-fertilization in a primary relationship. They pair off an unrelated boy and girl as a couple who will remain non-sexual as brother and sister in spirit. These two wed others for offspring, love, and economic support. Throughout life they share their spiritual development through insights, vision quests, dreams, conversations, and activities.

In the creative arts there are many examples of couples who've fostered one or both partner's artistry. Gertrude Stein and Alice B. Toklas, Thomas Wolfe and Aline Bernstein, Simone de Beauvoir and Jean-Paul Sartre.

Getting Into a Relationship   Good beginnings are worth more than any repair work done later.

As a rule, the longer the bliss period after a couple meets the greater the spiritual bond is between them.

Falling in love is mostly unconscious. Getting together and parting can become a way of life. There's no time to discover who the person is or why the attraction worked at first. In a culture where the old rules have been suspended and the new ones are as yet unformed, it is difficult to decide where to invest your sexual energy. Casual lovers, committed relationships, monogamy, and love affairs while in a committed relationship each have a distinct overriding energy. You must decide if you need constant stimulation from a new lover, or the steady growth of facing yourself in a one-to-one union. Committed relationships have different phases of sexual ardor, emotional closeness, intellectual fascination, and taking space for oneself.

When really in love, during the honeymoon phase of the relationship, common sense does not matter. The bliss period is a preparatory phase to strengthen the bonding of a couple whether they be gay or straight. Bliss should last for about eighteen months, with temporary interludes of reality when you can see your sweetheart's faults and good points clearly. An abrupt awakening much earlier in the relationship signals a coupling that ought to be given serious second thoughts before children arrive or other serious commitments are made.

You meet someone special and after six weeks, or five months, you begin to feel your gears don't mesh. Do not attempt to fix it, or change yourself for that individual. It's a clear signal that you will make better friends than lovers. Let it go. In the absence of having someone less than special to focus on, another more viable partner will be found. It's difficult to meet Mr. or Ms. Right when you're entangled in an unsatisfactory relationship that takes up your time.

To locate your best companion relationship, or your life-mate, you may need to do a bit of personal clearing of your own resistance. Affirmations may help you to delve into your own resistance to being in an intimate relationship. An affirmation gives you the lead time to adjust to having what you say you want or resetting your sights.

This is the affirmation I kept on my closet door, until I was prepared to meet the deepest love of my life. Under circumstances that can only be described as fated, it was love at first sight, a misnomer, as such meetings ought to be called instant recognition.

I AM READY FOR THE MARRIAGE OF MY MATURE YEARS, SINCE THEY ARE HERE,
A UNION OF TWO STRONG PEOPLE.
I WANT A LOVING, SEXUALLY ACTIVE, MENTALLY STIMULATING UNION WITH A SPIRITUALLY ORIENTED MAN. I DESERVE A MONOGAMOUS UNION WHEREIN WE RESPECT AND TRUST EACH OTHER.
I AM ABLE TO BE IN A CREATIVE INTIMATE RELATIONSHIP IN WHICH THE TRADITIONAL ROLES ARE SHARED BY EACH OF US EQUALLY.
I WANT TO BE MARRIED TO A CREATIVE MAN WHOSE OPEN POSITIVE ENERGY IS MANIFESTING IN THE WORLD.

When it becomes apparent what is holding up real commitment, a second affirmation can be created. No one else's affirmation will work for you. You can reword a good one, adding your own ideas and desires to it and deleting what you don't need, but affirmations alone are not sufficient to break down barriers and set up circumstances for a meaningful relationship. The highest forces of the cosmos are at work aiding and abetting you in your search. If you want a conscious union, pray for guidance. Sample affirmation:

I need a man/woman who will be able to stick with me and lead me through my resistance to loving. I want a woman/ man who'll urge me to greater heights of commitment to her/ him, while I continue to be me. I desire a man/woman who'll do that without attempting to diminish my career or my interests. A man/woman who supports me in the world and challenges me to grow with him/her.

To get into a relationship that is worthy of all the effort it will take for you to stay in it when the going gets rough, you first have to feel good about yourself. Withholding love when you feel unlovable detracts from your relationships, and your parenting. It's a nasty form of self-indulgence. Make drawings or journal entries of your feelings so you can see them in a distanced, less threatening manner. Writing them down or speaking them into a tape recorder and replaying the cassette, can clarify your thoughts on the problems at hand.

Marriage is risky business. Life is a gamble. If you don't take risks the rewards may not come your way. Marriage is always an educated guess and a challenge.

Men Who Use Women   Men who use women aren't always using them in an actively sexual way. A woman whose husband is flirtatious and bonds easily with other women isn't at fault. That's an old notion of the co-relationship, a holdover from the times when all a woman had to do in life was support her man and she'd be rewarded with economic security and abundant children. No one can prevent another person from behaving in an outlandish or foolhardy manner. No number of lectures or catering to his real or imagined needs will alter his addictions be they alcohol, work, drugs, or womanizing.

Men often commit adultery when they cannot allow themselves to go through the mental, spiritual, and emotional growth their spouse or long-term partner is demanding. Men are adulterous when they feel ineffective or dissatisfied with their position in the world. It's an ego boost to experience afresh the exhilaration of a new lover.

The mid-life crisis or the factor of aging is famous for sending older gentlemen to chase young maidens. "I'm still a satyr," he proclaims to himself as his love life centers on younger and younger females. Quite a few men discard their wives, remarry, and have second or third families in a futile pursuit of imagined youth recaptured.

The virginal male-female interaction, based on the woman wanting the man, while the man withholds sexual congress, is all the more powerful for him. Men who learn to practice this art do not have to deal with the tremendous bonding tug inherent in the sex act that eventually makes the relationship unmanageable. A real womanizer leaves the relationship at the point where the woman functions more as an equal, since he is unable to take her shakti from her without returning something. Politicians utilize this same energy to get their campaign workers to work more productively for them. They become a kind of father/ mother figure. Fanatics and charismatic religious leaders also have a similar hold over their followers.

Men who do heart bonding with co-workers get a deep loyalty, and later anger, for not producing the wanted results. If you remember back to adolescence, when sexuality was new, forbidden, and you longed for a certain unattainable someone, you'll recapture the distressing emotionalism within. This is what the usurious male does. He shares confidences with them, for the control this gives him. Women in the workplace have been furious for years over stolen ideas they were not given credit for. Sadly, the office wife is there to be used and places herself in that position by sharing her insights instead of utilizing her creativity for her own purposes.

The womanizer, as any bee wanting to nurture the hive, sucks juice from every flower he comes upon. Rarely is the woman the queen bee she believes herself to be. Like the real insect, her reign lasts approximately one year. After that it's all work for the woman producing the insight, wisdom, imagination, and productivity that free him to do whatever it is he wants.

Infidelity　　　　　Marianna Leppman, a retired pediatrician, once shared her philosophy on marriage: "The affairs you can live through." It is a very European attitude, from another century, I believed. Yet there is a bundle of wisdom in that statement. In an affair of the heart, the woman in the house cannot be dislodged unless she is insecure, or pained sufficiently to force the male to choose between her and his lover.

As the wife, a wise woman only has to affirm in her mind that she still loves him, wants him, and will go along with the better offers he presents to her. A wise woman reassesses herself, sees it isn't her he's rejecting, but his own fears and ghosts. A wise woman knows what he's up to and at the appropriate time calls him on it. Then she can be there without her own inner pain or fear of rejection and abandonment.

The woman he leaves his mate for is rarely the one he stays with. The interim woman may last a while, but he will definitely complete his transition at a later date, rendering him unsuitable for her or vice versa. All the classes, special weekends, best kept houses, and gourmet meals won't keep lovers close if their paths aren't compatible. The very things that attracted you at first may prove to be your undoing.

If you really want a blessed union, do not begin by being "the other woman." Far safer and ever more likely to be true to you is a man whose previous relationship has already dissolved without your presence. Freedom is the key to a healthy long-term union.

Life Force   Men need to learn how to draw in fresh lifeforce and shakti for themselves. Those who aren't able to learn this skill are doomed to sap woman after woman for it. As each woman becomes disgusted with the lack of intimacy the relationship actually offers her, she ends it. Men seeking to protect themselves begin to keep several lovers at once. Or if it's the inactive sexual type of bond where the shakti can be withdrawn, they switch from one woman to another.

It is the nature of the womanizer to get his energy from a woman. Women automatically draw down fresh energy from the cosmos and convert it into personal love or a spiritual dynamic that translates into power. Most give it away to a man, or their children, and then feel run-down or put upon.

A man can overcome his need to gather his energy from women. He can learn to pull it in from the Source. This is done by opening the heart chakra in the back and allowing the flow of universal love to seep in. With each inhalation you pull in some divine light, loaded with universal love. Automatically it is converted in your heart chakra to your personal vibration. You then send it out to others through the front of your heart chakra. It is preferable to receive universal love from the Cosmos rather than recharge yourself with another person's love energy, since the supply is unlimited and it gives you an independent source of love. Every person takes the unconditional love from the Source and converts it to their distinct vibration. When love is a shared energy exchange there is no difficulty; however if the energy is being sucked with little or no reciprocation you can receive the other individual's confusion and possessive desire along with it.

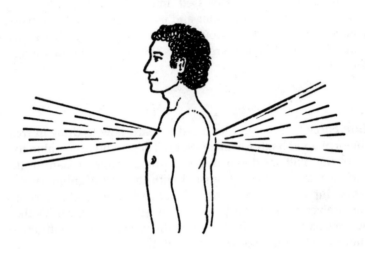

Women Who Use Men Women can suck on men in a financial way spending and spending, playing the role of a demanding child, a kind of spoiled brat. A man may give money in hopes of receiving love, nurturing, emotional support, or to buy his freedom. Women sometimes get cash, house, car, jewels, and kids in a divorce. The man is stripped of all the assets he's had, and left to start over. However, when the relationship ends, in most cases the woman is left high and dry without her accustomed lifestyle and no means of obtaining it again. As with any boom period, without substance, there will arrive a bust.

Women usually cheat on their partner when they're absolutely miserable in the relationship and see no hope for change. Looking for a replacement prior to ending their ongoing union is one common ploy. Another is to get satisfaction and relief from the heavy load of their unhappy marriage or live-in. Sometimes they do it just to spite their cheating spouse.

Relatively few long-term couples remain absolutely monogamous.

Dominance   In every intimate relationship the lovers battle each other for dominance. The one who can passively or actively put their mate down then has to deal with the sickness, mental or physical, the dominated partner develops. If you wish your consort who is mentally or emotionally more developed than you to be under your control, you can only do it by stressing them to the point where they become ill. Then you have to take care of him or her.

In some cases the man passively holds the woman back by never disagreeing with her, and then doing as he pleases. But he makes mock fights that appear real, on issues where he's willing to give in. Then she thinks she has the upper hand, unaware that she doesn't see the things he's secretly doing, be they investments or other women. She feels somehow off balance and betrayed, but thinks it's the last fight where he gave in to her over some petty household issue. The man, who has engaged in this battle just as vehemently as if he meant it, keeps her focused in his direction at all times. This type of man is very strong, for he knows exactly what he wants. She appears strong to the outside world but in actuality is quite unable to wield her power effectively. She may have many ailments over the years. If she knuckles under to his pressure and loses herself she may develop a chronic unrelieved condition where she dominates based on her illness. This gives him freedom outside the home and none inside.

Joan Hodgson's concisely written book *Why On Earth* (White Eagle Publishing Trust, England 1979), states:

> *Sometimes when in a previous life one partner has gained considerable power over the other a strange, magnetic emotional tie is set up in which he or she feels completely dominated and is forced to accept all kinds of bullying, mental or physical. In such cases it may well be that the down-trodden one has to find strength and courage to make a break, both for the sake of the children or for his or her own self respect.*

BREAKING UP

If a person cannot deal with your insecurities and you can only take care to cushion theirs—then it's not a worthy relationship.

Lianne Wolf

A general dissatisfaction with love relationships exists among a broad spectrum of the population. Forty-one percent of the marriage age population is single. This statistic covers the previously wed as well as the never married. For the majority, recovery from a broken relationship includes finding someone else to love. It is the magnetic quality of sexuality that draws on you so strongly that you're willing to risk everything in another union. Common wisdom says to part as gracefully and peaceably as possible, recognizing that you are two separate distinct individuals. The manner in which you end your previous relationship is the way the new one begins. A volatile, resentful break-up will not draw in a co-operative, enthusiastic, loving new partner.

Anger, sorrow, and other tough-to-embrace feelings will arise in any break-up. There are ways to handle these aside from calling your former beloved at three in the morning.

One year, when a particularly painful relationship had come to its final hours, I devised a technique called, "The tape of the tape." It prevented moot, unproductive, and vicious arguments that wouldn't resolve anything anyway.

Buy a ninety-minute tape. Place it in your tape recorder. Angry thoughts, repetitive reruns of unhappy times together, your dissatisfactions, grief, hopelessness, and despondency belong to an inner sound track in your mind that plays over and over again. It's a normal part of the bereavement and pain of separation. Lying in bed, or while involved with simple chores, the thoughts surge forth unbidden, taking you down dark tunnels of no return. Press the record button. Speak your mind. In three to eight minutes it's finished, and you can go on with your day in a better mood until the next episode overtakes your consciousness. In the beginning opportunities to use the tape seem unlimited. Within a couple of weeks you may not even react to bits of the material that were highly charged for you.

Some people quit repeating themselves, remembering that what they're about to say has been previously recorded. Others prefer to say it every time until they've gotten it off their chest. One woman played the tape back to herself until it made her laugh. Another option is to record over the material you've already told the tape or to insert a new tape when it's full. Deciding to insert a new tape means you have to dispose of the old one. Wrap it securely in a cloth rag, go outside with a hammer in your hand, find a hard surface and beat the tape to oblivion. Throw away all the tiny pieces. Large chunks of your anguish will dissolve in the cassette's fragments.

Parting Meditations   Affirmations and Gestalt cannot return lost love once the person is really gone. Any method will work if your ex-lover wishes to be with you again. The mutual longing gets you back together. But if your former lover has cut all ties of an emotional and mental nature, you'll not get him or her back. Affirmations work better for men than for women because women usually pine and grieve longer than men do, although men often ignore their feelings and put on a show.

Power spells can work, but they tend to wear off with all the attendant repercussions. You'd have to constantly be working and remaking them to keep your lover attached to you. That's not a real relationship, it's the impression of one, without any substance.

If you want to end the fighting in your relationship, or you wish for your lost love to return to you, send her/him nothing but pure heart energy for three consecutive days. Be cautious not to put any stops or conditions on the heart energy you are sending. Do one of these meditation techniques daily for thirty days. You may alter them to suit your individual situation.

Picture him or her inside a kernel of corn. The inner portion of the kernel represents the soul level where love is always steady and secure. Visualize the center as pink, and see your lover as happier than she or he has been in ages. See how pleased your true love is. Place yourself next to your lover and envision the love you are sharing together. See the merging of your souls and personalities, and feel the blessing of the Creator for your union. Then mentally send her/him a picture of your vision.

Another meditation is to visualize your beloved or hold a favorite picture of the two of you in your hand. Tell her or him out loud everything you are sorry about and what regrets you have. Say aloud what you would do to make amends and what you need in return. Send the energy mentally to him or her.

If you really wish to be rid of your former partner, nurture yourself very well. Whenever you think of something you miss about him or her, think of how you might replace that part of your relationship. If you traveled well and frequently together, look among your friends for a travel partner. Although you will most likely have another lover someday, she or he won't share the same things you and your ex-partner did. Visualize yourself saying goodbye to your estranged beloved and their acceptance of your parting.

Levels of the Soul and Incompatibility In Chapter 4 we discussed the levels of soul development an individual has achieved. Picking a partner who is in the same Mansion makes for an easier more fulfilling relationship than choosing one from a lower or higher Mansion. The partner who is from the higher Mansion is the one who suffers as the less capable partner holds them back and does disturbing things. Inborn in each person who is not of the same soul level as you are is a constellation of contradictory beliefs that lobby against parallel and compatible mergers.

One of the worst marriages I ever witnessed was between a Toddler/Child soul whose work was with the fifth rung of the ladder and his wife, an Old Soul who dwelled on the fifth story of her Mansion. He was a kindly, quiet, good-hearted gentleman, whose inability to take risks drove her to distraction. They shared a love of music that was legendary. He was exceptionally talented as a singer; she had no singing voice but understood the inner complexities and healing energies of sound. He lived by the book. A thing was either right or wrong by convention. He was tacitly religious. She, as an Old Soul, possessed great compassion, and viewed every situation as a potential for growth and development. As long as no one would be harmed, with proper precautions, it was all right to experiment. She was always flexible and cared more about human beings than conventions. Can you imagine the effect their attitudes had upon their children?

Theirs is a common union, since people are attracted to those whose interests are like their own. A nature photographer and an ecologist share their love of the natural world and its beauty. But can they see their comparative soul natures? Is one a Teenaged Soul given to fits of power mongering and acquisition for acquisition's sake? Is the other a Mature Soul who likes creature comforts but cannot argue over petty details? How will they fare in the long run? Eight months, the average time people know each other before marrying or moving in together, is hardly sufficient to assess the durability of a long-term commitment.

Lovers whose Mansions match, whether one is on the third story and the other on the sixth, will have a healthier, more pleasurable union than those whose Soul Levels aren't as well matched.

TRANSFORMATIVE SEX

The sexual bond is a very powerful one. It is a doorway to higher consciousness. The ingredients are surrender, physical intimacy without reserve, nonviolent sexual intercourse involving touch, taste, smell, sight, and sound. Your entire psyche, emotions, mental and bodily senses form a single energetic dynamic focused not on getting there, but in being here now in harmony and total rapport with your lover.

Three main categories of orgasm can occur during lovemaking. Mild body sensation and emotional satisfaction called valley orgasm, wild physical orgasm with immediate exhaustion, and the crescendo type where the couple merge their consciousness with the Creator. When you and your partner really let go of your individual egos you reach that third stage. At that moment you can't tell her arm from yours, the bodies are one. In women, the build up within a single sexual act can be from mild to intense orgasms to the peak experience orgasm that takes her to higher consciousness. Men do not experience the rise of the crescendo orgasm energy because they do not know how to surrender. They may actively experience it for about thirty seconds before ejaculation.

Tantra is a formula for going through the ecstatic doorway to the other levels of consciousness. It lacks spontaneity, which is the most potent way to enter the other worlds. The experience can produce bliss, knowledge and access to the Realms of the Source, Creation, and Formation.

Transformative sex, technically induced as Tantra, is a way to universal consciousness. Unfortunately, the religious dogmas attached to transcendental lovemaking are skewed so that the male's needs predominate.

Richard Alan Miller reveals many ways to cross the transformative gate via lovemaking in his exceptional book, *The Magical and Ritual Use of Aphrodisiacs*, Destiny Books, 1985.

Ancient China was a patriarchal society which nevertheless, believed that women were closer than men to immortal nature's primordial forces. Taoist magicians therefore alleged that sexual contact with as many women as possible (virgins were most preferred) would provide the sage with increased physical vigor, mental health and longevity.

People do not always know this doorway to higher consciousness exists, or tell themselves it isn't really there. Those who believe it's not cricket to allow their entryway to be sexual, or that there are other more advanced methods, are severing themselves from a share of the divine plan. Those who know that transcendental states of being can be reached via sexuality, but are too inhibited, or want a shortcut, turn to perverted forms of love, violence, sadomasochism, constant conquests, nymphomania, Priapus syndrome, or group sex to get the kick. They seldom reach bliss nor do they transcend, as the best and surest route to the cosmic doorway is in a committed, loving, non-usurious relationship.

Tantra is frequently usurious to women. Yet women like tantric lovemaking because the man has to spend two-and-a-half hours with her instead of slam bam and falling asleep. The rites of tantric sex forbid the man to ejaculate although he may do a "sperm sacrifice" if a baby is hoped for. Traditional tantra occurs just once per month, but modern non-religious couples partake several times a month for the sake of unity.

There is a method of restoring harmony to a chaotic relationship. Rather than making love to climax the couple engage in foreplay slowly and tenderly. When both are sufficiently aroused, they carry out a distinct form of tantric lovemaking. Lying on their sides, the man and woman embrace, her outer leg over his outer leg. Noses pressed together, side to side, he breathes through his right nostril and she breathes through her right nostril. The man enters the woman's vagina with the first third of his penis. They lie together, breathing without pumping. After twenty-eight to thirty-three minutes their energies are merged. The man removes his penis and they lie together until sleep overtakes them. This can heal even very difficult stressful unions, giving the couple a chance to love each other anew.

The breathing is crucial as the man breathes through the Pingala or male channel and the woman breathes through the Ida or female channel causing creative energy (shaktipat) to return to their union.

With a bit of adjusting for anatomical differences, lesbians can also practice this technique. One partner lies on top while the heavier or stronger partner takes the bottom position facing up. The important features are genital contact and one breathing through the left nostril while the other breathes through the right one.

Andrew Ramer, who claims to be a semi-recluse living in Brooklyn, New York, has written a sensible, warmhearted look at tantric love between two men called *Two Flutes Playing*. Andrew himself is charming, intelligent, sensitive, witty, and a good writer. This book is privately available through The Body Electric in Oakland, California. Much of what the author has to say applies to lovers of any gender.

> "Circuit integration between individuals is a gradual and delicate process. It can take as long as six or eight months for two to interface fibers through their sexual systems, and as long to disconnect. When sex is being used for soul information exchange, sexual connections with other partners will cause fiber blockage. Again, no more judgement here. This is a matter of human bio-electrics, not in function very different than the rules governing electricity and power lines and wiring. It isn't morality that guides an electrician, but an understanding of electricity. So too with electricians of the soul.
>
> "The purpose of sexual connection is information exchange. The more profound the exchange, the deeper the love felt. The purpose of sexual connection is not primarily reproductive. In truth, there are planets where reproduction and lovemaking do not make use of the same organs, as they do here. Species may have one set of organs for lovemaking and another for reproducing. As you become more and more conscious, more and more aware of subtle energy, you will

*understand this information more and more and come to rec-
ognize the purpose of function of love and sex in your life
and in the universe. Love and sex link individuals and
connect all sentient beings in a vast non-physical web that
ripples through physicality and has the capacity to flood it
with the total joy of beingness. Passion is not love, necessarily. Sex is not love, necessarily. Love is that shared reso-
nance between two individuals that allows for soul level
information exchange. Please remember that when you are
searching for a love-partner. Please remember that when you
are with your love-partner. Ask yourself if this is someone
you want to share soul information with, if this is someone
whose soul information you want to carry bits of yourself.
Sex connects, but it is not always an appropriate connection.
As you evolve, you will not always need to remember this.
You will come to function smoothly on all planes. And, sex
and love will happen harmoniously then."*

Throughout *Two Flutes Playing* the joyousness of loving is celebrated. There are exercises to clear your chakras and meditations
to prepare yourself for non-orgasmic lovemaking. One exercise,
the second sound meditation in the book, is profound.

*"Now sit again. For this the second sound meditation. Sit,
two, the same way. Face to face, relaxed. Now opening the
mouth wide, opening the throat, letting sound pour forth in
a single wide, thick, sky-ascending column. Make sound of
'Ahh.' Loud 'Ahh.' Full body shaking 'Ahh.' Feel sound rise
up between, surrounding you. In a vast sound column. And
then, when the body-breath expends itself, listen to the silence that follows it. The falling water sound of silence after
'Ahh.' Its descent. Dropping. Moving through the body.
Reaching a point of silent depth. Now, let sound rise up
again. Up through body. From pelvis to crown. Up above it.
Sound of 'Oh' this time Rising. Rising. Two flutes sound.
Two men. 'Oh.' Rising To highest point. Then falling into
silence, into 'Oh's' descent. Now, begin again. This time
with the sound of 'Eee.' Deep in the head. Chant rising.
Rising. then falling into silence. Slowly. With great spaces
of silence between chants. 'Ahh. Oh. Eee.' Rising and falling. Full bodied, full breath. This, the second sound meditation. Chanting these sounds over and over and over again.
Till the electric walls of flesh are aquiver with connected
sense of the man-man divine body oneness."*

Sexual Cycles From menarche to menopause women have a sexual cycle linked to the moon's orbit of 28 to 29 days. A woman knows when she is in her quiet point of the cycle, when she is ovulating, and when she is at her most attractive. She's aware of depression, upset, or mood swings in the days before her period, and finally that she is menstruating. The cycle doesn't totally cease at menopause.

Pregnancy is another sexual cycle. The woman is sexiest while she's gestating. Her hormonal condition changes from month to month. With it her desire fluctuates. If nauseated and out of sorts during the early months, a woman may not be sexually aroused. A fit-feeling, elated mother-to-be is often more amorous than usual. Most women feel their best during the second trimester of pregnancy, and may want frequent lovemaking. Many women stay sexually active until just before childbirth, while others are physically uncomfortable with intercourse as the third trimester advances. While nursing, the hormones connected with sexual arousal are suppressed in favor of lactation. Menstruation and its hormonal input are removed. This is nature's birth control. It's tough on a marriage when the woman doesn't feel like making love because her hormones aren't ready. Her partner feels rejected and further pushed out of the picture, since the baby is taking up ninety-six hours of her time per week. Statistics have shown that's exactly how much care each infant needs.

Some women deal with inadequate or unsatisfying sex in their lives by being pregnant, or lactating, both important parts of a woman's sexual cycle. Around 99 percent of all sexually active women don't become pregnant even in the absence of birth control, once they've reached forty-five years of age. Until that point, women married to sexually unfullfilling men can still experience sexual fulfillment by bearing a child. Women who have children simply to make up for what's lacking in themselves or their relationship will not have the strength to hold the children together once they wean them.

Although most men don't know it they have a cycle of fifty-six days, with sexual and creative peaks and valleys, as well as the accompanying emotional symptoms. They can't tell because no bleeding occurs. The husband of a friend of mine had drinking binges every two months like clockwork. She jokingly called it his PMS. Yet once informed of the male hormonal cycle, she realized it wasn't a joke. He eventually gave up alcohol and dealt with his bouts of depression and self-denigration.

All creative forces are sexual. During times of spiritual growth, sexual energy is diverted to the brain resulting in a low libido. The partner feels terrible. Women without a bonded relationship wonder, "Can't I find anybody?" not realizing that their hormonal output isn't sufficient to attract a new lover. Partners feel unloved and are unaware that the change is temporary.

Total Sexuality   Sex contains the same energy that it takes to go to God, that same orgasmic ecstasy. It's the ecstasy of the orgasm that is the energy that takes you to knowing God, to being with God. That's why it had to be contained and forbidden by the churches, so that people wouldn't put that energy into each other and forget to support established religions. Except for sexual tantra, which is a consciously channeled form of sexual expression, the churches played down sexuality. And in western culture, for many centuries, they forbade it outright except for procreation.

In this century the mass consciousness has been changed. So that the expression of the heart may open, we went through a sexual revolution which allows us to use sex as a declaration of loving, caring spirituality toward our partners; and the fallout from this new physicalness is that we are now allowed to be more publicly affectionate with our children and friends and to express appreciation and joyousness verbally and physically.

There used to be a bias in this culture that children were not to hear good things about themselves. It was thought that this would turn their heads. Nor was pleasurable activity generally thought to be good. "Idle hands do the Devil's work." The realization that sexuality is more than intercourse, and can open every human being to the fullness of their own developmental freedom and creativity, is fairly recent.

The appreciation of our cycles as women is part of this. We may now write about and speak about menstruation. We welcome and celebrate the menarche of our daughters, and treat menopause with the respect and dignity it deserves. And to be able to nurture those women passing from the menstrual cycle validating their reality, is a particularly impressive display of the change in sexual attitudes.

Likewise is the respect unfolding once again in our society for the wisdom of the aged male and female.

Another example of our recognition of the totality of sexuality is that men are now permitted to express their tender feelings and fully participate in the raising of their children with complete social approval.

These attitudes are more in keeping with the Cosmic concept of human interaction rather than the stiff distant fear of intimacy which was probably introduced to cool the passions of all forms of personal love.

Sexuality is much more than making love and mating. It creates a bond and an emotional field. Sexuality exists in friendships as hugs, non-intimate kisses, shared looks, and private jokes.

10

Friendship

Instead of loving your enemies, try treating your friends a little better.

Edgard Watson Howe

Friendship   Both friendship and romantic involvements begin as voluntary associations between two people. Given time, the relationships pick up obligations and depth. Marriage is the natural outgrowth of a blossoming romance, but friendships may fade, or become fruitful, providing the core of human contact for you. The ones with apparent magnetism succeed in the face of great odds. In all instances the Cosmos is at work bringing people together for a purpose greater than their individual journey. Friendships may also assist them with the exploration and unfolding of their Mission in life.

Every human being longs to be loved and accepted as they are. We are sociable creatures, who become recluses either for the sake of our spiritual journey, or because we've been wounded in our quest for acceptance.

You can love a friend. Loving friendships are very important to a rich, full life. Many people do not know how to be a friend and are therefore limited to superficial interactions with others. Anyone can learn to be a good friend, and also how to eliminate those who are backstabbing, irritating, and non-supportive.

A friendship is a freely chosen human interaction. Unlike family, with whom you are bonded by blood irrespective of your liking, friends are able to be together or not as desired. Family, if our language is a clue, quite obviously must be more important historically than your friends. Designations for half-sister, sister, sister-in-law, step-sister, foster brother, aunt, great aunt, great grand aunt, niece, father, grandfather, and great grandfather, include the relationship and the sex of the individual referred to. Only cousin fails to divulge the sex and requires a descriptive word like second cousin, first-cousin-once-removed, or girl cousin to denote who and how close.

English has no one word that conveys the depth of a single friendship. Intimate friend, close friend, casual friend, friend of a friend, a former lover, or lifelong friend are indiscriminately classified under one word, friend. The word friend must always be modified to clarify the depth or lack thereof in a non-blood relationship. The Australian expression "me mate" defines a close buddy, usually someone a man would be willing to defend with his mitts. Buddy can be a companion, comrade, or a small boy you befriend. A companion could be someone paid to live with and accompany you, your friend, or your live-in lover. In Shakespeare's time "my friend" was a euphemism for mistress. "Crony" means a good friend, but is usually derogatory unless preceded by old. "Confidant" has become a substitute for relationships based on women gossiping.

Contrast the ways casual and possibly involuntary associations can be announced: acquaintance, classmate, colleague, co-worker, neighbor, schoolmate. A schoolmate can be someone you knew well at school, an agemate you saw at school, not elsewhere.

Companions are usually in a superficial relationship. Fishing, movies, aerobics classes, it's the activity that's important, not the person. Friendships are different. It's not what you do that makes the time meaningful, it's that you are together. Friends share their thoughts and feelings, and hold in common a series of beliefs that are deeper than any single issues they may disagree on.

Seemingly close friendships are formed to further community projects, or because you live nearby, work for the same company, or your children are friends. They endure, or pass by the wayside when your children grow up, you move away, change jobs, undergo therapy, alter your eating habits, become richer or poorer than you were before.

Friends of many years standing do change, as you do. Your friend may have taken up an exclusive religious path that claims all those who do not follow it are to be avoided. Friends marry people you abhor and over the years become more like their spouses. Although you may grieve over the loss of your great friends, do not slam the door on them. They may become lighter about their religious preference, or abandon it altogether at some future time. Partnerships, professional and marital, have been known to collapse.

What is quite obvious, in the late industrial period, is that families are no longer extended socio-economic systems and they do not serve our emotional, mental, and social needs. Friends are the people you are most likely to share your free time with.

Marriage and living together are commonly temporal conditions, entered into many times. The culture has quickly invented terms for the condition of being no longer involved, "ex," "former partner," "the mother of my son." Along with giving up your spouse or lover you may divest yourself of their relatives as well, or choose to continue your friendships with "in-laws." Friends are frequently the closest family you have. They've lived through your successes and tragedies with you.

Letty Cottin Pogrobkin says it's harder to keep your friends when you're in triumph than in failure. My observation is that it's not only due to the friends dropping away, you drop them as well. Although society at large decries breakups or bad blood in a family, nary a ripple passes when a longtime friendship turns sour. Friendship is regarded as an association of convenience, without stipulated, formal obligations. In the Realm of Creation it is the deepest of commitments, one that endures death and rebirth.

Forever Friends   Kindred souls, who are your special friends of this lifetime, have been your lover, your child, your sister, your mother, your enemy, your intimate and confidant, your most trusted next to yourself. Your first meeting, whether in grade school or as new neighbors in a housing complex for the elderly, produces instant recognition, an intuitive feeling that you've always known them. There is no hesitancy or lack of immediate intimacy. The friendship has instant depth. Forever friends reacquainted early in life, whose careers and marriages interfere with constant contact, retain the feeling that no lost years exist when they come together again. These are your cosmic friends. These friendships cross age, ethnic, and economic barriers. Cosmic friendships endure despite political differences and spousal disapproval. They are often remarkable juxtapositions of dissimilar lifetimes joined by their endless love and attraction for one another. Forever friendship is strong love.

Loneliness   Loneliness is a big problem. The wrong way out of it is to marry. The loneliness inside a bad marriage is worse than the the kind you have when you're single. To avoid loneliness by associating with people who you don't really like, or whose behavior you consider inappropriate, is to be untrue to yourself. The young do it because they have no experience in the world and are learning about people. As you get older and sense who is compatible or acerbic for you, it's wisest to wait for those you really appreciate and who will appreciate you.

You believe loneliness will go away when you have a partner. Yet it hovers around, waiting to gain entry, to leave its cold hollow in your heart. Stoned or sober it follows you. It intrudes on your reading, everywhere at once it is bigger than you are whenever you allow it to separate you from others.

That loneliness which eats at you in crowds is gone quickly, transformed into solitude, if you choose to be alone. Through solitude and contemplation, in constant association with the Divine, comes bliss. Loneliness is not usually resolved by keeping busy, or having close friends. It is definitely not assuaged by superficial talk with acquaintances and untold rounds of partying. It ducks down temporarily, rapidly reasserting its presence in quiet moments. The way through is to merge with loneliness. To become it, and absorb it, is to know the Divine. Conquering doesn't work, only seeking your oneness with the Creator dissolves loneliness. Loneliness is separation from the Creator. Spiritual seeking through prayer and following your true Mission in life will alleviate it.

Ostracism   Ostracism, whether formal as in shunning, or informal as in keeping undesirables, women, ethnics, wrong economic classes out of clubs and organizations, exists throughout society. The informal type is dangerous as it exacerbates the economic and social injustices the outsiders are forced to bear. Yet the outsiders form a group of insiders that are socially viable and have their own distinct prerequisites for membership.

Being an outsider who wants to be an insider keeps you involved in a group. However, it prevents you from merging too closely as an insider and losing your values. It's the observer's (anthropologist's) role, held in contempt for being different once the group clearly sees you won't adapt to its rules and customs. Observers who do adapt still have to wait a long time for the group to accept them.

Ostracism has its own power. It leaves you free of entanglements with a group, unencumbered by their values and morals. It keeps you centered in yourself and your own affairs, as long as you don't want to be back in the part of society that has rejected you. It may happen that you become a central or peripheral figure within the group again, but in your own time and on your own terms.

Ostracism is self-imposed, even by those who've achieved the status by offending others. Most people who attain the status of outcast do so because they are miserable in the social groups they have access to.

Artistic and eccentric people frequently find themselves on the fringes of "normal" society. If you are that type and do not say much, keeping your discomfort to yourself, you will be accepted by everyone. Should your commentaries be ignored, or non-threateningly delivered, the group will still allow you access. But when your criticisms or blatant lifestyle abrasively contradict the group's beliefs or habitual behavior, then you'll be temporarily banished until you mend your ways or they become more open-minded.

Banishment can mean total exclusion, so that "nice" people no longer speak to you. Or it can be social slights, like being left out of parties, excluded from coffee klatches and so on. It can be in the form of a test, as in the case of a newcomer to a community who must break down the barriers to acceptance slowly. If the mainstream has been disappointed by other outsiders, they'll never quite let you in, unless many other new people move into the area challenging the old guard. You can achieve acceptance into a community by forming another socially visible group that is alluring to the established folks. Another way to beat down the doors is by serving on committees that aid the local hospital, volunteer fire department, and other causes.

Banishment can also signal that you do not belong in a particular segment of society, and your real friends can be found in another organization or community.

The downfall of every culture rests in its prejudices and self-indulgences. When the downtrodden use legal and peaceful means to strike back and win, all of society benefits. To right the world's wrongs, sing for your lives. An anthem can bring peace in the end. Revolution promulgates endless revolution. Considering that you will be born again and again as a woman, an Italian, a Greek, a Pakistani, a Jew, and a person of color, it's to your ultimate benefit to exclude no one from the mainstream. In your current lifetime, try to imagine a woman or a person of color having the knowledge and ability to solve our ecological and environmental ills, yet unable to get the information out because they are excluded from the right clubs or corporate structure. Whose loss is it?

Compassion   Compassion is one of the highest of goals, for with it you can understand and appreciate another's predicament. Compassion diminishes judgmental and critical behavior. Once you know you won't be drawn into another's drama, but can stand calmly by giving support and sound advice you have taken the first step toward compassion. When you can see both sides of an argument involving two people you really care for, and not jump to defend or condemn one or the other, you have developed true compassion. If you support each one and help them find the middle ground, or listen attentively allowing your friends to come to their own conclusion, you will be a really good friend.

Trust   Trust is a major ingredient in friendships and all other human relationships. If you have no trust, or little trust, life is always tinged or dominated by hopelessness. It's difficult to act as if the world is a friendly loving place when trust is small and injustice so readily seen. If you don't trust, how can anyone trust you?

Trust is a peculiar quality; you can't have trust until you trust enough to give your trust to others. And then you still have to trust yourself and your judgement even if that trust is violated. Trust involves trusting yourself first, believing in your own integrity and trusting that you'll learn from your mistakes and triumphs. Trust is more than confidence, although it contains that. Relatively few people have never had their trust in themselves shaken. As visible proof of the lessons that must be undergone, your trust will be challenged continually in new settings and on familiar turf.

Friends, those you share your secrets with and to whom you bare your soul, betray you out of ignorance or their own emotional turmoil. More people can explain betrayal than trust. Who can you always trust? Yourself and the Creator. Trusting the Creator is tenuous at best if your prayer power and meditative access have been held in check. Trust in the Source is easiest if you have faith.

There are those who have no trust in human beings, warily holding themselves aloof from any kind of relationship. Paradoxically, there are those who trust no one, but mix freely among their social milieu. Subconscious messages send some people trustingly into society. And these folks are shocked anytime their trust is betrayed, for it is an infrequent occurrence. The vibration of trust emanates from those who have it. Spend time with such people and you begin to have the courage to trust.

A big step forward is to be able to trust the Universe to take care of your needs and point you in the right direction. That's what finding your path and performing your Mission entails. Trust is sacred. To break another's trust in life and their trust in a loving, beneficent god is profane.

Past Lives and Current Associations

Believing in a past life unquestioningly, can make you react erroneously in the current life. Prior incarnations do not create an imperative for re-establishing the friendship in a new lifetime. The individuals responsible for your downfall, or for serving as the mainstays of your previous lives, don't necessarily remain in that capacity.

Two partners who play martyrdom and domination acts with one another can be affiliated lifetime after lifetime, as one and then the other of the unsatisfied duo rips the other off financially to even the score. They may have been brothers in a past incarnation, repeating the win/lose relationship they've had before. Does it really make amends and heal the wounds if they simply exchange whose turn it is to be destroyed by the other? Some unfortunate dyads never recover. Sometimes neither one recovers. Those who learn from the lesson will begin the repair work and recovery as soon as they assimilate the information. At this point they can pass their chapter test.

It's one of the best kept secrets of the Universe: Refining yourself is the way to change others. For as you change yourself, others change in the way they respond to you. Once they do, they can see another kind of possible interaction with others in their lives.

Do not hold out for the other to learn first. What you're holding out for is a truism expressed best by Tibetan Buddhist ideology, "If one becomes enlightened, all beings who have a relationship, either positive or negative, to that person share in the transmigration."

SECTION THREE
THE WAYS
TO ENLIGHTENMENT

11

The Elements

The first ingredient of life is courage.
Hahm Sok Han, 1965

Mystical people, and groups whose core religious practices worship or implore the four elements, have names for every one of the winds and the four directions. There is a sound, a chant, or a name to summon each element in societies where connection to these forces and spiritual practices are linked. Norse, Greek, Roman, and Egyptian mythology designated deities as rulers of an element. The Romans had Jupiter who governed the north winds that fertilize. To the Greeks, Aphrodite was the goddess of the ocean, and the mother/daughter team of Demeter and Persephone the earth goddesses. Poseidon was the ocean god. Kephisus, the Greek river god, represented the male principal of fresh water. To the Chinese the river goddess and rainmaker is Kuan Yin. Hindu religion credits Agni as the god of fire; however in Norse religion that distinction goes to Tyr in male form and Heartha in the female form. Tara is the fire goddess in

Tibetan Buddhism. In using the elements to attain spiritual wisdom, you are calling upon the Realm of Formation to teach you about Universal truths.

Everything in the Universe is related to the elements interacting upon one another. Each element has a characteristic—earth is heavy, water cool, fire hot, air active, and space mixed.

The cycle of the seasons is a parade of the powers each element bears. Winter belongs to fire, summer to the wind, spring to water, and autumn to the earth herself. The transitional seasons between the primary seasons (winter, summer, fall, and spring) belong to the element of space. [This fifth season, the transitional one, is hardest on living beings and most noticeable are discharging diseases: colds, flu, hay fever.]

Every two hours throughout the day the element that is the focus changes. This is comparable to Oriental medicine wherein every organ has a two-hour period of energizing activity per day. (See diagram in Chapter 14.) Every hour contains precise times for the elements. The first eight minutes belong to the wind, the second twelve minutes belong to fire. The third period, of twenty minutes, is delegated to water, and the fourth division of the hour gives fifteen minutes to the earth element. The final segment of the hour lasts four minutes and is for space. One minute comprises the changeover.

The elements as periods of learning can be divided into seven-year segments: young air (birth to six); young fire (7–14); young earth (14–21); young water (21–28); mature air (28–35); mature fire (35–42); mature earth (42–49); mature water (49–56); old air (56–63); old fire (63–70); old earth (70–77); old water (77–84); young space (84–91); mature space (91–98); old space (98+).

Each element has a color. Earth is yellow, Water milky, Fire golden-orange, Air light green or bluish, and Space sky blue.

Water teaches you about hydrotherapy, relaxation, healthy emotional discharges, and compassion. It also resolves fears and opens up the waters of your inner life. Fire leads you through the first spiral of enlightenment by setting your thought process straight. It clears the mind of worry and other confusions. Fire instructs you regarding power, self respect, how to turn a sword into a rose or a fight into love, human relationships, understanding, and negative pride. Earth as an element educates you on survival, managing physical life, and the courage to pass through successive gateways to growth and knowledge. Earth will show you healing plants, stones, and human nutritional needs. It will reveal telepathic communication with other life forms, and you'll come to appreciate the magnetic healing properties of the earth itself. Air trains the psyche, inner wisdom, opens the Source and prana. Stay clear of the wind until you have worked well into the Moon level and have done a full cycle with one other element. Space teaches everything that can be known. It is to be approached only after achieving proficiency with at least two other elements, and when most of your childhood traumas have been cleared up.

Mastery of an element commences in the Moon spiral. Healing is the way in. Healers heal others as they heal themselves. Healers heal themselves as they heal others. The more healing you do, the more adroit you become at it. Abuse your healing abilities and your skill shrinks. Cleanse your emotional and psychic wounds and all around you benefit. Proficiency in every spiral (moon, sun, star) of an element takes at least three-and-a-half years.

Inability to understand the basic elements of this planet is why scientific discoveries usually provide short-term gains that lead to disaster. A widespread illustration is timber industry blunders. Forests cannot have only one type of tree planted; nature mixes them for soil replenishment and disease control. Logging companies and the Bureau of Land misManagement ignore nature, hoping for quick profits. They plant only one type of fast growing tree in their reforestation programs. To fend off fungus and insects, they spray herbicides and pesticides, destroying watersheds and hurting wildlife in an attempt to protect thousands of acres of single species planted without regard for a forest's natural pattern.

Hundreds of other instances where nature has been tampered with to the detriment of the ecosystem are discounted by city dwellers who seldom notice the natural world.

EARTH

Earth is the name we call our planet as well as the terrain made of rock, sand, and soil we stand upon. We would do better to regard our orbiting home as a living entity, as do the Native Americans, Tibetan Buddhists, and other wise ancient lineages.

Treating her oil as the synovial that allows her to be comfortable in her body, the water as the blood in her veins, and the minerals as her flesh makes much more sense in light of the catastrophes environmental pollution has created. Mother Earth will survive us; she predated our existence. Ungrateful to our hostess, we despoil her body in the most disrespectful manner. Any guest in your home would be booted out for such boorish behavior. Since the beginning of industrialization we have injured her while killing ourselves. Descending into her insides demands a price, whether it is offshore oil rigs or coal mines. Technology, no matter how advanced, doesn't diminish the danger. We may wound her, but surely if there is a survivor in this war against nature, it will be Mother Earth.

Aside from volcanic activity, landslides, and earthquakes, earth is the most predictable of the elements. The other elements shape her more than she does herself. Sand can be windblown; water moves earth causing rockslides, avalanches, and gullies. Lightning fires can burn down entire forests or tear up soil. Wind and water together wear down mountains and carry away precious growing land.

Proficiency with the earth element includes deep communication and understanding about geological formations, plant life, minerals, and living creatures of all kinds.

The Formation Realm interacts most profoundly with human beings through the element of Earth. The realm has been well researched at Findhorn, in the Anthroposophic Society, and by devoted gardeners obscure and famous. Luther Burbank and others who worked with plants listened carefully and followed the suggestions of the plants themselves. Companion planting to achieve larger, healthier, faster growing vegetables can be observed. Potatoes grown near tomatoes do not do well. Peas next to potatoes make for quality and quantity. Crops that create favorable soils and smell good to the plants growing near them are fuller and mature more quickly.

Potatoes, planted in the waning or dark of the moon, have larger spuds than ones planted when the moon is waxing. Their bulbous roots number as many, but it's small potatoes, a poor harvest. Root crops planted before the full moon become flowery and bushy with leaves. Trial and error gardening methods are short-circuited by a person who allows the energies of the plant to influence them. Before foolishly removing a trillium from the woods to place it in a vegetable patch, they feel or hear it say "I only grow in dark dankish places."

Animals as well as plants communicate with us. Listening to animals can teach you many many things. A person who is really tuned in to animals will have all manner of wild creatures approach them peacefully. Animals taught humans how to domesticate them. Yet if animals told the herders how to limit their flocks to maintain the balance of nature, they were not listened to. Soil without adequate vegetation is washed away by the rain, then scorched by the sun and blown away by the wind. Did the animals not know this and wantonly increase their numbers once freed from the hazards of predators? Hardly. One possibility is that domesticated animals fell under the domination of people so that they no longer cared about anything that wasn't related directly to people. Tame animals respond to the desires of their owners.

Deer, raccoons, squirrels, and other species who live on the border of civilization let us see our attitudes toward the once great profusion of wildlife that occupied the earth. Overpopulation in Europe means you rarely see deer near farms aside from those bordering wilderness areas. Raccoons and beaver live mainly in an animal preserve on the Russian-Polish border.

Listening for the inner sounds of the earth is an essential part of mastering the element. The earth has a heartbeat which is a key into the mastery of it.*

There is another sound to the earth. The sound of things growing. It joins with the general hum or om of the Universe. Best heard early in the morning, before the day becomes strong, it's found in the deepest woods and high grassy places where little is disturbed. Swarms of buzzing insects imitate this sound although not in the same frequency range.

Ley Lines of the Earth
Ley Lines are a path of power extending around the globe. They are marked at megalithic sites on the earth by buildings and structures that accent the mysterious powers that occur where Ley Lines intersect each other. The pyramids, Glastonbury Plain, and Easter Island are a few of these.

---

*A full meditation to learn about the earth is in Sound Medicine by Laeh Maggie Garfield.

Nature also uses her own markers to show us where these power places are. The power of each landmark is different. These places rise up alone on a site where the surrounding land formations are far below them. Ayer's Rock (Uluru) Central Australia, Mount Shasta (Northern California), Mount Fuji (Japan), Mount Kailas (Tibet), Mount Rainier (Washington). The Four Corners in the American Southwest, an area 350 miles in diameter, is a power junction that holds the earth together.

Enchanted Rock near Fredericksburg, Texas, is a magical place. It is a natural marker, where the protective spirits guard the exposed base rock of pink and grey streaked hills. Intense winds blow across it, keeping it nearly soil free. Vegetation is sparse except in small hollows and crevices sheltered by balancing rocks and other formations. Climbing is an arduous task, left to the healthy and fleet of foot, or those willing to go slowly and laboriously, cautiously picking their way to the top. Filled with the exhilaration of accomplishment and the awe inspiring view from the peak, you stand on a spot connected via invisible lines of energy linking power places all over the world.

The dynamism recharges you. Splendid magic can be accomplished at such a site.

Go to the sacred sites nearest you and the faraway ones you feel drawn to, the Great Lakes, Mount Tamalpais, Lake Champlain, Machu Pichu, Jungfrau. Remain a few days in these locations far removed from cities. The spot itself will teach you. You don't have to live there. As a matter of fact, communities that have lived adjacent to a site on the Ley Lines oftentimes disappear without a trace, leaving only their edifices.

Sit without anticipation of what you will receive. Suspend all expectations and forget what others who sat there before you have written of their experience. Steep yourself in the energies of the sacred land, approaching it with respect. Prior to your pilgrimage, eat no meat, fish, poultry, nor foods made of animal products. Do not smoke cigarettes, drink alcohol, or otherwise profane your experience. View the place from far and near before actually walking upon it. Refrain from selecting a spot another has told you is "the magic one." Instead, allow your guidance to bring you to a *sitio* (small personal power site) that is truly right for you. You may lie down and merge yourself into the land from time to time provided that you do not fall asleep.

WATER

Water is a highly changeable element, but not as mutable as the wind. Wind blows on the water, causing high tides, and quickens the flow of rain or snowmelt. Water can drip slowly, or amass force to become a raging wild storm. Clogged by earth in the form of mudslides, water builds up behind a natural dam until it bursts through. Rocks, stones, uprooted trees, and plant debris cannot contain it; water surges more rapidly around such blockages. Water can change the rhythm of its inner sound and thereby its vibratory rate. The underlying sound in water always travels downstream. Each place where you go to concentrate on water will show you something new about its essential nature and your own life pattern.

Water rules the emotions. Logic and emotion are not compatible. One does not cancel out the other; both are human capacities each with a role to play in your life. Western logic stifles the emotions, sending them back inside, disavowing them, preventing you from working out the discomforting patterns of behavior. Fear of the emotions paralyzes your ability to rationally examine them, and forbids feelings to arise to be appreciated and explored. Every exercise you do with water will free your emotions, including tears and laughter. Personal health problems in the kidneys and bladder will be released by water meditations. Water will allow the water you are to merge with it, rediscovering your own spontaneous feelings.

Ocean Listening   Wind and water manifest as God's breath in the ocean's roar. On a clear or cloudy day, in fog or sunshine, you approach the water's edge. Watch the weather; you cannot perform this meditation in the rain. As a beginner, spend only twenty minutes meditating on the waves and listening to the sound. Increase your time over a period of months until you can sit for an hour and a half without becoming ungrounded. Once on the shore, ascertain whether it's an outgoing or incoming tide. Seat yourself accordingly, far away if it's high tide, close to the water at low tide. You may sit on a rock or on the sand.

There is a pattern to the waves, and within the overall pattern is a second integrated rhythm. You may watch and listen a long time, even over a period of years, before you hear and see what is obvious. This is a hint: catch the longest wave. And, when you have it, you'll still only be at the beginning. Count the pattern as you listen carefully for it. Notice when the wave pattern fails to repeat, and above all do not let your eyes deceive you. Transformation requires of the seeker to seek and do the work of seeking. Jumping to conclusions will distract you from the actual pattern. Keep looking even when you think you've gotten it.

The wave pattern of a sea is consistent within itself. No two are exactly alike. Even if an ocean and several seas contain repetitious patterns of seven waves they won't be the same. Nor will the lull pattern be equal in each. The lull pattern and the number of waves per cycle are individual for that ocean or sea. The wave pattern doesn't necessarily have to be a seven series. There are others depending upon the ocean or sea you are listening to. One has a nine-wave pattern that builds on three distinct rhythms until it reaches twenty-seven waves in a row.

Another sea has a pattern that begins on an extra short wave followed by two short waves, then a medium wave. The fifth wave is as short as number one. The sixth wave equals the fourth, the seventh is short, and the eighth very long. Examining this sea on its eastern border, where it meets land to the north and where its western face kisses the land, shows the consistency of the eight-wave pattern. On the last eight-wave cycle an extra long wave, longer than the eighth wave, appears just before the lull cycle. Listening to the ocean with eyes closed you hear its underlying rhythm as distinctly different from the one that pulls the Pacific.

You will also see spirals of energy descending from the heavens to drive the waves. Do not let this phenomenon throw you off from listening to the waves and watching for their pattern. Standing above the ocean on a cliff you might see the wave pattern once you've heard it.

Oceanographers speak of the world ocean, although human beings have conveniently divided them and named them the Atlantic, Pacific, Indian, Antarctic, and Arctic Oceans. Wherever you travel, you'll have to test the seas yourself to see if the patterns you've discovered doing this meditation are the same from sea to sea. The Caribbean, Baltic, Mediterranean, Adriatic, and North Seas all have memorable and unique wave patterns and underlying sounds.

Whenever there is a severe storm, a hurricane or a cyclone, hundreds of miles away the corresponding polarity in the ocean will be calm like a lake. Miami beaches have tiny almost imperceivable waves while hurricanes lash away at the Caribbean Islands that have the opposite magnetic pull. This is true for any section of the ocean.

Two of the locations the seas meet at are: the North and Baltic at Skagen, Denmark; the Atlantic and Pacific Oceans at Tierra del Fuego, at the tip of South America where the roughness of the water makes sailing hazardous. The waves break against each other over an invisible barrier, then roll back into their own ocean without mixing. What magical process exists, if any, to keep the oceans from exchanging waves? The waves are moving in a circular motion rather than a linear one. The answer lies in the wave patterns and their primal sounds.

Wisdom exists behind these patterns and sounds. Eskimos standing on an unfamiliar shore can draw an accurate map of the coastline 150 miles upward in latitude from where they are. An aerial photograph will confirm their map made by listening to the sound of the waves alone.

Grandmother Ocean   The ocean and seas each have their own grandmother guardian who oversees the energy. Once you have learned the wave pattern of the sea or ocean you are closest to, an underlying sound will surface. That sound is what drives the waves, and it can reveal the presence of Grandmother Ocean residing in the foam. Repeat the sound, chanting or humming it, and you can cleanse the water of pesticides and other contaminants.

After you've made the acquaintance of one Grandmother Ocean she'll tell you how to approach the others in other oceans and seas. The Grandmother's colors and looks are distinct in every sea. Grandmother Ocean does not have one name, for she isn't one entity. Every one of the Grandmothers of the oceans and seas will tell you her special name to call her with. The oldest Ocean Grandmother is the Pacific, and the youngest is the one who guides the Baltic Sea. This one I call Oma Ocean. The Mediterranean, the Atlantic, the North Sea, and the Caribbean each have a Grandmother Guardian and a mixture of colors that are expressly their own.

Sincere rather than curious people are rewarded with the unique wisdom Grandmother Ocean has to offer. It takes long dedicated practice to learn the wave system and underlying sounds that drive each ocean.

Work with water until you've mastered the element and know its essential sound. Water is the key to all of life and you must have a connection with it before you move on to the wind, or confusion will result.

Controlling Storms The simplest way to send a storm away is to use the prevailing wind currents. If it is a dangerous tropical storm, pray to its spirit to keep it moving quickly or use your developing powers to spread it out over a wider area thus dissipating its energy. No waves can exist without wind, no rain comes in still air, although there is a calm front before a storm. The dominant wind currents change seasonally in some areas. Remember all storms flow from the west to the east following the pattern of the earth's rotation. Seasonally, rainstorms arrive in the north from the south along the Atlantic and Gulf coasts.

Another technique is to sing and leave instructions for spirits who guard water, to help much needed rain get to the right location. As each new storm front arrives, send it on at the correct velocity to have sufficient rain at the destination. Sending a storm at a steady, even pace removes flood danger. Rein it in tightly to avoid horrid floods washing out fields and towns.

You might have an overabundance of rain. In that case visualize an opening in the clouds and disperse them in all directions. Be careful not to send it only to the next county, which is as saturated as your own. Focus on where the need is greatest and redirect the rain there.

Rainmaking itself must wait until you understand water fully. As you gather proficiency with water, you can pull together droplets in the sky to make a cloud that produces a quick shower. Later on you'll be able to create a deluge. These skills must be used with great discretion, for if you use them for vengeance, or as a parlor trick to brag about your prowess, the water spirits will desert you. Or maybe worse, they will cause a flood that sweeps you away. Respect the elements, at all times.

FIRE

Fire is an alchemical, etheric, living substance. No wonder the ancients worldwide claimed it was God's representative and kept fires burning in temples. To this day, to keep the Deity close by, Hindus perform Arthi, Jews keep an eternal flame lit, and Catholics have votive candles burning.

Of the elements in constant and readily noticeable flux, fire is the most easily merged with. Fire is magnetic. It responds to your thoughts. Your energy and breath can slow or speed up to match the fire.

Other elements are present in fire as well. The crackles are the fire of fire, explosions in the form of chemicals meeting the fiery force. The hissing sound is the water in the burning material. The whipping sound is the wind of fire. Thuds are not the fire itself, just the earthy material (fuel) falling. When the fuel is gone so is the fire. Listen for the sounds of the other elements within the fire. Sparks flying upwards, showers of fiery wood splinters, and resounding hot spots either punctuate a thought you've just had, redirect your attention, or signify an energy change within the fire. (The pops and crackles have meanings and the underlying sound of the fire is to bring you into your own center as part of the art of mastering fire.) The goal is to be at one with the sound of the fire, allowing it to be your teacher. The sound of the wind in the fire can bring up your kundalini and instigate the production of Tumo, the art of warming yourself without a heat source. I caught the practice of Tumo when it jumped into me in the midst of a fire meditation.

To the initiated, the firetender's habits, patterns, and emotional life can be read like a book.* Quite often the fire person immediately responds in an obedient manner to an instruction from a living teacher, reverting in half an hour to their ordinary methods of poor observation and misinterpretation of the fire's fuel requirements. Watching yourself closely when you are the fire tender can teach you more about yourself than years of psychological counselling. It'll show you how you fuss too much, or lose your concentration, let your mind wander, become uncentered and overreact. Until you merge with the internal dynamic of the fire you'll be a less than perfect firetender.

An apprentice, not having much discrimination, used the singsong word he got during an earlier fire meditation to call fire. The fire mantra, or sound, is invoked solely when a fire is

---

*For fire tender's job and the fire meditation, see Chapter 11, Sound Medicine by Laeh Maggie Garfield.

too low or it dies down. A person who tends the fire and has misunderstandings about the powers they're summoning can disturb the health, both mental and physical, of other meditators unless there are at least seven sitters present. An improperly tended fire can result in a headache or a generalized malaise. If this occurs more than once with the same firetender, the fire meditators are incompatible with the tender's energy. Choose another person to care for the fire. Gather more than seven people to meditate on fire, and the firetender's influence diminishes.

Each person has to follow their inner clock when participating in a fire meditation. Don't be a sheep turning around in conformity with the others. Take no tea or other liquid during the short fire meditation.

Knowing your fireplace is essential as each one has a definite personality, which may cause it to smoke when logs are stacked too far forward, jammed against the back, or too close to one wall. One fireplace may draw well, while another is dependent upon a bellows to get it to blaze nicely. You can observe the magical interaction between meditators and the fire provided no toxic chemicals have been introduced to help the fire along. Pressed logs purchased at supermarkets and convenience stores are not healthy as they emit poisonous fumes. Neither is painted, creosote preserved, finished, or treated scrap lumber. Kiln dried wood is okay, as is natural wood or coal if you have a coal burning stove that can be left open. A talky fire helps you to know the fire element in fire. It clears thoughts. If you tend to think too much, or do an amount of problem solving while meditating, it's best to make a talky fire. This is accomplished by stacking the logs at odd angles and using a variety of woods. Mixing wood types also aids in seeing colors in the fire. Redwood makes a yellow fire. Madrone produces violet flares. Part of your pleasure in mastering fire is to discover what colors different kinds of timber yield.

Fires can be blue tinged, purple, violet flamed, red, orange, green hued, bright yellow, or pale tinted depending upon the intensity of the burn and the amount of air, water, and earth in the fire. The chief colors in the flames announce the fire's main element. An earth fire is a combination of yellow, golden-orange, and green. A fire element fire is orangy or red. A watery fire is magenta and green. Air fires are predominantly blue and green. A spiritual fire is blue, pink, and purple.

Tumo   Tumo is the art of warming yourself without any fire. Teenagers and young children have this ability naturally. While their parents shout at them to cover up, they are able to walk out into the biting cold and stay warm although hatless, gloveless, and otherwise underdressed. The practice of Tumo is best known as an austerity to train young monks. It can either be a sacred or non-religious mystical activity. Amazingly simple to perform, few realize it can be mastered without retreating to high altitudes of frozen ice. Naturally this is not done except in cold weather or drenching rain. Visualize a fire of orange and golden orange flames, no smoke. Make it a large blaze. Once you have it going in your mind's eye you can breathe the flames in with each inhalation. Breathe in the fiery orange flames and feel them warming you. Breathe out and quickly inhale. Repeatedly hold the warmth in your third chakra. In a short time, perhaps as little as twenty minutes, if you remain focused, you shall have flaming red cheeks and a warm body.

WIND

Energies and thoughts travel on the winds. They remain in the air permanently, occasionally landing some bit of good or ill luck on a community or an individual. Asthma and emphysema are disturbances of the inner wind. Learning the outer wind helps to understand the potential of the inner wind, called prana or breath. Air is needed for nourishment. It is the most essential element for life. Breathing fresh, unpolluted air leaves several impressions per second on your brain. Minds without these impressions quit functioning.

The lung is your prana channel. Do not put smoke in it. Smoking cigarettes or anything else and breathing dirty air will clog your pranic force. These three main components of the subtle body all bring in prana: Tigle = energy, Tsa = body, Lung = speech and inner air.* Doing pranayama yoga breaths and asanas clears all three. Chanting also clears the inner air.

The wind is the most changeable of the elements. Merging with it, you must be mindful of the essential nature of each of

---

*In Tibetan Buddhism, Tigle = The Realm of the Source,
Tsa = The Physical Realm, Lung = The Formation Realm.

the four main winds that may blow separately or in any combination. Still air does not last long. Unifying yourself with the wind means going behind it to the core, the Source. North is the strongest wind; East is next in strength. West has a steadier, firmer, more friendly pace than the others. South wind is gentle or like the Föhn or the Santa Ana's doldrums with a vacuum behind it. South wind as the weakest, can be very yin. Any wind can become wild and threatening, although north winds have the worst reputation.

The Creator is the force behind the wind. The sounds beyond the internal wind sound is God, the Great Spirit breathing. To know the Source is to undertake mastery of the wind. To know the wind you must seek the Source. The force of all Creation is in the wind. Do the wind meditation* daily for an entire week on a high mountain, in the desert, or on an open plain. There is no spot more sacred than any other, only those with more wind or privacy.

Holland has wind and open sky. The landscape isn't much, but the wind blows exuberantly. To begin to control the wind, it is a good place. The prairies and deserts without landmarks to stop the wind give it permission to be itself. Here you can synchronize your breath with the wind, and experiment with its velocity.

Wind moves in spirals, either tight or loose. Any temperature change is caused by it. Whether it stands upright floating in a spiral gown of clouds or circulates in billowy horizontal shapes, the pattern determines the direction and velocity. Winds 40° N 40° S of the equator are called "the roaring forties." The winds here are formed by air warmed at the equator and cooled at the poles. Earth's rotation from west to east causes the phenomena as it carries the winds with it. Air gets heavier as it cools. It descends there at 40°, creating strong winds.

The winds and their properties were very important to ancient peoples. Tribal dwellers, especially the shamans, knew the names for all four winds. The wise ones had songs or sounds to call each wind when they required its assistance. They also knew how to send a storm away by speaking the name of the responsible wind, and frequently made offerings to the troublesome ones.

Wind meditation is on page 157 of Sound Medicine *by Laeh Maggie Garfield.*

In her book *Prayers of Smoke* (Celestial Arts), Barbara Means Adams, an Oglala Sioux, tells her tribal names for each of the four winds and the legends about them. Every ancient culture you look into has an indigenous secret name for the wind. Related tribes, even those whose languages are akin, may use a dissimilar sacred word for the same wind. My Pomo teacher gave me special sounds to call each wind and send it back.

The North wind cannot blow backwards. This may account for the fascination native cultures around the world have had with the North wind. Other winds roll forwards and fall back regardless of the fierceness with which they blow. The retreating wind is felt as a lull or calm. Winds change direction quickly, calling upon their sisters to the east, south, west, and north to chime in with them. Traditionally, north is claimed to be the direction of the wind. South is the wind of summer, East belongs to spring, the West wind to autumn, and North wind to winter.

The Holy Spirit is literally "breath." From this we can deduce the direction of the Holy Ghost to be the north. Anantvayu is a name for the Goddess of the Wind. She is predominant during pregnancy as the space element. The totem animals associated with the north wind are the hawk, the sow, and the goat.

According to Welsh wisdom, listening to the wind in a sacred grove induces trance states. Cardea is the ancient Latin Goddesss of the four cardinal winds. Cardea rules over the celestial hinge behind the North Wind, around which the mill-stone of the Universe revolves. Boreas is the name of the north wind in Greek mythology. A star behind Corona Boreas is the origin of the wind. It is here that death dwells. Hyperboreans, back-of-the-north-wind-people, formed a priesthood concerned with the northern other world.

These ancient myths concerning the source of the wind— other stars and galaxies containing wind—have been given scientific credibility by the instruments currently available. "Scientists have found evidence of a wind swooshing about a galaxy called M82, 60 trillion miles away from our cheery little planet. The wind, composed of hydrogen, is propelled by supernova star explosions." The analysis by two researchers at the Institute for Astronomy in Honolulu was reported in the July 7, 1988, British journal *Nature*.

The very chemicals that comprise the universe are thought by scientists to create the winds that travel through space.

Believed to be an empty vacuum, space actually has neutrons, atoms, and other energetic particles bouncing around in it. Perhaps there is even an intelligence directing its movements in a relatively orderly fashion.

The Test Wind takes a long time to master. You have to keep at it even when it seems you're making no headway. Throughout, as you advance in competence, you will receive small tests. When I was about four years into mastering the element, on a windy Sunday night in March, the door at my friend's house blew open. Becky and her teenaged son Eric were on one couch, facing me, with their backs to the door. John was in the kitchen.

"Close the door Laeh," one of them shouted. And, to my own surprise, I got it two-thirds of the way shut just by merging my mental energy with the wind. Then John came walking towards it, putting me down, saying "Come on, Laeh, close the door." The wind evaded me although I tried. Resorting to something I already knew, I used his body energy as the transformer to slam the door in his face as he got closer to it. Becky, Eric, and I cackled in delight and amazement. John opened the door to go outside, ignoring what he'd just witnessed. I felt good about my growing mastery of the wind. The door vividly showed me I was two-thirds of the way there.

The wind will teach you many of its secrets if you take the time to play with it. Little glyphs of colorless light that you see as you look into a strong wind are prana in the wind flying in the air. Breathe the fresh flowing prana and you'll feel an immediate lift in your energy. Stand outside on a windy night and allow the pressure of the wind to clean your psyche. Take a ferry boat ride—alone on deck, the wind will sing to you. Once you get cold go inside, warm up, and go out again to learn from the wind. To walk against a strong wind, cross your legs one in front of the other to angle yourself against it. This balances and propels you forward in high winds. It's the sailor's deck walk. Listen for ancient songs still flying in the wind.

The Inner Wind One of the most common and workable meditations is to focus on your own breath, the wind that flows through your body. You can meditate upon your own breath regardless of whether or not you are attempting mastery of an element. Sit quietly without altering your breath's natural flow. See where it is long, where it is short. Notice the internal cycles your own breath produces. One inhalation will go into your back, and the next may be centered in your pelvis; a third enters your neck and shoulders. Sans judgement, just watch your own breath pattern and the emotions and thoughts raised by a single cycle of inhalation and exhalation. Observe, do not muse over what you identify. Keep watching your breath for at least twenty minutes.

You cannot control prana with the mind. You can control it by combining breathing and concentration of mind. If you are doing a particular type of profound inhalation in a position which isn't favorable for that kind of breathing, it doesn't help.

There are seven different breaths in each breath cycle. You can practice doing the seven breaths, using the seven correct poses for each of them. Concentration is necessary for prana to circulate. A series of poses regulates and develops every variety of breath. Yantra yoga contains movements and counts for all seven poses. A teacher is needed to learn the technique properly. Books cannot impart the correct inhalation, exhalation, and accompanying movements. However, one book worth your time and effort is by Namkai Norbu Rinpoche: *Yantra Yoga: Yoga of Movements* (Verlag TSAPARANG Graz, Austria, 1988 [in English], ISBN 3–900890–01–3).

A Tibetan mantra, for use in a strong wind, is good for purifying the mind and regaining clarity. Repeat it 108 times.

Om Eho Shuddhe Shuddhe
Yanho Shuddhe Shuddhe
Bamho Shuddhe Shuddhe
Ramho Shuddhe Shuddhe
Lamho Shuddhe Shuddhe
E Yam Bam Ram Lam Shuddhe Shuddhe Svaha

Here is a breath and mantra integration, to help you understand the nature of sound and the elements. You must do it daily for several months before you get more than surface results.

OM	AH	HUM
inhale	hold momentarily	exhale

SPACE—The Star Level

Space, a vast uncharted mystery slowly revealing its secrets to scientists, is well known to mystics who've explored it intuitively and telepathically. The rings around Uranus, found only in the late 1980s by photographs from an unmanned spaceship, were never a secret to the mystics. If the university educated scientists would ask knowledgeable mystics, they could guide research in astronomical, physical, and chemical discoveries without incorrect theories and predictions.

When you undertake the examination of space you are entering the wise ways of vacuums, gravity, electromagnetism, space travel, and life on other planets. Electromagnetic fields guard the orbits and movements of the galaxies, stars, planets, and their moons.

Via contact with UFOs and the Beings of Light who flit facilely over our landscape once they have landed, you can uncover a formula for entering the Star stratum of enlightenment. The Beings of Light are breathtaking, luminescent colored shapes—fluid, changing, moving along in a fluttering, hovering way or with great speed, using high pitched whistling sounds to communicate with one another. How close they will allow you to come is a matter of your own trust and fearlessness. And, it depends upon whether they believe you are ready to see them. Should they dim their light, attempting to put it out altogether once you've seen them, it's a signal that they do not welcome your intrusion. If the light stays relatively steady they trust you will do no harm and may even come closer to you.

Where is Heaven? Every child asks that question. Usually there is no acceptable answer. Yet there is an answer. In back of our three-dimensional world, hidden behind the curve in the black holes in space, is the place we commonly call heaven. Light reflects back to us from there, in a boomerang effect. Time runs backwards and space seems to have no place further to go wherever one of these black holes appears.

Heaven is the pairing of the Realm of Creation and the Realm of the Source, where we go once our physical body has been dropped.

Revisiting the Earth as an element can spark much knowhow about the Star spiral. The same elements as exist on earth are available throughout every galaxy. Through fire hotter than any iron pot can withstand, alchemical changes occur. Iron becomes gold and if the gold is too hot it becomes lead. In the burning of stars the elements silicon, oxygen, neon, carbon and helium mix with interstellar gases.

Robert P. Kirshner in "Supernova Death of a Star," *National Geographic*, Vol. 173, No. 5, May 1988, gave some scientific evidence for mystical traditions: "In the same manner the generations of stars that lived and died in our galaxy before the sun was formed created an inheritance of heavy elements that was bequeathed to us. The carbon atoms in the ink on this page, the oxygen you're breathing . . . the calcium in your bones and iron in your blood are the products of stars."

The death of stars is part of the origin of life.

Meditation of Space   Space has its own meditation, practiced to hear the sound of space and unify your consciousness with it. Meditation of space is another avenue to The Source.

The weather must be warm and without rain. Preparation: Arrange for a cabin within walking distance from the site you have chosen to meditate at. Fast for four days, drinking only pure water. On the fourth day you lie out in an open area like a high mountain or an uncluttered plain and stare into the sky from sunup to sundown. From time to time you will sip a bit of the water you've brought. Walk to your sleeping quarters, speak to no one. Rest, remain quiet, and think little. At daybreak return to your location with water sufficient to get through the day. At sundown return to your dwelling. Stay calm and quiet. Continue fasting. On the sixth day repeat the process. If you haven't gone crazy, on the morning of the seventh day you will have real knowledge of space.

Should it begin to rain at any time when you are out meditating return to your cabin at once. Damp clothing and this meditation are a deadly combination. Yes, this meditation is dangerous and not for the faint of heart or spiritual tourist. WARNING: Do not do the meditation of space if you are in an unbalanced mental state or have suffered a recent broken relationship or the death of someone close to you.

Now and then people ask if it is more effective to attune to the elements by living in a wilderness area. The truth is, only if you pay attention. A well insulated house in the woods, with its laundry and dishwasher, won't be any different than a suburban home. Snowmobiles, farm machinery, and dirt bikes do not help you to know the elements. Walk in nature, sit by the creeks, listen to the wind, sing to the trees, and wildcraft plants in season. These activities will make you wise in the ways of the elements.

How the Elements and the Chakras Are Integrated

Within each Mansion an individual may select any element to express the story of their life. As souls progress from Mansion to Mansion they gain insight into their own peculiarities and strengths. They pick an element that complements their needs, or tests their flexibility with those things they've already learned.

The elements and the Mansions they belong to are: Survival Mansion—earth, Mansion of Emotion—water, Mansion of Power—fire, Mansion of Love—air, Mansion of Sound—space.

For lifetimes traversing the first floor of any Mansion, earth is the best and easiest element to choose. Water, when combined with the root chakra, is fairly difficult. Air is the hardest to mix energy with successfully. Fire as the element of the first chakra is fine since it lends itself to bringing up energy and keeps it flowing. If your Essence Self decided upon the fire element as the format for the root chakra, all you have to do is keep from burning out too quickly.

Fire, as the element for traveling through the sacral chakra lifetime, might cause the individual to be barren, abundantly fertile in every way, or communicate clearly each facet of their emotional life. Air as the element to accompany a second chakra assignment might make the person too open and give them more impressions than they can absorb. Yet air, via its mental nature, lends itself perfectly to establishing a balanced emotional state. It is a kindred element since the astral body, the wellspring for your emotional states, feeds on air. Earth always adds balance to a stint in the second chakra. Water can make the personality overly emotional; therefore it warrants control of the emotions.

An Adult Mansion lifetime focused on the tasks of the second chakra may choose to do the air of water; potentially a turbulent or suppressed emotional life accompanied by intense learning. The air is the Mansion of Love's own element, and water is the second story of every Mansion. Air already contains water molecules. Earth as the element of choice could totally obscure the work of an Adult Mansion second chakra lifetime.

However if the Essence Soul already knows they are far too likely to be swept away by the tenor of the times, earth can be exactly what they require to slow down.

Fire as a lifetime task for the third story of any Mansion is a natural, with the exception of the Teenaged Mansion where it leads to explosive situations. Water for a third chakra lifetime can give locomotive power or inertia. Air here makes for thinkers and philosophers rather than doers, while earth adds strength and durability to the individual's Mission.

Adult Mansion or fourth story lifetimes work best with air or fire as the main element. Earth poses the most difficulty while water actually complements. In the Mature Mansion water extends the most problems and all the other elements are helpful.

In the chakras that have no connection to the body's functioning, the elements provide a balanced backdrop. For the Mansion of Knowledge or the sixth story of any house, the element fire produces excellent intuition and insight. Fire for a third eye incarnation fuels quick thoughts and powerful visions. Water makes for sensitivity, air pulls in intellect and fantasy to help interpret clairvoyant images. Although earth is the most arduous element for the sixth story or Old Soul Mansion, a Source Self who is unable to concentrate or absentminded might be wise to utilize it as a method of staying grounded while transiting the third eye.

With the crown chakra, or seventh story of any Mansion, the elements work this way. Water moves into a lower chakra, often the second. When you are sublimating in this way you are susceptible to drug addiction. The most usual pattern is for the water element to block the throat chakra. Fire and air are better choices for seventh chakra lifetimes when you are doing the toughest story of any Mansion. Volunteer Souls will not have serious interference no matter what element they decide upon for an incarnation. You have no choice, once born, over the element you've been assigned. You must live with it and do your best.

Your Personal Element   The key to conquering the diseases that ail you is to study and meditate upon the element that will integrate your entire task in life. It is a positive way through your path. In mastering the element you need to, you complete your Mission. There are many levels of mastery, from small skills to great mystical depths.

If you want to figure out your element, just watch your behavior. Are you always merging with others, then raging or fading away? Extremes of this nature are under the emotional sign of water. Do you ponder over things from every angle? Do you intellectualize everything? Then your predominant element requiring attention is air. Does a fiery or depressed nature make you act hastily or sit inertly for prolonged periods? If this describes you, the prescription is to explore the fire element.

Do you jump into physical activities and competitive sports? Are you super woman or man, or the exact opposite, dragging your heels at every turn? You'd best look into mining, planting, building, or carving, to develop the elemental experience of earth. For balance yoga, Tai Chi, gardening, and physically challenging activities are a good beginning.

Earth can be self doubt, lots of pessimism, no faith in yourself and a strong sense of responsibility. Water is gut level responses, psychic, telepathic, easily freaked out. Water can gravitate toward emotionalism, varying forms of hysteria, and constant emotional turmoil. Fire is communication and thoughts. It is the great clarifier and purifier. It is also imagination, where it would rather live than get down to the practical aspects of making a living. Air gives detachment from feelings, substituting reason or logic as ways of dealing with life. Airy individuals must be mindful of their water intake.

Some individuals have an astrological chart that stresses three elements. It is up to that person, in that lifetime, to integrate those elements. When the elements are **Air, Earth, Fire,** the integrating process is done by *Fire* mastery.

In a **Water, Fire, Air** mix, water cannot become the mediating element, because it does not mix well with fire. The element of focus must be *Air* as there is air in water and fire cannot burn without it.

Your mixture might be **Fire, Earth, Water,** in which case the unifying element is *Earth* which absorbs water. Earth is the source of the fuel of fire as Mother Earth, grower of the wood for the fuel, in whose body dwells coal, gas, and fossil fuel.

The connection of **Air, Earth, Water** is made by integrating yourself with the element *Water.* Water is in air and earth.

The way to integrate yourself is to master and remaster the element as you work from one spiral of enlightenment to the next.

12

Color and Sound

Wonder, wonder!
How marvellous is the teaching of no words.
It cannot be grasped by hearing with the ear,
For that voice is to be heard with the eye.
                                        Zen Master Tozan

Sound and color are two methods used from time immemorial to heal and rejuvenate the human mind and body. Color is seen in meditation. Sounds and color are experienced in visionary states. Healers and spiritual leaders have been aware of the power of color and sound to influence the mind and emotions. Usually the two energies are employed separately rather than as a fused unit of color and sound, since the natural talents and emphasis of the medicine person or healer captures the essence of one and not the other. Color healers may play soothing music, but seldom do they integrate the two factors. Musical therapists sing or play without augmenting the sound with a related color.

Color and Sound together have fascinated human beings for centuries. Zen practitioners have died to understand the color in sound while striving to hear the color and see the sound. It's far too great a task unless you are willing to explore and master the three levels of enlightenment one by one.

Color and sound mixed in a sensory crossover is the star spiral of enlightenment. This area is in its infancy as far as scientific and written material goes. Many people have this form of synesthesia, but insufficient research has been done to correlate the omnipresent nature of color and sound. Colors, music, and other sounds are correlated with another spiritual factor, the Clan you come from. Every Clan has its own system of interlocking colors and sounds.

COLOR

Color alone is the moon spiral of enlightenment. The more you love and appreciate color, the clearer the colors become in your meditation. The color you see is an indication of your soul level and the Clan you belong to. As your search along the moon spiral progresses, the better you will understand the function of color and how to apply that knowledge.

Colorology is the study of color in its invisible and visible state in relation to people, living things, and the universe. A theory runs through most cultures that color is a cogent, penetrating force shaping human behavior. Color contains light in the form of wave lengths (vibrations) and matter (photons). Color produces sensations in response to the mental and emotional interpretation of what the eye perceives. Colors represent destructive and constructive emotions: purple is a spiritual color, but in excess it brings out fear. Color causes a chemical reaction. Foods chosen and consumed for their color are used by the body for healing. Hues, tints, and shades you wear become infused with your electrical and magnetic qualities, attracting others according to the strength of the color.

The colors you choose are regulated to some degree by fashion. Buying a mustard yellow shirt that disagrees with your energy field simply fills your closet. Once confident enough to abandon what is chic, people gravitate toward colors they resonate with irrespective of what's most available.

Color as a healing agent has been popular in the United States since the late 19th century. With the advent of electricity, color healing in the form of light became generally available. Prior to that time, in churches throughout Europe, capable priests placed sick people under the stained glass window of the "saint" who could cure them of their ailment. Those requiring healing for low appetite, arthritis, poor circulation, depression, pancreatic disorders, or skin diseases sat under the predominantly yellow window depicting Daniel in the lion's den.

Capturing sunlight in much the same way, water infused with color is used to heal those who haven't the time nor the electrical apparatus to achieve similar results. Color healing can also be accomplished with food, flowers, clothing, and redecorating the home. Color affects every aspect of our lives. In well documented studies it has been found that the highway patrol reacts first to red cars, second to yellow ones, and hardly at all to blue ones traveling beyond the speed limit.

People otherwise immune to intuitive experiences give reports of a hue or shading that makes their heart soar, initiating a feeling of well being and comfort. A specific color can make you feel physically exhausted, or provoke nausea. Everyone knows somebody who is addicted to a color they never seem to tire of. Is it the sound inside the color that is perceived beyond your ordinary consciousness? Or is it the color alone? Will the reaction to the color fade or become greater when seeing it accompanies a musical form you are fond of? Our language encompasses ideas like loud color or soft shade to define the feeling a color sends out. These expressions actually refer to the inner sound of the color.

Language can add to the confusion over identifying color. Until the twentieth century, the German language made no differentiation between purple and violet. Both were called *purpur.* Red-violets are indeed different from blue-violets in the way they affect the human psyche. Some Mexican tribes have few words for color identification, placing all shades and tints under a general classification. Green and blue tones fall into the green family; the reds and oranges are all in the red grouping; yellows and golden hues are all yellow; blacks, greys, and browns are all referred to as black; and any light color falls into a category they call white.

You may find in healing someone that a color appears and is superseded by several tints until it changes into another color. You might also notice that as you sing or drum for someone, the healing colors approximate the rainbow, changing from red to red-orange, orange to a golden yellow, a pale yellow that turns lime and then bright green, fading into a sky blue and then a periwinkle. The color or hue that remains at the end of the healing is the one the person needs to be healthy. Silvery shades and bright luminescent white may also appear. In the midst of a healing, seeing black and white mixed means the person requires a reality check. Their inner vision may be way off base. It is a good sign if the favorite hue of the individual appears.

In sending messages or in absent healing, trying to reach someone through the vibration of a color they don't like is using the wrong wave length to connect with them. It serves to keep your energy from hitting them. Conversely, you can't send them anything negative through their right shade of blue, turquoise, purple, red, orange, green, or yellow. Tints and tones in harmony with a person's own favorite colors protect the wearer/user.

Every color has a specific function to perform in relation to the body/psyche. When someone is too young for their chronological age, yellow-greens appear in their auric field. These can be anywhere from bilious to apple green to greenish yellow. The auric hue adapts to the mental condition of the person, changing to its true splendor when the bearer's mind is in harmony.

Browns, greens, and blues represent the thinking creative mind, interpreting insights whether of primary or secondary channeling, giving them dimension and meaning on the physical plane.

Brown is the categorizer, compartmentalizer, which acts to neutralize the emotions. It has a calming effect, although when used to excess stagnation occurs.

Purple stands alone, polarized between blue and red. It is the buckle of the circle of sound and color. As a family of colors it moves from raspberry to periwinkle. We have hundreds of ways to describe it because it is so important in our culture. Purple represents the true integration of our male and female selves which can only occur in the grandparenting stage of our lives, after age fifty-three.

Red-purple soothes the emotions.

Blue purple sends information from the mind to the brain for storage. It is a creative color, bringing down information or images from the cosmos to the individual who will interpret it as art, music, dance, spiritual revelation, scientific theory, or other forms of wisdom.

Turquoise is the color of brain-mind connection. The mind uses the brain as a storehouse, retrieving the information at a later time. Alice Walker, whose book *The Color Purple* received plaudits and praise, had a case of writer's block so severe she forced herself to come up with a unique solution. She hungered for turquoise and coral as colors to ease her writer's block, so she painted her entire house in those two hues. As a result she has produced another very special novel.

Bright Red-orange denotes resistance. HUM is the sound that removes it. What notes are sounded to bring it into the proper or balanced perspective? Resistance is only a symptom. Removing the resistance without resolving the bigger problem cannot be accomplished except by repression. It'll crop up elsewhere in the person's life causing difficulties or illness.

Pale yellow has to do with issues of abundance and the lack of it.

Color Healing   Color healing has been extensively studied, and systems that work are known. Yet the systems don't seem to agree. One may claim miraculous cures for burns using green, while another says orange works. In fact, they both do. Orange takes away the swelling and green causes rapid regrowth of skin and other tissues. A third system advocates the use of red with burns because fire fights fire. However, I find drinking water infused with blue works better than red to soothe and heal chemical burns.

To make color-infused water obtain one-liter (quart) jars in clear true colors. You can also place stained glass panels in front of the clear bottles. Select the colors as described later in this chapter. Pour pure spring water into the jar and allow it to sit at least eight hours in the window, whether the day is cloudy or sunny. Cover the top with a piece of paper or loose lid, to prevent insects and debris from contaminating the water.

The water will not be colored and will look like regular water, nevertheless, purple infused water will taste like fungus and lemon permeated water will taste citrusy. Drink an eight-ounce glass of water charged with the color you require. You may sip as much as you have on hand. It is not necessary to leave the water in the colored bottle once it has been permeated by the color. Pour it out and keep it in a clean thermos that has not been used for coffee or tea. Refill the colored jar with spring water to prepare another day's treatment, or to use as needed.

One November the dog came in while I was washing dishes. I gave him a bone which he proceeded to enjoy on the carpet ignoring my entreaties. I took him by the collar and led him and the bone outside. On the way back to the sink I must have touched my eye before scrubbing my hands. The next day the poison oak from his coat sprang to life on my eye and proceeded to work its way down my face until I looked like a chipmunk. It itched and burned, causing much pain. Every evening, upon my return from work, I drank eight ounces of cobalt blue infused water. Within minutes the itching ceased and the redness quieted. After three days the swelling remained, but my skin no longer hurt nor itched. Due to the use of blue water the rash was confined to my face. Poison oak is a chemical burn that can spread from one area of the body to another making for weeks of itchy outbreaks.

The Spectro-Chrome Tonation System was given to me over a dozen years ago by Arthur Whitcomb of Portland, Oregon, who was eighty-seven years old at the time. For more than fifty years he practiced color therapy using special visual equipment with rotating glass filter panels which the AMA forced the United States government to ban in 1948. Although such machinery is no longer contraband, at the time its prohibition interfered with the proper administration of color therapy. Therefore, in its absence, Mr. Whitcomb and others devised another method for color healing. He wrote it up and distributed it everywhere.

"Build a wooden box large enough to hold a very heavy, bright light bulb (500 Watt). On the bottom side of the box put some sort of grooves or catches to attach panels of color. Purchase or make panels of only the purest color—this is important. Suspend the light from the ceiling using the appropriate color panel."

Stained glass cut to the size of your box may crack from heat and prolonged use. However, stained glass is the best medium in most instances because plastic panels will eventually warp and theatrical gels melt. The shade of magenta that settles anxiety states and emotional turmoil turned out to be made by Kodak for use in darkrooms.

The selection of the color is of the utmost importance. Choose a tint or hue that is clear and not dark, like a true orange, rather than a burnt orange. Glass without designs, pebbling, or ribbing is best. If you cannot buy a smooth panel in the correct tone, buy one with the least imprinting for immediate use and keep shopping for a plain surfaced one. Sheathe the glass in padded mailing envelopes when not in use. This is the best and least expensive way to prevent breakage.

In my practice I have found Arthur Whitcomb's Spectro-Chrome Tonation System to be highly effective when used exactly as he instructed. The person being treated sits under the lamp for only one hour, no more, at a stretch. For burns or broken bones a person may sit one hour out of every four under the colored light. Emotional problems will clear within an hour as will respiratory illnesses.

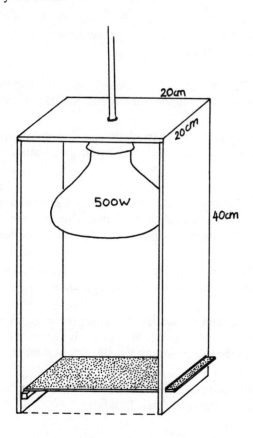

Here is the list of colors and their uses as he presented them to me.

SPECTRO-CHROME TONATION SYSTEM

RED—Sensory stimulant, Liver energizer, Irritant, Vesicant, Pustulant, Rubefacient, Caustic, Hemoglobin builder.

ORANGE—Respiratory stimulant, Parathyroid depressant, Thyroid energizer, Antispasmodic, Galactagogue, Antirachitic, Emetic, Carminative, Stomachic, Aromatic, Lung builder.

YELLOW (bright)—Motor stimulant, Alimentary Tract energizer, Lymphatic activator, Splenic depressant, Digestant, Cathartic, Cholagogue, Anthelmintic, Nerve builder.

LEMON—Cerebral stimulant, Thymus activator, Antacid, Chronic alterative, Antiscorbic (prevents scurvy), Laxative, Expectorant, Bone builder.

GREEN—Pituitary stimulant, Disinfectant, Purificatory, Antiseptic, Germicide, Bactericide, Detergent, Muscle and tissue builder.

BLUE—Counter-irritant, Anodyne (soothes pain), Antipruritic (stops itching), Vitality builder, Demulcent, Diaphoretic, Febrifuge.

INDIGO—Parathyroid stimulant, Thyroid depressant, Respiratory depressant, Astringent, Sedative, Pain reliever, Hemostatic, Inspissator (promotes evaporation), Phagocyte builder.

VIOLET—Splenic stimulant, Cardiac depressant, Lymphatic depressant, Motor depressant, Leucocyte builder.

PURPLE—Venous stimulant, Renal depressant, Antimalarial, Vasodilator, Anaphrodisiac, Narcotic, Hypnotic, Antipyretic (high fevers, hot flashes), Analgesic, Sex builder in supernormal.

MAGENTA—Suprarenal stimulant, Cardiac energizer, Diuretic, Emotional equilibrator, Auric builder.

SCARLET—Arterial stimulant, Renal energizer, Genital excitant, Aphrodisiac, Emmenagogue (promotes flow of menses), Vaso-constrictor, Ecbolic (uterine contractant), Sex builder in subnormal.

Mansion Colors   The Mansion the soul is from and the system of color and sound a person utilizes are basically unknown. However, members of various Mansions readily show magnetic attraction to the colors of their soul level. Some even carry it as their Ray. As an example, when you are an Adult soul on the seventh story of the Mansion you may resonate best with cobalt or azure blue and that will be your Ray.

Infant Mansion or 1st story   Yellows, pale to dark, golden and lemony

Toddler Mansion or 2nd story   the orange family

Teenage Mansion or 3rd story   variations of reds, scarlet, and crimson into pinks

Adult Mansion or 4th story
   1–4 story of the Adult Mansion   pink to magenta, pale pink to dark rose

   4–7 story of the Adult Mansion   green all from spring green to emerald

Mature Mansion or 5th story
   1–3rd story of the Mature Mansion   red-violet, magenta

   4–7th story of the Mature Mansion   turquoise to sky blue

Old Mansion or 6th story   purples, lavender, lilac

Volunteer or 7th story   indigo from navy to glowing baby powder blue, cobalt blue to azure blue

The Ray   People often want to see their Ray, yet do not know where it originates. Your Ray is the color that is always with you. It doesn't change as the aura does. The color tonal quality remains steady irrespective of illness, emotional trauma, age, or steps to spiritual growth taken or avoided. The Ray's tint or density is a good indication of the soul level you are operating from, and its color corresponds to the chakras you are growing through this lifetime. The Ray enters the body in a conical shape, descending from the ether into your pineal gland which distributes the energy throughout your body.

Of course the Ray has nothing to do with your racial or ethnic birth group, as these change freely each time you're born. Men can have feminine colors in their Ray, and women masculine ones, because the Ray has nothing to do with your gender.

In a combined Ray such as red/white/blue, it is the measure of the Mission you are performing to integrate these components and move onto the next phase within your Mansion. If your Ray is yellow, you might assume you are an infant soul. However, you could take on a yellow or lemon-lime Ray when you are doing some major first Mansion work in Teenaged, Adult, or a later Mansion.

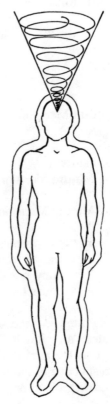

How to Find Your Ray For seven nights in a row go to bed requesting to see your Ray upon awakening. The first color you see or think of as you arise is the one you must note. It is unlikely that more than two or three hues would come into your mind. The one that most frequently appears is the one that belongs to you. It is possible to have two, in which case you'd hear, see, or think of each hue at least three times out of the seven days, immediately after or just prior to opening your eyes.

Your Ray resonates with others who have similar or compatible Rays, due not only to the color but to the inner sound it emits. A lemon-lime Ray is terribly uncomfortable around people with purple, raspberry, magenta, or lavender rays, yet settles down happily next to green, blue, yellow, and gold. A soul with a gold Ray is in rapport with all others, including the brilliant reds and oranges. A gold Ray can be paired with a delicate azure blue or other pale tint without overwhelming the bearer. Rays which do not integrate, as in the latter case, signify a double sided Mission for the one who carries it.

Bettina, a client in her mid-thirties with a magenta Ray, was analyzing her unhappy relationships, expressing problems of incompatibility through the color Ray of her former partners. "The reason my man trip doesn't work out is that I am fascinated by the red white and blue Ray which is a high use of power with demonic attributes. I called my guides and asked them to assist me. I decided to be a good witness and watch people with red white and blue rays to see how they operated and learn via that route what I need to know. I needn't take them home to bed with me to get the lesson.

"I fear involvement with a man because I always pick that Ray which does not go well with my own. My former husband has a purple Ray and he bored me because it's one that blends too quietly with mine. Maybe orange or lemon/lime would give the right stimulation and warmth. Orange knows how to have fun which is something my Ray needs to express."

Bettina had explored her situation rather well. She required only a modest amount of counselling to help her further. I suggested she take some classes with Tibetan spiritual masters because they utilize the red, white, and blue in their meditations. Perhaps her craving for it wasn't personal but spiritual. I also advised her to look at the words she'd chosen to describe her relationships. Involvement isn't the commitment she craved. Bettina limited the potential of a developing union.

Clan Colors The color of your Ray is usually not the same as that of your Clan. The Ray of your Oversoul is habitually an indication of Clan affiliation. Should your Clan have a blue-white Ray, it will seldom appear above you. Yet you will long to see that color, for its inner sound calls forth a unity and sense of belonging in your soul.

The Clan you belong to is usually symbolized by a particular color or tint of a color. The colors people are always trying to define or assign sound and other symbols to are abstractions for the major tribes we come from. In meditation you can sometimes get a glimpse of your Clan. Whether you see lilac, peach and silver, or purple, true orange and gold, or the blue-greens, yellows, and white, the combinations and their intensity tell you what Clan you belong to.

Clans are sometimes referred to as lands, with the color used as if it's the country's name. A small boy wanted to encourage his mother, who was hoping to have more children. "I wish you would hurry up so my sister can get here from the turquoise land. And then my brother can come from the purple and blue land." About ten months later his sister was born. After she was a few months old, he told his mother, "My little brother may never get here. It's taking so long, he might not come."

Within a Clan, sub-groups exist denoted by the change in color from clear true blue to cobalt and down to palest blue. Representatives of a Clan that has pink and blue will shimmer and switch their color from one side of the spectrum to the other while communicating with you from the spirit world.

According to reputable mystics, all saints and archangels are assigned a color. The colors have become traditional in Christianity. Daniel is yellow, Gabriel blue, Raphael red, Michael green, and Uriel violet. St. John of the New Testament is white and represents the White Eagle Clan. Not all the archangels named in the Bible are heads of clans. Not all archangels are named in the Bible.

SOUND

Sound belongs to the solar spiral of enlightenment. Hearing sounds like a running brook when far from one, the music of the spheres, or a favorite theme in your head is a signal to pay attention to the moment. Such phenomena become commonplace to people who are working on the solar level of development. Your Clan has its own sounds in chords and vibrational attunement that call your attention. Those sounds resonate with every member of your Clan.

In 1987 Celestial Arts published my book *Sound Medicine.* Most everything you need to know about healing and the prophetic use of sound is covered in it.

Various healers avow that chamber music will cure heart disease. But if you don't like it, your blood pressure might rise. One fine method of healing with sound is to tone for the client, letting the sounds come through you. Toning is dynamic and idiosyncratic, and its power occurs in the moment. Toning produces harmony realigning the body's molecules and restoring the inner sound of an individual.*

The type of music we are accustomed to is cultural. Chinese musical notes aren't Western ones. African rhythms and Amerindian drumming do differ. In the satellite age we're likely to be familiar with any type of music that has ever been recorded.

You might be highly influenced by sound beyond your awareness. The mother of an eleven-year-old who starts his day with a screaming radio may believe she is irritated only for the moment, yet her entire system can be disturbed enough to bring on a late afternoon headache that she blames on her job.

Eating in a cafe where the acoustics are bad and you have to shout to be heard drains you and throws off your natural vibration. Additionally, if the cafe is painted a jarring green hue that makes you uncomfortable, you will be upset by two negative factors whose combined effect will more than double the disjointed energy.

Inharmonic relations can be cured by the right utilization of sound. There is a spirit that rides between two people which contains a sound complementary to both partners. Reach for that sound; that's where you find your unity. If it's impossible to do it with words, do it with sound.

Music and DNA   Dr. Ono of UCLA, a geneticist using advanced research techniques, assigned notes to the DNA

Toning is covered in Chapter 5 of Sound Medicine *by Laeh Maggie Garfield.*

molecules. He found musical notes in combination that matched the genetic codes for many ailments. There are echoes of DNA coding from inside the composer's life in the compositions of Bach, Schubert, and Chopin. Chopin's later concertos reveal the genetic code for cancer, not consumption, which it is commonly believed he died from.

A student inquired, "Will listening to Chopin heal or cause cancer?" I wouldn't advise it as the sole method to heal cancer. You don't have to worry about the music planting a cancer in you. The composer wrote in a homeopathic manner, under the laws of similes: like cures like. Beethoven wrote music that works as a curative on the kidneys. People with predispositions to these ailments are attracted to the compositions, in the same manner as the body craves foods seldom included in the diet to heal itself.

Color and Sound   You can learn how to heal using these two elementary, magical forms of creative energy. There are forms where they overlap readily. Quite a few color and sound healings are remnants of ancient ceremonies and techniques passed down from teacher to initiate within a spiritual lineage. Ceremonies exist wherein songs are sung that aren't used at other times, and the priests and dancers wear colors symbolic of the invoked transformation.

Elaborate rituals have evolved around solstice and equinox observances. Most familiar is Christmas, a celebration that ties pagan symbolism about the rebirth of the sun to the birth of the Christ child. The two bright shades of red and green used at Christmas are seldom seen together under any other circumstances.

In meditation, a color visualization becomes a *yantra* (image symbol) for an absent healing or purification ritual. Chanting is a normal accompaniment to this type of meditation. At the end of the meditation, the color is sent to the person, place, or realm you intend to influence or add merit to. You may be doing a prescribed mantra with a preset visualization that refuses to stay static. If you are attempting to follow a form, such as a Goddess meditation for a transformation, and the color you usually have no difficulty visualizing refuses to appear for more than a few seconds, let it be. Having seen it momentarily is good enough.

There are inner meanings of specific sounds and colors that repeatedly seem to blend together to destroy or heal living beings. Using the right set can alter your life positively, and the resulting harmonics can make your family and friends simpatico at all times.

Synesthesia   Synesthesia is the intermingling of color and sound, as well as form, memory, touch, taste, smell and/or sight, a common phenomenon to those who retain the ability of sensory crossover. Usually two unrelated phenomena are paired in a single individual as taste and touch, or smell and sight. You may also enjoy an episode of synesthesia under optimal conditions. Exceptional experiences usually occur as you listen to an ostinato, a short melodic phrase repeated by the same voice or instrument in the same pitch. Ostinatos are a hypnotic, haunting musical form common to the compositions of J. S. Bach and popular singer Tracy Chapman. An ostinato acts as a bridge, triggering memories of past events more powerfully than ordinary memory. It can also place you in a time warp where your future is revealed.

People who have synesthesia frequently report seeing the same colors while listening to symphonic works. Ravel's Bolero is seen in a variety of bright reds. Brahms' Symphony #4 produces a dense medium blue that undulates swiftly like a river. Popular music, jazz, rock and roll, give off colors and patterns that are linked to the sounds of each piece. People repeatedly see equivalent colors and forms in the same song.

Natural sounds also transmit energetic dynamics in color. A nearly inimitable sound is that of a deer giving warning. Some synesthetes who've heard the cry of a stag claim they see vibrating waves of brown in many tones, aside from the reddish browns. Others say they've seen widening concentric lines in silvery white from the same sound.

Finding little research in the field, I began interviewing artists since many have the sensory crossover I am most familiar with: color and sound. Artists I've spoken with say they can hear sounds when they spread paint on paper. Notes and squawks that vary from one color to the next is the way a water-colorist put it. Another artist told me of seeing names and places in color when she hears them aloud. Several weavers and painters have told me that Thursday is purple and Tuesday is brown. They've seen the days of the weeks and the months in colors since early childhood. To explore fully the intermingling of color and sound and how frequently individuals receive the same data from synesthesia will take years of interviews.

I am not a scientist, a mathematician, or a musician, therefore my interest in this field stems from my own synesthesia. I have a second type of synesthesia, smell and memory crossover, which is totally unrelated to the color and sound. Sound does not trigger smells, nor do colors. However, sound does take me to the other worlds of knowledge.

Since I am not a musician, I've researched systems devised by Paul Foster Case, a Tarot expert; a theoretician, Peter Guy Manners, M.D. of Britform Trust; mystical mathematician Hans Cousto; and Kabbalistic linkages of color and sound. Your soul level is the best indicator of which system works for you. It might not be any of the systems below.

This first system is from Paul Foster Case and is linked with the Tarot, a mystical method of divination. It misses something because the cycles per second aren't known.

C	red
C#	red-orange
D	orange
D#	orange-yellow
E	yellow
F	yellow-green
F#	green
G	green-blue
G#	blue
A# (or Bb)	violet
A	blue-violet
B	red-violet

Lists of Cousto's and Manners' systems are below. Each uses frequency ranges to correlate with the colors.

These systems do not match one another. Yet each method works in and of itself. Cousto's and Manners' color and sound application is with tuning forks. Listening to the forks is different from placing the vibrating fork against the body. As the tuning fork vibrates, you subliminally experience the color it emits as well as the sound.

MANNERS' SYSTEM

Note	Frequency–cps		Color	Organ
	octave			
D+	584.2	23"	Blue-Green	Circulation
		46"	Green-Blue	
C prime	256	53"	Green	Personality
B	493	28	Yellow	Adrenal
F	349.2	39	Indigo	Bladder
E	329	41	Violet	Kidney
F	174.6	78	Indigo	Colon
E	164.6	82	Violet	Gall Bladder
G	196	69	Magenta	Liver
A	220	61	Orange	Lung
B	123.25	110	Yellow	Spleen-Pancreas
A	110	123	Red-Orange	Stomach

The system that Peter Guy Manners formulated is highly effective. The colors are the very ones I've used with a color lamp, color infused water, and foods, for the same diseases or imbalances. At a class in Munich an elderly woman who'd been sick with the flu for a few days brought me the A 220 fork. It worked like a charm on her cough. It also helped a person who'd suffered all winter with bronchitis. If all you have is one chronic or recurring problem, purchase the fork that suits your needs. Then strike it once and listen carefully. Repeat again until you don't want to hear it. You can also momentarily place the fork on the meridian for that ailment.

Another person who correlated sound and color using tuning forks is Hans Cousto who has written a highly readable book, *The Cosmic Octave*, published by Liferhythm.

He has matched the frequencies of the colors to their vibrational rate within a specific octaval range. Using mathematics, Cousto matched the wave length of the note and the color to each other and to the planets in our solar system. His method works, but some care must be taken. The tuning forks do work, but they are so subtle that you might be drawn to keep striking them over and over and place them on your body as he describes. Once is enough for a couple of days, more can do damage. For healing, listening to the forks repeatedly is helpful.

COUSTO'S SYSTEM

Note	Frequency–cps*		Color	Planet
D	423.34	72	Blue	Mercury
A	442.46		Orange	Venus
C#	432.10		Blue-Green	Earth
D	433.67		Blue	Mars
F#	436.62		Red	Jupiter
D	443.04		Blue	Saturn
G#	439.37		Orange-red	Uranus
A	422.87		Orange-red	Neptune
C#	445.26		Blue	Pluto
G#	445.86		Red Orange	Moon

*cps = cycles per second

Both the perception of color and the hearing of sound are determined by the ability of the eyes and ears to distinguish between different frequencies.

The color orange-red, for example, has a frequency which is considerably lower than that of blue, while a G of 194.18 hertz (or vibrations per second) is lower than a D of 290.94 hertz. Unlike the ear, which can distinguish between tones spanning about 10 octaves, the human eye can only recognize a range of about one octave. The lowest frequencies that the eye will react to lie in the region of 375 trillion hertz (375,000,000,000,000 hertz), which corresponds to the color red, while the highest frequencies lie in the 750 trillion hertz range, which corresponds to the color blue. All the other colors have frequencies lying between these two extremes. By applying the law of the octave, each color can be correlated to a respective tone:

purple-red	F
yellow-green	B -
red	F#
green	C
orange-red	G
turquoise	C#
orange	G#
dark blue	D
yellow-orange	A
Prussian blue	D
sharp yellow	B
violet	E

(From *The Cosmic Octave*, p 14–15)

The amazing thing is that all these systems work in and of themselves to heal the entire body/mind/spirit. They don't appear to mix well, so the novice is advised to experiment separately with each one. There are also other frameworks for the interrelationship of color and sound that have existed from antiquity. One system that comes from the Kabbalah contains within it twenty-two integrated colors and sounds, which have held true for thousands of years. Many spiritualists from the last century claimed to know the system, but their writings do not indicate the full number of colors and sounds. I assume this is because they were unable to read Hebrew. The best way to learn the Kabbalah sounds and color correlations is from a Jewish mystic. The sounds work quite efficaciously to heal and revitalize stagnant energies and alleviate difficult situations.

13

Death and Life

. . . death is an eternal companion on our left, watching us at arm's length, always with us . . .
Carlos Castaneda quoting his mentor don Juan

She stands at death's door,
asking, nay fighting for one more reprieve.
Death grants her request.
Death has time, death can wait.
Death always wins.
Death is the final, unbeatable caller in life.

To confront death and live through a major illness or a serious accident, or to be fortunate enough to avoid these calamities, is not the same as undertaking to know death's secrets. To know all about death, you make it your ally. To live with experiential knowledge of the mystery of death is a major goal of the solar spiral. Death and life are part of the initiations into the Second Tier of Mysteries. To know it, you will have to confront death.

You would be ill advised to undertake the secret practices for contacting death before you have mastered two of the four elements, and have worked several years receiving and testing knowledge received from trusted spirit guides. You must also be well attuned to the spiritual nature of sound. To do otherwise invites your premature demise.

You may read this section irrespective of your own development. All the exercises in this chapter are safe for you to do. However, they can lead you to levels of knowledge you aren't prepared for. Heed the warning. Do not attempt to master the second level of enlightenment until you are well accomplished in those skills belonging to the Moon spiral of enlightenment.

Every religion has its own name for the Angel of Death. In the Old Testament and in Rabbinical writings there are many names for the Angel of Death, who is always in God's service. The most common Hebrew name for the Death Angel is Malach-ha-Mavet. Others are Adriel, Apollyon, Azrael, Hemah, Kafziel, Metratron, and Gabriel as the guardian of Hades. Leviathan is associated with shakti, Yama is Sanskrit for the Angel of Death, and Yamanthanka is the Tibetan deity of death.

Hayagriva is the wrathful Tibetan deity of compassion, as well as a guardian of death. He may be invoked in making death an ally. Hayagriva works with frustrated anger, turning it into useful work. Anger is energy in its bottled form. The wrath helps to stamp out obstacles standing in your own way, in your own life. Hayagriva is invoked by Tibetan physicians when mixing medicines for a patient's healing. A mantra for Hayagriva exists. You can do it once a Rinpoche imparts it to you or gives you Hayagriva initiation.

Yama and Hayagriva are both magnetic entities. Knowledge of them is shrouded in mystery and initiation rituals. They each are held with respect and awe by the cultures where their names originate.

Serving in two capacities, the Egyptian deity, Selket, brings forth every soul's human birth as the midwife-goddess and also assists them on their way out. Selket, depicted with a scorpion headdress, is the guardian of the gate between life and death. Pyramid tombs, including King Tut's, contained her golden statue to protect the vessels that held the corpse's intestines. One of Selket's duties is to lead the deceased into the afterlife and offer instructions in the customs of that realm. In this capacity she also embodies the rebirth that follows death. Hence her dual function as the midwife.

The goddess' image still works to comfort, assist, and enlighten these total transformations. In cases of infertility, her statue kept in the bedroom often provides the spark of life that permits a soul searching for rebirth to choose parents who lack the ability to call down a child. Without Selket's help they would remain childless.

Unlike the feared Angel of Death, Selket, as scorpion goddess (Selkit, Selkhet, Selk, Selquet, Serk), is known for her healing powers, especially in the case of poisonous bites or poisoning. Selket's image has been used to represent the spiritual marriage between a couple and the Creator. Additionally, she is the protectress of the thyroid gland which has a major effect on reproduction. In Egyptian mythology she is the guardian of the throat chakra and therefore the voice.*

After death an individual's voice remains the same.

PHYSICAL DEATH

Life is a learning experience that includes your death and dying. How you die is a learning process. Any attachment to either life or death is negative and surfaces as suffering. Victory for one person is failure for another. A person may live following a bout with a life threatening disease, yet the rest of their life is dull, blank, and uninviting.

Another may find every nuance of existence invigorating once the ailment has been tamed or vanquished. An individual may die of their sickness, although the time from its diagnosis to death is the most meaningful and healing they've encountered.

A prominent healer in his thirties was dying. In the final ten days of his life he performed an extremely valuable service, mirroring all who were around him. Through his illness I saw my own destructive blueprint. His pattern of self-neglect, sporadic healing attempts, stop-gap measures, and postponements brought about his death. The way he died was more telling than his intermittent treatment for a systemic cancer.

On a wintery Friday he asked me to do a meditation that would allow him to forgive himself and others he'd had difficulty

---

Refer to Chapter 2, Sound Medicine by Laeh Maggie Garfield.

with. Monday he awoke, saying to his mother "This is a good day to die." By evening his journey here on earth was over. His body was not as sick nor as ravaged as most people with the ailment he had. He was done suffering, his decision firmly and irreversibly made.

To comprehend death you must be willing to let others die, as well as to save them. The real gift is to know when they've let go and not insist they reconsider and live. Either service is good, to help someone to move along their rightful path in life or to let go and be reborn at another time. Even young people and those still in their thirties and early forties go through an unmistakable old age in dying of cancer or AIDS. At the onset, their decision is clearly indicated in their physical body. The more youthful they appear, the more likely they are to recover. Do not mistake the freshness of those about to die, who've given up their daily and long term concerns, for this youthful glow. This is an entirely different manifestation.

Life Cord/Chord   Death comes first, then life. There's a point inside the anus, below the first chakra and attached to it, that holds the cord (braided tri-color of red, blue, and yellow) and the chord (sound) that grounds you to earth. A painful first chakra is undersized and overly contracted. The place under the anus cannot be decommissioned unless the person agrees. If it's not your time to die and there are disturbances in the cord/chord, accidents and illness may occur giving you an opportunity to reassess your life.

When this spot is off balance, the grounding of an individual is not good. Some manifestations of this difficulty are eternal adolescence, lack of common sense, a disruptive sense of timing, inability to provide enough for themselves, fears and phobias, or blocked memories.

The final transitions begin when the Angel of Death and appointed helpers pluck the cord to your inhale mechanism, disengaging it. Then they squeeze your heart, like two hands around it contracting it in opposite directions, to release the soul. If the soul floats up through the sixth chakra, a healer, CPR person, nurse, or anyone who knows a method to do so, can bring the person's soul back into the body. Exiting from the seventh chakra means the individual has made a perfect transition and cannot be revived without spiritual intervention. The Angel of Death and your Source Self are the only entities, other than the Source, who can return your life to you. No matter what has happened to institute your death, they can send you back without a recovery period, with your vitality completely restored.

It's the half-baked save from the grave by rank amateurs in the spiritual or medical arenas who do the worst damage. If you can't totally pull a person back from a stroke or major catastrophe, don't touch them!

Organs   Only a personality, or Learner who leaves through the sixth chakra can be a heart donor. Hearts of crown chakra departees are unable to function in the new body because the bearer is thoroughly removed from any attraction to their former life. The organs, blood, skin, and all other tissues carry with them characteristics of the person to whom they belonged. The recipient and the organ are alive only if the former owners keep their attention on it.

Each organ also contains the sound of the individual within it. If the sound within the organ doesn't match the internal sound of the recipient, rejection is certain. Incompatible notes or chords cannot resonate health in the new body. Patients whose body does not reject the organ have an internal harmonic close to the organ they received. Those who reject the well matched tissue are placed on drugs to make them accept the organ. However, the drug cannot alter the internal sound of the organ. That inharmonic note will eventually cause rejection of the transplant, or the death of the individual.

Crucial organs like the liver, heart, and kidneys never take on the vibrational sound of the recipient although bone marrow and other fast reproducing cells do. Blood transfusions, the transplanting of a liquid organ, take only thirty days to integrate, but other internal body parts like blood vessels may be completely yours only after seven years. When a portion of a healthy living regenerating organ is transplanted from a living grandparent to grandchild and the internal sound matches well it will last as long as the grandparent's love for the child thrives.

Mismatched sounds cause changes in the personalities of organ recipients, which are the donor's energy and personality. Nurses, physical therapists, and family members notice these changes which become permanent in the case of major organ transplants and disappear quickly in blood and bone marrow.

When adequate research is done, those with the internal sound of A-231 will most likely be found to be universal donors for every organ.

The Death Sound Death also has a sound, never heard anywhere else. It is whirling whistling, like a lasso, with a sireny overtone. It's a captivating, droning sound, that leads you on a swirling tricolored umbilicus, out of your body. The chord winds you back, into the cosmos, from the earth. If you follow that sound you're likely never to occupy your physical self again. If you can make that sound, or repeat that sound, you can call down death on someone. This is one sound whose notes are not to be repeated to anyone, once you know it. They are hypnotic and seductive as they disconnect the braided grounding cord that keeps the first chakra on a survival course.

This sound is not to be confused with the buzzing or ringing in the ear so many people have. That is the sound of creation urging you to go on, unleash your creativity, cease obscuring your personal and emotional growth, and allow yourself unlimited horizons. Once you use the sound of creation to walk your path fully and live up to your potential, the buzzing stops.

Before death you will see a clear blinding flash of light. I saw its undefined shape, prior to the explosion. Caught in the act, the light moved away, still in its semi-solid state. This same energy also appears as a fire, burning without fuel, smokeless, odorless, and silent.

The colors in the braided death cord are a muted silvery grey, white, and an orange-gold closely resembling 23-Karat Egyptian gold jewelry. The glowing orange has been consistently reported by individuals who have had premonitions of death and are in the throes of deciding whether or not to go on. White represents the Source. The silver is well-known from antiquity. Mystics in every culture report its presence during death.

Ageing No discussion of death nor life is complete without a thorough examination of ageing. Old age is preparation for death. Many do not ever reach that stage in life, having died earlier. Westerners, with their eternal pursuit of youth, ignore the passages time commands them to make. Without spiritual practices or initiations for almost all their transitions, or the awareness to communicate with other realms of existence, they fear and resist death.

Aged individuals frequently renounce worldly positions and goods they once held dear, liberating themselves for the transcendence of death. Others, in equally freeing fashion, dedicate themselves to causes and ideas they want to leave as a legacy to the world. These people may be producing the final, or first completion, of the three branches explored in Chapter 5. For a substantial number, elderly status is a time of regret over lost opportunities and a pitiful loss of their mental and physical faculties. This need not be the case. Retirees can count on ten to eighteen years of healthy active life after their wage earning days are done. Not everyone becomes feeble before dying. People can stay healthy until their final hours. Deep spiritual practices, that spring from the heart and are not imposed from the outside, serve to keep the body/mind alert and lively longer.

Plan your older years while you are young by cultivating the interests you say you wish you had time for. Take up the paint brush or the sailing jib sheet, make the quilts, garden, do walking tours of your area, act in the little theatre. Begin whatever is necessary to give you happy memories and lasting pleasure.

Every year go see something you've always wanted to, like the pyramids or Lake Champlain. Get box seats to see your favorite performer. Make many goals, and as you meet them add new ones. The main thing is to enjoy life. Admit pleasure in the everyday things—a sunset, the way the wind blows across the grass, your favorite food being in season. That's the best preparation for old age.

The hardest thing to befall a person in old age is senility, especially during the time you know you've lost your memory. It often begins early in life with short term memory loss, forgetting what you're saying in mid-sentence. It's a form of dyslexia resembling senility except you recover quickly and go on to the next subject backtracking to the original one later. Your thought process is interrupted by movement, but when you reverse your actions in the order you did them, the thoughts frequently return. If you have this difficulty it's good to exercise daily, as movement will stimulate your mind.

BREATH

The breathing place, the spot where the impetus to breathe is located is directly under the shoulder blade. Refrain from breathing, and it itches to signal the breath mechanism to kick in. Inhalation is automatic. Faulty exhalation is the origin of irregular breath and troubled breathing. Paradoxically the inhalation sequence has to be adjusted correctly or the exhalation will be irregular. In healthy people who aren't exerting themselves or undergoing emotional distress, a series of seven to eight breaths are taken per minute. The length of each breath varies, but the rhythm repeats itself in the ongoing series of breaths per minute.

From a secret place underneath the shoulder blade, well out of reach of human hands, the Angel of Death pulls out the final cord to sever your life by heart and lung failure.

Basically, that is how you live or die. An extremely competent shaman can reset the breath from under the shoulder blade by "blow doctoring" the right spot under that muscle tissue. This realigns the pattern or respiration and can cure all ailments. While healers can repair damage, only the Universe's emissary can eliminate the breath process.

There is an unbuttoning process in death. One: inside lowest rib; two: third rib, chest side of body on the lung point; three: fifth rib in the area usually covered by the arm. Any intuitive or able healer will begin by readjusting points one two and three as noted on the illustration. These in turn will restimulate the fourth point to vibrate in harmony.

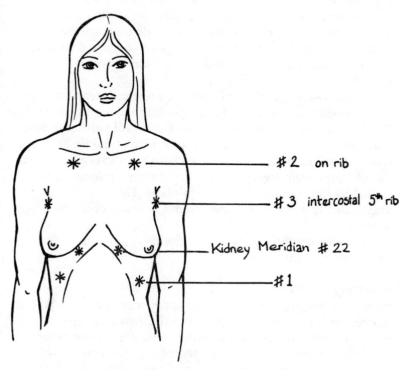

#2 on rib

#3 intercostal 5th rib

Kidney Meridian #22

#1

Those points will be
a bit tender

Excessive crying dislodges the special prana point, jamming it into the wrong frequency range. As the child cries without let-up, the breathing spot becomes stuck and inadequately restores itself. Labored inhalations become characteristic of the child's respiration. That is why, in many instances, colicky babies are later asthmatic.

The cosmic alignment (astrological) of the Forties, for breathing difficulties that affected an entire generation, was brought to fruition by doctors who declared that babies ought only be fed on an inflexible schedule. If the babies didn't adjust, they were to cry it out. Mothers ran from the room and covered their ears just as pained until feeding time. No wonder a generation was born that hates doctors.

To make sure that newborns were breathing properly, doctors slapped them on the behind, shocking them into taking their first breath. It works by unbalancing the breath pattern impulses that gently activate the prana spot under the shoulder blade. In this manner, millions of individuals have been violently thrown out of their dream bodies, into the cold three dimensions accepted by the majority on the earth plane. This practice, long in vogue, disrupts the normal flow from one plane of life to another.

Extreme laughter can also damage the pulsations of the pranic mechanism.

Resetting the Breath Pattern

Resetting of the breath pattern must be done by an experienced person who has worked with ever increasingly sick or disoriented people over the years. Blow doctoring can kill healers who don't know what they are doing or who cannot protect themselves adequately while readjusting the breath and lifeforce of another individual. Harmonizing the breath may cause a person to recover completely, or to die peacefully. It depends on the contract they have made with the Universe.

Revitalizing the breath pattern is accomplished by blowing along the golden or silver cords that hold the body and psyche together. These lines pierce the aura interconnecting the body along the front and the back. It is safest to learn blow doctoring as the apprentice of someone who is accomplished in the method. If you are misinstructed, you can upset your own breath pattern, calling down serious ailments that only you can cure yourself of. A mistake in blow doctoring could kill you outright.

Choosing Death   Death is a cessation of the winds of change within the life that was being lived. The entire soul not only chooses the time to die, but has lots of latitude in resetting the moment.

Every death is a suicide. In death each person goes out due to a private evaluation. The resurrection is the denial of death. Death is denied because it is considered a defeat, except with the elderly-accomplished-in-life, who are venerated. Those with Mission accomplished, who followed their star, go home in peace.

Many of us know that auto wrecks, sudden death by shootings, violent encounters, accidents, and heart attacks are immediate decisions agreed upon between you and your Advisors as the means by which to terminate your life. The malingerers who can't make up their minds get wasting diseases and have about eighteen months to make their final decision. Failure of an individual to make contact with their well of health leads to the small prana button being deactivated. There follows a short or prolonged comatose period—depending upon the individual's attachment to the life that is ebbing and how long they refuse the next one. They lie neither dead nor alive until the peace of death is victorious, or they muster the courage to make their own miraculous recommitment to the body they are in.

Death often occurs because a person is unwilling or unable to pass through the gateway into another segment of life. We are all too familiar with the memorial service at high school graduations for a member of the senior class, often a prominent, accomplished student or athlete who dies accidentally, or from a sudden fatal illness. The drowning victim, in his prime between thirty-eight and forty-five years of age, and the new mother-in-law with a life threatening ailment, are each protesting against growing older, moving on to the next phase. In former times it was common for women with too many children and those in a bad marriage to die of complications following childbirth.

There are people who cannot face the next cycle of time, be it a yearly event or a personal landmark. To die at Christmastime or within a few weeks of your birthday makes your demise all the more noticeable. The college professor emeritus who passes away in the days immediately after graduation ceremonies held at the university where she taught, the newly retired person who suffers a fatal heart attack, the man who has a debilitating stroke after a committee rejects his master plan and he wastes away thereafter, and the individual who accomplishes a lifetime dream and dies once it is sufficiently savored—all are examples of this death phenomenon.

Losses　　　　A sage was asked, "What is happiness?" He replied, "Grandfather die, father die, son die." Would you have it any other way? When your parents die you lose your past, when your children die you lose your future.

Even a mother whose child has raised his own children to adulthood suffers a loss of her future comfort in her old age provided by her child. But she does not lose a total dream as the parent of an infant or teenager does. A daughter with small children is a great loss as her children very likely will be reared by their father who might not include the grandparents in the children's lives.

Loss of a spouse, while devastating, rarely causes endless grieving. Healthy people tend to restructure their lives within a couple of years. Widows or widowers who were happily married tend to pair up a second or third time. That is true for all but the suicide victim's widow. To become a widow by suicide is an indication of not being really loved or treasured. Unlike her male counterpart, she habitually feels remorseful for every little abrasion that ever came between them. Society in some way blames her and she in turn blames herself.

How to Help　　　　Acknowledge the grief of the dying. In long deaths they are slowly letting go of the life they lived, oftentimes losing capacities they once prided themselves on. Each diminishing bit of independence can be a cause for grief. Some will be angry at themselves for becoming a burden to family and friends. Others may be angry that they aren't receiving the love and attention they expected from longtime friends and relatives.

The physically infirm have much grief and many adjustments to make. Those who remain mentally alert and philosophically cheerful are likely to be visited by younger friends and admirers seeking a good script to grow old with. Those who become bitter frequently face abandonment.

Ordinarily women become the caregivers, whose patience is sorely taxed as they care for ageing or ill relatives at home. The caregiver may deny many needs of their own and be guilt struck over the resentment they feel for the sacrifices. Sometimes they may be angry that the dying need so much from them.

In either case, the correct thing is to listen with respect and suspend judgements about their feelings. You may be the only one they trust to share their doubts and sorrow. And, if you hear gossip saying what a complainer the caregiver or the dying person is, remember you might be filled with the same emotions in a similar situation. It's no shock that they wish to be finished with their current circumstances. Be empathetic. Dissuade them from hurrying the end before being actually called and from prolonging their agony. Life support for the hopelessly ill is as derelict as performing unasked-for euthanasia. Just as there is a correct time for being born, there is one for dying. Neither ought to be manipulated mechanically as this interferes with the Cosmic order.

Is euthanasia, a socially accepted practice much in vogue at the moment, correctly following the Universal plan? The question is not, is it moral—for morals are made by human beings. The question is, does hurrying death cause as much trouble for the reentering soul as hastening life, via induced labor or prearranged Caesarean sections? Delaying death with medical strategies often means a dying man misses his appointment with his takeaway persons who are repeatedly sent for in vain.

Beyond listening, be of service. Simple things are best. If you can read to the frail one while the main caretaker has a few hours off, that's a service. You could cook a meal, deliver it, and share it with the family unit. If you have been a close friend or a near relative, assuming some of the responsibility is a great help, particularly if you do it routinely.

If your friend permits, while they're asleep provided their illness is not contagious, lay a cloth on the bed and lie down next to them placing your hands gently on their back. The majority of seriously ill or dying people suffer from a lack of loving touch. Your hands can heal and console them.

Meditations   Many good guided meditation tapes can help souls making the final transition in life. The sweetest and most loving ones are the guided meditations friends and relatives speak aloud to the individual, whether they are conscious or not. Every so often, someone resists the taped version while embracing the spoken one offered by a familiar voice. Speak with a moderate to slow tempo, in calming tones.

Each person requires visits to the other side to allay their fears of dying. We all want a peaceful death rather than a painful prolonged suffering one.

The meditation given here is a sample. Use the parts of it that your loved one finds most reassuring. The meditation like the prayer needs to be neutral, urging neither death or recovery.

The family might object to meditations while the sick person appreciates them. Enlist the dying person's confidence and do them only when you are alone if the family is uncomfortable. Volunteer to "babysit" your relative or friend so that other caregivers have free time.

The person may be in a long decline and then be roused due to the meditation. This can create an emotional or psychic breakthrough that will give their remaining time here, be it six days, six months, or six years, more meaning.

The meditation below is one you can lead someone in. It is very effective. Your friend might want a recording to do it alone. Speak slowly and deliberately in a soft audible voice. In meditation, the inhalation is always automatic.

Meditation for Reintegration of the Self   Get into a position that is comfortable for you. You may lie on your back or sit up in lotus pose or tailor fashion (legs folded but uncrossed). Once you are in an easy pose, begin breathing deeply letting waves of air enter your abdomen and move up to your chest and shoulders, as you continue to inhale. Allow these waves of air to leave your body, shoulders first, chest second, and abdomen last. This is the relaxed breath of sleep. It is also the natural form of breathing yogis and enlightened people do.

Breathe in and feel the wave of air travel through you. Breathe out and feel the wave of air leave you taking with it all the emotional patterns you want to give up. Repeat three times.

Now imagine yourself as a wave upon the beach. Each molecule of the ocean is adjusting and readjusting itself to accommodate that wave.

The wave re-enters the ocean and becomes the ocean once again. And then, every little molecule that will be the next wave hits the beach forming the next wave which is you reformed again.

(Pause briefly.)

With each outbreath you are a landing wave, with each in breath you are a rejoining wave.

Breathe in deeply. (Pause.) And breathe out, totally letting go. (Repeat twice more.)

Breathe out and you are a landing wave. Breathe in and you are a rejoining wave rejoining the vastness of the ocean. (Allow 20 seconds.)

Breathe out and you land upon the beach. Breathe in and you become the ocean once again. (20 second pause.)

Breathe out and you become the ocean once again. (20 second pause.)

Now let your wave become a wave of light. Make yourself a wave of light, flowing to the farthest reaches of the Universe on the out breath. (8 seconds.)

Breathe in and take the farthest reaches of space into yourself, into your very being. (15 seconds.)

Breathe in and become all the the universe inside of you. Breath out and become all of the universe again. Breathe in and out at your own pace. (15 seconds.)

Breathe and become the universe inside. Everything in the vast reaches of space can come to you. Breathe out and you become the farthest reaches of space. (20 seconds.)

From this vantage point you can know every planet in the universe. You can visit any star because as you are breathing out you are there. And, as you are breathing in, you are bringing it into yourself.

Breathe out and look around to see what there is in the furthest galaxy. Breathe in and bring that galaxy inside of yourself. (Short pause.)

Just as there is incessant movement in the universe, there is also a stillness. Become that stillness. (Silent moment.) For that is the place where The Creator lodges. (Long pause.) That stillness is unconditional love and acceptance. (Short pause.)

Now as you breathe out in your ocean of light you are the stillness, the repose, and the silence of the Universe. (Medium pause.)

In that stillness you will know unconditional love. You can accept yourself, the way The Creator accepts you. You will see that your personality is but a gown that you have donned for this existence and for no other. You lose the attachment to that personality. (Pause briefly.)

Once you have done that, once you have accepted that your personality is not you, just something you are wearing for the moment, you can love it all the more. (Pause.) You can accept who you are just the way you are. (Medium pause.)

Take that stillness into your body and remain with your eyes closed. (Quiet moment.) Return to your body. (Pause.) Through your closed eyes, as you breathe out, beam the light you saw when you were in the presence of the Creator. That light, coming through your eyes, will look like headlights on a car. (Short pause.)

When you breathe in you will bring more of The Creator into you. And when you breathe out through those headlights which are the eyes of your Creator, you will send more of the Source into the world around you. Breath in and breathe out. (Repeat four times.)

(Silent time.)

As you breathe in from your crown chakra there is a fountain of luminescent rainbow colored light. Breathe in and absorb it. Breathe out, and it becomes headlights of multicolored rays illuminating the world.

Breathe in from your luminescent, ever shining fountain of light in your crown chakra. That illumination will fill your headlights as your eyes beam out into the world around you.

Your third eye takes in light from the Universe as you breathe in. It is an astral beam entering as a beacon of indwelling light. (Quiet space.)

Breathe in and bring in shining bright colored light from the Universe. Allow your third eye to be filled with astral beams and let the light that has become you allow your godliness to fill the world. (Pause.) Fill the world with light. (Long pause.)

With this extraordinary consciousness you have, merge with someone you love and become that person. (Quiet moment.) You can feel what that person feels and experience what that person experiences. (Long pause.) Observe your loved one as they see themselves. You will know them better once you have merged with them in a clean clear way. (Long pause.) From now on you can see everything with your headlights and illuminated fountain.

You may open your eyes but do not let ordinary consciousness enter. Only allow your crown chakra still flowing as an illuminated fountain, your third eye as an astral beam of light, and your eyes as headlights of holiness to be the functionaries of your consciousness in the ordinary world.

(Silent time.)

As you slowly open your eyes and let in ordinary reality, viewing it through your enlightened fifth, sixth, and seventh chakras, you can begin to deal with one of the blockages to happiness. That blockage is resentment. This resentment can be long standing harm that was done to you by a single person, or it can be treatment you received from a group. Lay aside your resentment at the person. Resent only the treatment you received. As you look at your resentment from the point of having been merged with The Creator, you realize that we are all part of the Source. That person you are resenting is an instrument of The Creator. Could you be resenting the Source as well?

Be honest with yourself. Let yourself feel that resentment. Be honest about the fact that you do have that resentment. (Pause.)

Go see the one you resent through their own eyes. Permit yourself to be totally free to experience that person. See them as they see themselves. (Long pause.) Now see yourself through their eyes. It may be painful, but absolute honesty is the only clearing possible. It's the only way you can form healthy relationships and allow yourself more and deeper spiritual experiences that expand you as a person instead of keeping you closed in. (Long pause.)

Forgiveness is an opening to a new life, to health in relationships and to clarity in the etheric levels. Now that you have recognized the resentment, forgive that person. It is very difficult to forgive the person who may not have changed much and may still harbor unfortunate feelings towards you. Remember you are forgiving them for your own sake. If they have died they can feel you concentrating on them and offering up forgiveness. (Lengthy pause.)

There is another blockage to growth and that is guilt. (Medium pause.) To deal with guilt you must make amends. (Short pause.) Recognize that you have erred. It's irrevocable. The time has passed. There is nothing you can do except to let the other person know that you are aware and you have remorseful feelings about the incident or long term condition. Outside of meditation write them a letter, go and see them, or phone to tell them that you are sorry. Make your plans and realize in the very core of your being that this must be done to free you of guilt which keeps you from higher consciousness and from being a totally free human soul.

(Long pause.)

If the person you feel guilty towards is dead they will hear your thoughts traveling through the Universe. (Silence.) Once you have taken care of the matter forgive yourself. (Pause briefly.) Forgiveness is the greatest key to growth. The One forgives everything. Because you have merged with The Creator, because you are in part The Creator, you too can forgive everything. (Pause.)

Now you may begin to come back to your regular consciousness. Open those headlights your eyes have become. Your rising awareness will keep them beaming in all your contacts with everyone.

Use your fountain of light and you will always be in meditation. You will always be in contact with The Creator, and with your Source self, and with the forces of love and caring. (Long silence.)

You may sit up and move around very slowly. Acclimate yourself to your new condition. Looking at any reality through your illuminated crown chakra, your headlights, and the astral beam in your third eye, will eliminate much pain and suffering for you and all who come in contact with you. You are now at peace inside and out, ready to face whatever you must with reawakened consciousness.

Rituals from the Heart   Burn a candle twenty-four hours a day, lighting each candle from the previous one so as to keep the flame alive. White candles or those in your loved one's favorite color are best.

Say prayers for your loved one to exit peacefully. The prayers begin by thanking whoever you pray to for the love and friendship you have had with the ailing or dying person. If it was a difficult relationship state what you gained from it. If you still have grievances against the individual, resolve them separately with suggestions given in the next section, making amends. Ask in your own words, keeping them neutral, for your heart friend to be given the strength and courage to live their true and rightful path and make whatever transition is necessary. Bless them and all those whose lives they touch. You may end by saying "Ho!" which in the Native American tradition, simply means "I have spoken," or say the more traditional "Amen," or "Hallelujah," whichever feels most comfortable to you.

Making Amends   You must make amends to release your relative or friend, and you can do so. Should they be geographically distant or unconscious they can still hear your thoughts. Have a heart to heart chat with them, mustering all the sensitivity and caring you can. Begin by telling them how much you liked, admired, or loved them and felt they did not reciprocate the feeling. How much that disappointed you. What it led to: separation, gossip, lack of contact, or severe emotional dependency on one another and resentment from each of you. If you believe you were betrayed by the individual, tell them how and what that made you feel like. Whatever the cause of your grievance, let it out and leave time for a reply. You may hear them say things that heal you like balm to the heart. Or you might get one that cuts you to the emotional quick.

Usually, this mental/spiritual message transmission works like televised pictures being sent from private studio to private studio. There are people who hear it clearly, others feel it. You may not get an answer back if you block it from coming in.

If the person rejects contact, it may be that they have already cut you loose in order to lend wings to their next step. Most dying people decrease their attachments by seeing a diminishing circle of visitors. This happens very quickly in sudden death, although on careful examination you might find that the person had been moving away from friends and family they considered extraneous. At the same time the inner circle weaves itself tighter and tighter around the one about to die, subconsciously trying to get enough of them, until they too are ready to let go.

Those who die are in an atmosphere of unconditional love. For the survivors there are other lessons, some bitter, some illuminating.

Author Peggy Eastman, widowed after a long childless marriage, wrote in *New Age Journal*, July/August 1987:

"I am different now: I have been to a far place and see through different eyes. I learned a bittersweet lesson in that far place. I learned that suffering does not stunt; it spurs growth. I would never willingly have paid such a high price for growth, but I have grown-into a more acute understanding of mortality, into a more acute awareness of the need to celebrate those we love while we can. For they are not ours to keep; they are only lent to us for a while to keep us company on what ultimately seems to be, for each of us a solitary journey."

Calling Your Oversoul

Provided you have regular, active contact with your spirit guide, this way of helping is open to you. If you do not, read it for future information rather than attempt to practice something you will more than likely perform ineffectively.

The correct link-up is through your Lifeguide to your Oversoul, and from your Oversoul to the Oversoul of the person you're helping.

Whenever you are called upon to help another person transit the corridor of death, to life beyond the gate, you can call upon your Oversoul for guidance. To do this, you will have to have had prior contact with your own Oversoul. If you are facing an immediate death, it is too late to set up a full-fledged conscious relationship with your Oversoul. If you have a few weeks to prepare yourself, it may be possible to make sufficient contact with your Oversoul. A description and illustrations about the Oversoul is in the Who's Who section of this book. A fuller account of the Oversoul relationship appears in *Companions in Spirit*.

Calling the Dying Person's Oversoul

To send for another individual's Oversoul, begin with a prayer asking that this contact be for their best and highest purpose. By turning it over to their Source Self, and their Oversoul, you allow the person, if conscious and receptive to the idea, to meet with their Oversoul while still alive. This will make their final journey all the more comfortable. It's conceivable that they may be able to renegotiate the contract with their Oversoul and live a fuller life in whatever time they have remaining, be it long or short. Once you open the lines of communication with the Oversoul, you are pretty much in the position of a knowledgeable Learner, who is coaching the dying.

Listen carefully for messages from the Oversoul. Those near death are uncannily able to walk the bridge between the living and the spirit worlds. A consciously dying individual will readily assume responsibility for their own conversations with their Oversoul, once the original contact has been made. Your job is to assist and reassure them.

Should the individual be unconscious, you'll be making requests in their stead. Your position is either neutral or positive towards their recovery or death, clinging to no specific outcome. The Oversoul knows everything already, including thoughts you or the person you're helping have never voiced. In spite of this, select your words very carefully, weeding out ambiguous phrases. If a negative thought pops into your head while you're working with their Oversoul, just say "Cancel that," and proceed as if it never erupted. Ask that everything you do and say in their behalf be used to their highest benefit.

The Take-Away Person   No one is permitted to make the passage from life to death unaccompanied. A take-away person is assigned to assist you on your journey. The very ill, even those who've been comatose, can be heard to call out a name immediately prior to death.

"Nurses in many hospitals have noticed that, at the time of death, a patient who has been weak or even comatose may suddenly start to speak quite loudly and lucidly with someone not visibly present. Those whose loved ones pass away at home often observe the same phenomenon, a phenomenon that can also affect a family member who is senile or semi-conscious due to accident or illness. In most of these cases, the family member is heard talking—or mentions having talked—with someone, now deceased, to whom they were once close: perhaps their mother, or a sibling, or a childhood friend. In 1842, Ralph W. Emerson's son Waldo died of scarlet fever at age five. In 1882, when it was the father's turn to make the transition, his friend Bronson Alcott heard him call out, 'Oh, the beautiful boy!' just as he had done at little Waldo's deathbed forty years before.

"The conversations that the dying have with their take-away person are deeply significant. The take-away person is a discarnate being whom the dying one trusts, being able to provide reassurance during the crossover period when personal and acculturated fears can combine to hamper natural acceptance of the transitional process, a being who can pick up the nuances of the dying person's emotional condition, mental state and level of energy. The two enter into an intimate confidence. Information is funnelled into the person about to be transformed (how to move through walls, for example and how to travel astrally)—various kinds of preparation for life without a body. For those whose death is swift the take-away person acts as an anchor amid the confusion of the initial adjustment period."*

On the Other Shore   Immediately, as a soul begins the journey through the tunnel to the "greeting room," beliefs about the afterlife, impressed by the personality's religion, are released. They arrive freed from the fears and phobias earthly society has placed on them. Those who scramble the messages they received in their recent incarnation are greeted by people they trusted and are familiar with, who passed over before them. These friends, now in spirit, tell them the truth about the Realm of Creation. A soul who ignores this process and fails to realign itself with its Oversoul and Source Self, literally becomes one of the living dead. The real purpose of the prayers the living say for their dead is to alleviate any distortions in the transition from life to afterlife.

Your Oversoul, your Advisors, Spirit Guides, and others who care for you will come to debrief you during the three to five days when you transit from earthly life to spirit. You might attend your own funeral—in spirit many do—observing your friends and family, listening in on conversations, unobtrusively and unseen. Should you have left unfinished business that will stymie relatives, friends and associates, you are allowed to send them messages in dreams, visions, and telepathy that will help their transition to life without you. This form of guidance, lovingly done, can continue for many years, possibly as a spirit guide or in occasional contacts. Those still living are able to send you messages via thought waves and in their dreams, prayers, and meditations.

---

*Companions in Spirit, Laeh Maggie Garfield and Jack Grant.

The funeral over, you might settle into a routine that includes several visits a day from your teachers who debrief you concerning your lifetime and help you examine your accomplishments and failures in your Mission and its tasks. They will also help you re-establish a perspective about your human interactions and relationships, from the Universal vantage point.

Messages from the Other Side   After death an individual pays visits in dreams, visions, flashbacks and daydreams that seem real. They deliver messages that comfort or make completion with friends, co-workers, neighbors, and family. Each one will receive the message they need to hear. Everyone's afterlife contact is reminiscent of the person you knew in life. Your relative or friend often brings you answers to questions you may never have discussed with them or simply reassures you that you are still important to them. The connection isn't broken by their exit from physical reality. Be considerate of your loved one's commitments in the afterlife and yours to life in the Physical Realm; do not continually call them back. Use discretion, or you may be unable to elicit reasonable responses when you really require their intervention.

A religious man in his middle years, married to the same wife for eighteen years, put up with her idea of a union although the fad for open marriage had long since faded. She continued having lovers long after he was weary of the exploits. Ted, the husband, dated other women simply to have something to do when his wife was head over heels in love with yet another man.

An elderly member of the church, a pillar of the community whom the husband had grown up knowing, was dying a lingering death that made him less and less able to function. Ted's lifelong contact with the elderly man, who was an enduring, intimate friend of the family, had influenced him. In adult life, Ted had become the backbone of the religious and civic community too. The old man died. Within a month Ted had a dream. In it the old man said, "Ted, since I'm over here I found out God does not care who you are lovers with." He was shocked as well as relieved by the dead man's statement.

In a meditation, held following the death of a woman of advanced years, she told her daughter, who is open to such things, "I've had my check-up. Everything was okay, I can go on with my work." She also confided in her daughter that she had many things to settle with her husband and one of her sisters. She went on rather brightly about seeing many old friends, her brothers, sisters, and cousins who'd passed on. "It's been like a party," the mother stated. And then more newsy like a telephone call, "Uncle Henry reincarnated about 10–11 years ago."

14

Time and Time Again

This time, like all times, is a very good one if we but know what to do with it.

Ralph Waldo Emerson

REAL TIME

Two types of time exist in our lives. Eternal Time, which we touch upon when dreaming, and World Time, a linear progression of events suspended in irretrievable time. Eternal time could also be called Cosmic time, Star time, or natural time. Ancient Egypt worked on Star time. Eternal time is a spiral that follows the spiral travels of the ever expanding universe. World time is based on the movement of the sun's orbit. It is calendar time, with a fixed yearly cycle of seasons and astrological rendezvous, and a daily round of twenty-four hours from sunset to sunset. World time can also be moon based. Thirteen moons make up a solar year.

The fixed aspect of the stars sets Eternal time. Stars have an orbit to maintain in relation to other stars within their constellation. A single human lifetime can only utilize mathematical calculations to chart a constellation's movement in correlation to nearby constellations.

Eternal time, or Cosmic time, has no set dates or hours that match up with World time exactly. Occasionally these two types of time cross over one another. If the dates synchronize, we acknowledge foresight, telepathy, and a multitude of other phenomena as having validity. Learning that a friend, at a distance, dreamt of you the night before your impromptu visit raises questions about sending messages and receiving them. You may believe this type of dream contact is normal, or consider it paranormal. If you planned the get together in advance, as a surprise, your friend might feel she was picking up on your thoughts telepathically. This will not interfere with your linear notions about World or passing time. If you wound up in their city due to a snowstorm that rerouted your flight through it and suddenly had seven hours before departure, both of you would be amazed at the crossover between World Time and Eternal Time.

If your friend's dream included what you would tell her, or where you'd go together in exacting detail, each of you would acknowledge the depth of the connection you have to one another. But, would you see the linking of World time and Eternal time as represented by your friend's dream? What if you had the same dream a month ago, noting it in your dream journal? Is it *déjà vu* or something even more extraordinary?

Whenever you do a fully competent healing or a truly channeled reading for someone, you enter Eternal time. This is where formation and reformation of events, situations, and the conditions of an individual's or a community's life exist.

The crossover point of World time and Eternal time is seldom noticed and usually denied. If the two events do not occur in the same sequence as they did in World time, you'll discount the validity of the mental or psychic contact you have made with the other individual. Yet your pets have no such separation of Eternal and World time. They seem as overjoyed at your return after a few hours absence as they do after several weeks.

Small children only learn to make the distinction of passing time because their elders teach them they must. They do not know how many days are in a week. And, if you think about it, to have divided our time into segments of seven days, four-and-a-half weeks to a month, is a relatively arbitrary accounting of time. The number of days assigned to a week is based upon a lunar cycle of 28 days, with thirteen months or moons to the year. Ancient peoples, world over, hit upon this method of reckoning passing time.

Solar time divides the year into six-week segments. We are most familiar with the four cross points of the solstices (winter and summer) and the equinoxes (spring and fall). The other four demarcations are May first, which is the beginning of summer; August first, the initial day of autumn; November first, the onset of winter; and February second, the start of spring. The solstice is actually a midpoint if you remember the Shakespearean play "A Midsummer Night's Dream". All these dates are magical and many are celebrated around the world. Halloween, a vestige of such festivals, is the eve of winter.

Other than the seasonal changes and the amount of daylight we receive to leave us clues, without calendars we would only know that an event occurred recently, or some time ago. Therefore, the two friends in the dream cycle example cited earlier, might perceive nothing extraordinary in the time frame. Our calendar is a mix of lunar and solar time.

A prophet lives on the three levels of time daily. There are the lunar level where the immediate and near future emotional cycles of the people, animals, plants, and earth can be felt and predicted, and the solar level where the cycle of change is elongated into six-week segments. These two make up World time. The star level is where Eternal time functions. Each planet in every solar system has a different reckoning of passing time. When we are able to do interplanetary travel we will confront the same problems that affected our globe in the previous century.

Until the need for mass communication made a single calendar necessary for the entire planet, many nations and religions lived by their own calendars. The Gregorian and the Julian calendars are noted historic examples. A person emigrating from Russia during the 19th century would have to re-estimate their date of birth according to the Julian calendar in use in the United States.

All religious calendars reckon time from the date of their founding. According to the Christian calendar, the present year is 1991. The Hebrew calendar, comprised of thirteen lunar months, counts 1991 as the Jewish year 5751. Their new year always coincides with the new moon in the Hebrew month of Tishri. The Chinese Buddhists' calendar lists 4688 years since they began their lunar linear system. Twelve years designated by animals (snake, rabbit, pig, rat, rooster, dog, horse, buffalo, tiger, goat, dragon, and monkey) make a full cycle. All months have 29–30 days. The fifteenth day of the month is always the full moon. Every three years they have to add a month, and they are short two months every five years.

Sunrise and sunset are natural designations for the beginning and ending of days. Moslems and Jews begin each day at sundown. Western calendars measure the new day at a prearranged hour, midnight. When it is 7:00 AM in Hawaii it is 10:00 AM in the far western United States, 1:00 PM or 1300 hours on the eastern seaboard, and 6:00 PM or 1800 in England. The time zone in England is Greenwich Mean Time, the yardstick by which navigators, shortwave broadcasters, and others count their day. From this short sample it is possible to see how arbitrary measures of passing World time can be, no matter how accurate they are scientifically.

There is a third type of time which is unnatural. It is created outside World time and Eternal time, by an individual or a group. False time is like a gridlock between World and Eternal time. False time destroys the cooperation between World and Eternal time by being heavy and cumbersome.

False time occurs whenever you won't let Eternal time take its course and you rush off doing things to activate future events, instead of seeing each activity for itself, occurring in the right framework, as the future unfolds into the present. We in the West have been so dominant in our ideal of setting goals that we make and carry out these ambitions, all too often against our better judgement or our intuition. Many are, in this way, derailed from their rightful path in life and live out a lifetime of disharmony, despite their considerable achievements. These goals are often limited in their scope, and individuals who don't fit into the mold become society's throwaways. The lucky ones find their destiny anyway, as eccentrics and innovators.

Time comes in bands. People who can see into the past or the future see across these bands. Time is similar to a Moebius strip. To make a Moebius strip cut a strip 1 inch wide from a standard sheet of paper. Give this strip a half twist and fasten the ends together. Your finger slipping along the band will traverse both sides before returning to the starting point. This is an approximation of how time bands function. Many such bands are linked together in wave-like formations. Making a strip will enhance your comprehension, by giving you a three dimensional image.

INTERLOCKING TIME

The merging of World time and Eternal time is best explained by examples. These will jog memories of moments when the two intertwined in your life.

A woman student, Angelika P., from Northern Germany, educated in the life sciences, came to me incredulous. She'd had a dream, early that morning, in which I held up a blackboard. On it I'd written her future career and the date, May first, for its inception. Whenever we met, over the past several weeks, I'd attempted to tell her that her current transition would be complete in about a year. She unfortunately was stuck in false time, pushing the river, to make change happen when only patience would do.

"Do you remember consciously that you came to me in my dream this morning and told me this?" she asked. As a very intelligent and insightful person, Angelika required more than a knowing smile. Patiently I explained the concepts of World and Eternal time and that I'd been sending her telepathic messages over the past few weeks to help her relax and let go of false time.

"But did you know you actually came in my dream to tell me?" she pursued her original line of thought further.

My response was, "I've tried to let you see that this career change you've been anxious about will happen, but you cannot image how it will. All you need to know is that it will. The message was sent from my Source Self to your Higher Self. You received it in dreamtime."

"But did you know you actually came in my dream, this morning, to tell me?" she persisted, wanting to know if I'd been consciously aware of her dream as an active participant.

This question, too, could best be answered by an anecdote. I told her the story of Merrilee, an American student of mine. In the fall of 1981 I was on an assignment in the northeastern corner of California where the borders of Oregon, Nevada, and California meet. It is a very powerful area spiritually. The high, semi-arid, mountain plains make for excellent transmission and reception of dreams, visions, meditative states, healing power, and other skills of the shamanic path. One is very close to the Realms of Creation and Formation there. During my first three weeks in the area I'd experienced astral travel, wherein those I visited remembered our meeting in exact detail, although my physical body never left the room.

On my last Sunday in the area, I accompanied the entire crew on a tourist journey to some caves, and then to a special lake with magical powers. It was a fairly long drive. I had been working fifteen-hour days, rising before 5 AM, seven days a week. I'd formed friendships with the women and the four of us chose to picnic alone, down the beach from the men.

Something urged me to lie down and look at the sky. The others thought I was dozing. Although I could hear every word of their conversation, I was also far removed from it. Every twenty minutes I'd open my eyes, respond, and drift off. I was checking on my body, as well as making certain no one actually knew what I was up to.

I traveled through areas that can only be described as chaotic pictures and images of things familiar to my third eye but never seen in this lifetime by my optic apparatus. Scenes slipped into scenes, and knowledge was revealed.

During one informational portion I was quite astonished, and then horrified, to see Merrilee slipping by. I knew she shouldn't be there. She wasn't developed enough. How had she slipped in? Breaking off my astral teachings, I went rushing through the Universe, with Merri in hot pursuit, begging me for assistance. In an earlier sequence a cobalt blue bottle had floated above me. I rushed off after it, reached for it, and poured the contents into her head. Merrilee returned immediately to the earthly time frame she belonged in. I released the bottle and resumed my travels somewhat shaken.

In the end I remembered the teachings but not the cause of their interruption. I forgot what had offended me, retaining only the image of the blue bottle and my horror once the journey was over.

As scheduled the following Tuesday, my contracted hours on the project completed, I left for home. That afternoon Merrilee's sister Janis, who was a great friend of mine at the time, came to help me warm my frozen house and share our adventures over a cup of coffee.

Without warning Janis asked, "Laeh, did you meet Merrilee when you were away?" "No," I answered defensively, thinking only of physical meeting.

"Well," she went on "Merri says she saw you. She was out of her body and couldn't get back in, last Thursday. You came and poured something from a blue bottle into her head and she landed fully conscious in her body again."

I began screaming and jumping up and down all at once. "The blue bottle, the blue bottle, that's what I used it for, Merri." Then more calmly, I said, "She shouldn't have been there. Why did she go without a teacher, or a trusted capable spirit guide?"

"So you did see Merrilee," was Janis' reply, "When was that?" "Sunday afternoon," I said, stating the approximate hour as well.

Thursday and Sunday, before or after an event, have little meaning in Eternal time, where all things are always suspended outside of our Worldly time. Ponder the meaning of this wisdom. Ask yourself, is time a teaching of the solar level of enlightenment, or the star level? Can you understand the final form of enlightenment if you are unclear about time?

Body Time   Eternal time is linked to the pituitary gland. The pineal gland is solar in function and is linked to solar time as it affects earth time. This is calendar time. When you use your mental energy solely in a linear way the power of the spiral pineal gland diminishes and its capacity and output falter. That's why it's alive and vital in children and mostly calcified in adults and elderly people as shown by X-Rays.

Scientific research has shown that animals react to sunlight. In dark wintry periods, the pineal body behind the crown chakra slows its activity. After the winter solstice the pineal gland sends a hormonal stimulus to the sexual glands. When the build-up is adequate it's mating season. The pups, whelps, kids, foals, fawns, goslings, and birds are born at a time when conditions are most favorable, spring and early summer.

In human beings the function of the pineal body is little known or understood except for a few vital hormones it secretes. Catholic monks shaved the spot over the pineal to let the light fall on the pineal gland. That's as much exposure as the gland can take to light and the elements. Orthodox Jews cover the pineal gland to protect it. An M.D. who had a portion of his skull removed over the pineal body went mad.

When your soul urges enlightenment, the pineal body stops sending sexually stimulating hormones.

The thyroid is linked to the moon and is influenced by lunar time cycles of twenty-eight-and-a-half days pertaining to the earth. If you follow the tidal patterns you can easily fathom lunar time, which has a profound influence on your mental and emotional health.

Bodily organs are stimulated, according to Chinese and other Oriental forms of medicine, on the basis of a twenty-four hour timetable. The wheel shows which organs are focused on during each two-hour segment of the day. At 3 AM, the body's hormones are at their lowest level. Beginning at 4 AM, the hormones are emitted on an hourly basis beginning with the hypothalamus.

Daytime   People, animals, and plants each respond to light. Your inner clock is set by the movement of the sun. A pineal gland that has a total absence of light doesn't continue on its natural clock. After missing daylight for twelve to twenty-four hours, your internal clock is operating without outer signals. Lack of movement for prolonged periods without the visual stimulus of sun, moon, or stars upsets your innate order. This accounts for jet lag. Movement restores the body's inner clock by stimulating every organ and gland.

Modern life, ruled by industry's unreal schedule, takes no note of seasonal changes. Therefore it is totally out of synch with healthy, cyclical time. Electric lighting, closed blinds, and windowless rooms effectively throw off the body's rhythms.

The clock you operate under is also unreal. The daytime hours mimic equinox when day and night are tidily equal in duration. Clocked hours bear no resemblance to natural time. People do not waken with the first light of day, nor do they sleep following sundown. Cities live on twenty-four-hour time, in world capitals: New York, London, Tokyo. University professors,

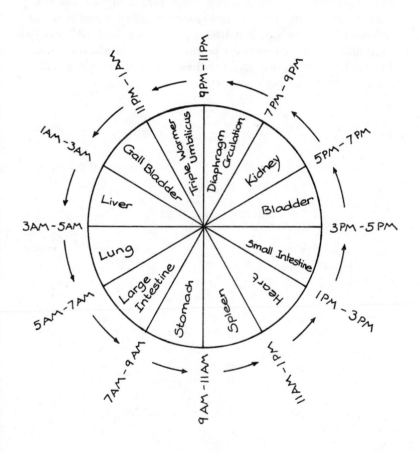

researchers, nurses, students, operators, phone and power company maintenance crews, can work any shift that agrees with them. Any one of you can choose which segments of the twenty-four hours you want to be your waking and sleeping periods.

Inside insulated houses you cannot see nor feel the subtle changes of the day. Dawn doesn't move into early morning, mid-morning's light and the accompanying bird songs are taken no note of, as late morning arrives. Noon replaces it and is in turn followed by afternoon, late afternoon, sunset, and twilight. Twilight and dawn are crossover points between World time and Eternal time. Regularly missing these magical moments is destructive to the seeker's journey.

15

Dreamtime/Vision Quest

I see this life as a conjuration and a dream.
Great compassion rises in my heart
For those without a knowledge of this truth.

Milarepa

DREAMTIME

Dreamtime: Entering a mythological time frame centergirding a culture through dreams and visions. These dreams have dream figures in them common to the culture, others are from antiquity. In our day and age an underground parking garage may take the place of the subterranean tunnels or caves visualized as the labyrinth of choices a soul has to discriminate between. Department stores represent magical places to the person cut off from nature, whereas someone who goes camping regularly or who is familiar with the natural world would see herself in a sunny glade or a sacred grove.

Each of you is privy to universal consciousness, sometimes called racial memory* and therefore can have visions of things beyond what we have learned or seen within this lifetime. Modern folks frequently resort to the mythology and legends of more ancient cultures for understanding of figures in their dreamtime experiences. A raccoon to the Eastern Woodland Indians was a trickster animal who could not be duped. Unlike coyote, who could have the tables turned on him, raccoon got away unscathed regardless of his tricks. Turtles, snakes, deer, bear, and other animals can be found in the stories of many cultures. Themes central to your own vision are the ones to explore, not those of a culture whose description of the animal or dream figure doesn't match up with yours.

A visualization of a beautiful woman or yourself (if female) in your late teens, imprisoned underground, would lead you to explore the Greek myth of Persephone. In it her mother, Demeter, roams the earth caretaking the crops and her father, Hades, rules the underworld. Through this adventure Persephone became the guardian of the seeds. A woman burning or carrying fire could symbolize Heartha the Norse goddess of the home and hearth. In a contemporary vision, to see a refrigerator in dreamtime would also indicate nurturance, food, abundance, and the home. Colors and shapes that appear may be of great significance to you personally, but mean little to a dream expert attempting to help you interpret your dream.

These dreamtime experiences can come from a special trance dream, a vision, or an abrupt departure from standard reality while in the midst of an otherwise normal day. There's a type of dozing that produces a memorable form of dreamtime. You are aware of your surroundings and immersed in an altered state fully cognizant of being on many levels of consciousness simultaneously. The entire time you are dozing/journeying you see, feel and hear with all your mental, emotional, and intuitive faculties at the subconscious and conscious levels.

You don't release a dream or a vision to the Cosmos until you have digested it. This includes your nighttime dreams. An unreleased dream sticks in your consciousness until you

---

*Racial memory is the accumulated knowledge of millions of lifetimes lived by all souls who have incarnated. Everyone has access to it.

understand it. Portions of it may reoccur in the midst of an unrelated dream sequence. You will be struck with a feeling of *déjà vu* or consciously remember having dreamt that particular scene before. A segment that repeats itself can force you to integrate your waking and sleep consciousness for a fraction of a second while dreaming. Until it becomes customary, you'll even awaken somewhat astonished recalling the phenomenal blending of conscious states.

Repetitious dreams occur most memorably to children between the ages of four and seven. These informational dreams, sent by their Essence Being and spirit guides to steer them to their correct path in life, may at first be very scary. The best help parents can give is to direct the child to walk through the frightening event in the dream, because it is only a dream.

One girl had a recurrent dream of a cave filled with fire. She got up screaming in fear night after night. Her father lovingly restored her perspective over time, until she just came to the table saying, "I had that dream again last night." Finally her father, determined that a way be devised to resolve the daughter's dream, advised her to walk through the fire into the cave. By then she had grasped his reasoning that it was not ordinary reality and therefore she wouldn't actually suffer physical damage, which was exactly why the dream threatened her. She followed his suggestion and on the other side found her "instructor" (spirit guide) for this lifetime, who told her what her life's Mission was to be.

Dreamtime Events   Some forms of vision quests can occur spontaneously. A few of the more notable ones are astral travel, journeying through the tunnel to the Akashic records, a clear message in the midst of a repetitious task, a daydream that turns out to be true, and dismemberments. Drumming is a common method of inducing these visionary, sensory, and auditory intuitive states, as are chanting and guided meditations. Ask your trusted spirit guides to provide you with the type of dreamtime you could benefit from. A living teacher, long experienced with these phenomena, is the optimum way to journey.

Astral Travel   You go out of your ordinary reality through a field of color. The shade and its intensity is an indication of the type of journey you will have. The color or its tone may change during the voyage, indicating an alteration in the format of the astral journey, or a new theme.

The trip may be to actual places and people on the earth, or to other planes of existence that are hard to explain in words. You will feel sensations of oneness with every living thing, an aliveness beyond the ordinary senses. It's quite like active dreaming wherein you know you are dreaming, witness the sequence of events, and are inseparable from them.

Flying is only one potential impression, not the sole bellwether for an astral journey. You may feel the touch of someone who is not present, as if there is a protective arm around your shoulders. Should you feel this it is possible to open your eyes, briefly returning to mundane reality to check, and finding no evidence, quickly revert to your travels. You might feel as if you are floating or tumbling, until you reach your destination. Another possibility is to wish to be somewhere, and within seconds you are. Although it's not your physical body that is at the new location, people, or spiritual beings in those surroundings will most likely notice your presence and respond to you.

The Tunnel   A student, delighted she'd found her own way into the tunnel, described it in detail. "Down into the tunnel we went to inner earth which has life in it just like the surface. The shafts where knowledge is stored are bronze-brown and look something like organ pipes. The tubes are all around an open space that has luminescent black liquid at the bottom. We entered a shaft on the upper level where the knowledge (Akashic records) is stored in picture form."

You can go to this source whenever you require prophetic information. The imagery will take you there. First picture yourself entering the tunnel, which is safe as thousands have come this way before you. Know that you will resurface in your customary reality with another perspective which will allow you to "see" more and provide you with information keyed to your spiritual growth. As you get further into the tunnel you will move quickly toward the entryway to the Akashic records.

Dismemberments   Dismemberments are a form of reconstructing your life by throwing everything away and taking back what you need. These usually take place unbidden. You can

be terrified, horrified, shocked, or befuddled by a dismemberment, especially the first time it happens to you. Remember this
is not mayhem, it's a mental/spiritual rather than a physical experience. While a dismemberment is in progress, it may be difficult
for you to determine that the event is transpiring beyond ordinary reality; it can be very real. Many people feel the episode,
see it, hear it, smell and taste it. Conversely, you might have
only one or two forms of sensory input, yet have a complete
experience.

Dismemberments tend to strip away layers of ingrained ap-
proaches to life and lifelong strategies that impale rather than
free you. You may come out of it stunned or elated, but either
way your body will be safe and sound. In the former reaction
you can feel as if the electrodes in your body have been incorrectly reconnected. A long shower or warm bath will realign you
and remove any inharmonic bodily feelings. Mental exhaustion,
trying to put it into the perspective of ordinary reality, and Monday morning quarterbacking are best dealt with by a nap and
regular dreaming.

One man being guided into a dismemberment via meditation
seemed to be an observer at first, but as it went on it became
more real to him. He saw himself enter an elevator in a large office building. The doors closed. There was a loud grinding sound
right before the elevator plummeted. He began to check his pockets to make certain he had all his documents, so that his body
would be rapidly identified by the rescuers. He was not afraid,
only concerned that he not cause others any trouble. The elevator
plunged to the bottom. He saw only darkness. He became aware
of other bodies pressing on him. Crawling up through them, not
knowing whether they were unconscious or dead, he reached the
trap door, opening it just as the rescuers arrived. He then woke
abruptly from his trance state.

Talking about his experience later, he claimed to have seen a
very unfortunate habitual pattern he was stuck with, making life
convenient for others at his own expense. Within a couple of
days his conversations turned to how much he needed to challenge his tendency toward isolation from others. He addressed
his fear of intimacy as contributing to his failure to nurture himself and others.

A woman in her fifties saw herself torn to shreds by hungry
dogs in a spontaneously induced dismemberment. Nothing was left

except scattered bones. With quite a bit of difficulty she started to reassemble herself. She knew the problems of gathering and restructuring her body to be a mirror of her inability to sell some property she'd been holding onto, and to make a long needed transition from one career to another. She was a fine healer, but afraid to be known for her work. So she stood in the shadows, helping the families of schoolchildren she taught part-time.

Most impromptu dismemberments occur to seekers along the path who are holding themselves back in some manner. Shamans have developed ceremonial dismemberments to help the initiate deal with these problems. The Tibetan lamas have an ancient ritualized dismemberment called Chod. By singing the words of power that create the dismemberment experience, the pilgrim is relieved of many emotional, karmic, and mental burdens and is thereby freed for advanced development along spiritual lines.

Moon Visions and Transformation   Choosing the right time for the type of change or spiritual insight you seek is as important as deciding what you want to look for. Small or grand visions done in the correct phase of the moon will yield the most favorable, demystifying results. Dark of the moon rituals are for opening the intuitive channels; waning moon rituals are to give up something; full moons are for making wishes, setting prayers, and doing vision quests.

Cardinal signs are very good for beginnings. A full moon in Aries, Libra, Capricorn, or Cancer serves new projects and undertakings best. Usually the seeker is looking for long term goals. To work magical or transformative visioning you must know whether you require organizational intervention, Virgo; immediate insight, Pisces, Sagittarius, Gemini; or to make certain the energy is long lasting, Scorpio, Taurus, Aquarius, or Leo. When making requests for world peace the Aquarian full moons are the most potent.

Full moons occur when the sun is in the opposing sign. These signs are: Aries–Libra, Taurus–Scorpio, Gemini–Sagittarius, Cancer–Capricorn, Leo–Aquarius, Virgo–Pisces. An astrological calendar will help you find the exact time for the full moon in your area and what sign the moon is in on a daily basis.

Full moon is the time of the greatest magic power. Wishes or prayers made while the moon is full have the best chance of being granted. Worldly or spiritual, the quality of your devotion means more than whether your request is worthy. One wish per full moon, not a string of them, is the rule for full moon visioning.

Preparation   On the day of the full moon prepare yourself by bathing, washing your hair, and putting on all fresh clothing. If you haven't kept track of the moon's progress and the hour is near, burn some tobacco, sage, mugwort, juniper leaves, or cedar to purify yourself. Any one of these herbs is equally effective.

A full moon after daybreak requires that you do your visioning the night before when the moon itself is visible. Clouds will obscure the vision and rain will cancel it altogether, but the power is available whether or not the night sky is clear.

If you are able to fast a whole day before the full moon and up until the actual time of your vision quest you'll increase your preparedness for the journey. Whatever you devise to increase your concentration prior to going off on your moon vision will free your mind of extraneous details and attachments. For some this can be a thorough cleaning of their home, for others the completion of a long delayed project. In any case, some kind of preparation for the journey is called for.

In cold weather it is better to be overdressed than to freeze or become so chilled that the visioning experience is obliterated by your chattering, shaking body. Adequate and appropriate clothing for the season and the weather is important to the success of your moon vision.

You will need to be away from streetlights, houses, traffic, and other buzzing or lighted places. Transformers, pumps, and other equipment will distract you and lend an element that diverts from your journey. Plan to be in the country, or alongside a body of water where there are no lights. This kind of visioning can be done with friends if all of you agree to remain silent and not to disturb the others unless there is an emergency.

Men seem to have a harder time doing a moon vision than women. Perhaps it is women's cyclical affinity for the moon through their menses. It may be that men who normally watch the moon for tides and planting times, living close to nature as gardeners or fishermen, have the same openness toward the moon.

Bernard, a man who lives in the country, decided to have a vision quest with the moon. He came to speak with me about the prospect, choosing the Cancerian full moon in January. I told him to select his location and not to move from it no matter what. He was so enchanted by the moon's movements and the clarity of the night that he kept changing his site as earth's rotation obscured his view. At one point he climbed a tree sixty feet high to keep the moon within his sight. All his moving about destroyed whatever concentration he may have begun with. Additionally, he did not have a clear idea about what he was seeking, and therefore chose the wrong full moon for completions.

In moon visioning you absolutely must stay in the same place, even if another unrelated party visioning near you sings or rings bells, interrupting your concentration. You'll get past that. Squint your eyes so that the moon comes down on her golden gown to your feet. If the gown splits, watch where the points land. The gown will appear to retract and advance in your direction, depending upon your attention span and the manner in which you assimilate what you are being told. If the moon is concealed due to clouds, wait it out—it will come into view sometime during the night. Remember, the moon is known for changeability, secretiveness, and revelation. Cloud cover will part, and you'll glimpse the moon through beautiful rainbow colors and a purple haze. On an intermittently rainy night you may have to abandon sitting out-of-doors, but you can view the moon through an open window. Window glass and screens distort her gown and obscure your sixth and seventh chakra connection with the moon.

A Dream Becomes Reality   For an individual, the amount of lead time between a vision and its actualization can be a week, eighteen months, or half a lifetime. You will come to know your own pattern. Spirit doesn't lie, so the vision will come true precisely as shown and work best if you don't accept a partial implementation. For example, if you saw a house in a meadow surrounded by trees and the one you are offered is on a hillside covered with trees, it's not the place.

Within a society it takes five generations, with some plateaus and backsliding, for a full change to come about. Four generations lay the foundation for a dream to become the new standard by which the society lives. The fifth generation lives the dream and usually is given credit for inventing it. Each generation implements a specific change that becomes the key that unlocks the next generation's change, until so many modifications have been made that the culture has been completely altered.

A perfect illustration is the smaller families Suffragette women advocated and bore as a way of breaking the yoke of women's oppression. This caught on, becoming the norm as each successive generation parented fewer and fewer children. At present, the average family in Western countries consists of two children. The more assimilated an ethnic group becomes in our society, the faster the number of offspring born to each generation drops. Women educated in the United States, coming from non-European countries, bear as many children as is acceptable within the norm for our culture, usually two or three.

The original dream was to be freed from the oppression of too large a family and burdensome household duties, and by that to have choices and chances to express other talents. While it was not acceptable for Suffragettes or women reaching adulthood between the two world wars, afterward a climbing divorce rate showed the way out of unfulfilling marriages. The majority of women born after 1940 opted, whether by design or happenstance, to become single mothers as divorce became socially acceptable. That generation instituted another more dramatic change. For those born from the second world war onward, women have the choice to be mothers whether or not they are married.

And while this vision of the future may never have occurred to you as you were growing up, in adulthood you discovered a lack of community services to deal with the situation, placing you in another difficult position. Society always catches up with the dream later. Perhaps the dream can be completed by the time those born in the 1980s raise children, with paid maternity leave for either parent, job sharing, neighborhood, or on-the-job day care centers.

These are possible solutions to freeing women from the fate of those born 120 years ago. A future goal, whenever feasible and desired, is keeping the family, including the father, together. This objective requires that the men have the same vision of equality as women do. For only when agreement is reached on the scope of the dream will it be implemented. Since men as equal caretakers of children is still a hazy notion, and househusbands have to have some other complementary career to be able to stay home while the wife is the main breadwinner, we aren't there.

VISION QUEST

Not knowing what obstacles lie before you or clutter your life is a lack of clarity. A set ideology and fixed attitudes are impediments to spiritual growth. Old beliefs no longer practiced but still cherished as a keepsake, or a reference point, must be revised or removed.

Two formats exist for vision quests. The inner, usually referred to as journeying, and the outer where the body is stressed to its endurance by fasting, sleeplessness, and exposure to the elements. The more popular route is the inward quest. Both bring you to a state of dreamtime reality in realms beyond your physical limitations. Respectively, they deliver you to the introspective process which is especially difficult for the outer directed person. Logic and deductive reasoning aren't of much use during the quest. They can help you gain perspective in the weeks that follow, so long as you don't try to shrink the experience you've had to fit your former lifestyle or beliefs. Cerebral work is only a small portion of your life, but unfortunately you've been taught to rely on it almost exclusively. What ascends in the vision quest is love, the universal, everlasting love you can plug into anytime. Love as a renewable reachable resource.

Most of you have not had your life vision. Perhaps you have had a vision that suits you for a time or opens you up to new avenues of growth. One of the requirements of a vision quest is that someone watch over you or be informed that you have undertaken it. That person will either fast for you, or pray for your success, as a way of keeping you stabilized on your journey between the cosmos and earth.

A wise elder to instruct you is a great help for the true seeker and brave novice alike. Preparation begins once you become aware of your need for an outward vision quest. Natural settings, unfamiliar to you, sever your comfort zone and day to day existence.

Everyone of you who undertakes a vision quest will know physical discomfort as part of the rite of passage. Self-doubt and questions arise about your sincerity and your sanity for embarking upon it all together. You will also have to gather courage, for in every vision quest fear of the unknown is a factor. Information derived intuitively will come forward about previous situations, relationships, and events in your life and those of people you know. You'll have instinctual clarity about things that have shaken you in the past. Alone in the wilderness you'll discover your essence. You'll identify the gifts you have been granted for this lifetime. Upon your return to society you'll be able to use these gifts as a giveaway, your contribution to the positive forces and the greater good that girds the world.

Your first successful vision quest will definitely not be your last. Everyone has a special place or set of circumstances that yield productive visions for them. Your teacher, if you have a wise one, will know whether you would do best in a cave, on a hilltop above the woods, sitting on a high branch of a tree, placed next to a waterfall, or walking from dusk to dawn. Your teacher will also know whether you are ready to do four full days and nights alone, twenty-four hours, or simply sunrise to sunset. A capable teacher will come waken you via astral travel if you fall asleep, and see whether or not you are doing your assignment. Occasionally you will have spontaneous vision quests when camping or walking in the woods, and obtain information for yourself.

More than a dozen years ago, on an afternoon hike with my dog friend Kyote, I had a unique encounter.

Deciding upon privacy, to avoid meeting people on the usual pathway to the top, I chose to climb the steeper, unimproved back of the holy mountain located right outside the town I lived in. The dog had no difficulty negotiating the rough, rocky terrain. I scrambled behind. Unsure of foot, I used my hands as well, to ascend. Suddenly Kyote stood still and would not move.

Needing a break, I sat down to wait for the dog to go on. As soon as I was settled, my spirit guides came to me delivering a long complicated message filled with images and knowledge. It must have taken an hour, but as I had no watch and it was a cloudy day, I could only guess. Conversely, it seemed like only minutes had gone by. As soon as the guides were finished, the dog stood up and hurriedly began to climb again.

People have reported spontaneous vision quests while traveling, fishing on an unfamiliar stretch of a river, or in their own home. The scene may suddenly switch and you enter into Eternal time. It may last a few moments, several hours, or days. The type that goes on for days often produces an outward delirium that mimics or is caused by a severe illness. Pubescents and adolescents whose Mission is revealed to them in this manner seldom pick up the conventional scripts floating around among their peers. They are headed for excellence, provided they seek the pattern and lifestyle "spirit" has shown them in a compassionate, reverent way.

Journey by Design Nearly everyone wants to have firsthand knowledge of the Cosmic secrets. Spontaneous, unexpected visions catch you off guard and are all too brief. You may be so startled, scared, and unprepared that you won't be able to digest the information you get. Commonly it's so shocking that you land back in ordinary reality with more questions than you had before. You may be bewildered by the experience of crossing into another realm without preparation. The meditation offered here aids your psyche's flexibility, and sets the stage for a positive, fulfiling journey.

Crystal Meditation Hold your most treasured crystal in your left hand. Bring the crystal to your forehead. Lay your favorite side of the crystal over your third eye. Your hand firmly, yet gently, cradles the crystal.

Let go of all your self-loathing. Send it into the crystal to be transformed into self-appreciation. Breathe in, allowing love to flow from the Universe into your heart center. Exhale self-depreciation, inhale self-acceptance, appreciation, and love. Every in breath contains love, acceptance, and self-appreciation. Each out breath removes self-depreciation, loathing, and criticism. Give it to the crystal to be transformed. Continue breathing in this way until you feel relaxed and loved.

Enter the crystal. Inside you will find a crystal lined tunnel. Walk through the tunnel. You will find yourself moving faster and faster, until you reach a huge room whose doorway is filled with blinding light. Your eyes can safely look at it and through it, for these are your inner eyes you are seeing with. Gaze at the light and sail through it into an immense room. Your greeter is standing there to take you on an adventure of the mind's eye. Feel the universal love pouring forth toward you from your greeter. Notice the non-judgmental nature of this individual. Your greeter will serve as your guide for the rest of this journey.

You may ask any questions you desire. Your adventure will be uniquely yours. You will remember everything in minute detail.

When it is over your greeter will take you back to the crystal tunnel. You will travel back through it, out into your own precious crystal. Jump now from the crystal to your third eye. Slowly open your eyes.

You are in the reality you briefly left, filled with new information and knowledge. Lie there quietly, breathing in the universal love you found during your journey. Rise and remove the crystal from your forehead when you feel totally willing and able to do so.

16

Truth

Of what avail is an open eye, if the heart is blind?
Solomon Ibn-Gabirol

There are several types of truth—honesty with yourself and Truth as in true wisdom or knowledge. The first type is the one people have great trouble with. The second form has two branches, primordial or ultimate truth, unchangeable forever, and fleeting or conventional truth. Conventional truth changes with the times. Ultimate truth is the true nature of reality on every plane of existence.

All spiritual doctrines contain true truths. Each one has prescribed methods for reaching truth, although none will let you find out a truth that undermines their religious dogma. To seek true truth you'll eventually have to abandon even the basic tenets of your chosen religion, for each has doorways that are closed. If your Mission is to go through that doorway, don't abort it because you've found a key the church says doesn't exist. The Kabbalah, Christian mysticism, Yoga, or Tibetan Buddhism may still actively support your struggle to find the Truth.

To come to true wisdom the Dalai Lama says, "Any point of view, even a mistaken notion, has truth in it. By following the truth, wrong ideas will be discarded. Inference becomes direct experience. True knowledge will arise out of continually seeking and changing your viewpoint."

Awareness is the key aspect. Apprehension is one key to whether an idea or a channeling is illusion or true knowledge, as the latter occurs without doubt. Doubt is what brings a seeker to Truth.

You can fool yourself into thinking you are listening to your higher self when all you are actually doing is following your egotistical impulses. Being unselfish, compassionate, and truly ruled by the heart is a commitment to service that most people haven't mastered. In an individualistic society like ours it's easy to misunderstand a command of the heart versus a demand of the ego.

Baba Hari Dass of Mount Madonna Center is a savant whose words are few since he speaks only through his chalkboard. This is an aphorism from his book, *Fire Without Fuel:*

> *The heart is an emotional mind and emotions are triggered by desires. When we say, "I have to listen to my heart and do whatever the heart says," we can very easily misguide ourselves because the language of the heart we are listening to is polluted by desires. But if the mind is purified and devotion and dispassion are attained, then the heart tells the truth.*
>
> *The mind doesn't want any discipline; it always makes excuses to avoid it. So most people say, "I have to listen to my heart," and they stop their efforts to purify their minds. In this way they trick themselves and can't progress in their spiritual life.*

Saintliness Christian saintliness is a much misunderstood concept. The real saints were human, utilizing all the human emotions, including anger, to fulfill their objectives. Saint Francis had to have strength and will power to stave off the church fathers who objected to the religious order he was building.

Ahimsa is a yoga principle which is often mixed up with our unrealistic viewpoint of what constitutes saintliness. The best explanation of Ahimsa is a quote from Gandhi who inspired civil disobedience as a method of political change.

"I cannot practice Ahimsa without the religion of service and I cannot find truth without practicing the religion of Ahimsa. I am striving for the Kingdom of Heaven, which is spiritual deliverance. For me the road to salvation lies through incessant toil in . . . service . . .

"The yoga of Ahimsa consists in the devising of means and doing of acts . . . to check the evil effects . . . of such acts from human society."

Ahimsa as a hiding place to avoid conflicts and appear more spiritual is a false position. Quakers, Martin Luther King, Gandhi, and Jesus confronted and continue to confront others on their prejudices and the perpetration of injustice. Allowing someone to abuse your good graces or to play on your love for them is not Ahimsa.

One year, a woman I'd known fairly well at one time, came to me with her new husband who'd been diagnosed with a fatal contagious disease. Prior to their marriage he'd been evasive when she asked him if he'd taken a test for the disease. He'd kept his illness a secret until he suffered a serious attack a couple of months after their wedding.

The fact was he could no longer deliver his half of their financial obligations, and he said he had no energy to make love or be affectionate with her due to the disease. She claimed responsibility for his care and denied to herself what her friends saw. He'd only married her for the excellent healthcare benefits she received from her employer.

Every marriage has its illusions. She ignored some crucial facts to stay in hers. He'd hidden his illness from her, exposed her to it by his secrecy, and endangered her life. Security and the children she'd hoped to have all fell by the wayside. My friend is a member of a religion that sanctifies the development of compassion. She was convinced that her salvation rested on how compassionately she handled his illness. She was practicing a form of spiritual deception.

Self-deception   Many people are spiritual camp followers. They move through one path and then another seeking what's right for them. All too often, all they find is what is in vogue this year or this decade.

Yuppies in Australia are called trendies. When you don't know yourself, you follow all the trends in fashion, activities, current beliefs, and a host of other things you claim as your own. If it's in vogue to go to a Hindu Guru you are the Ashram Princess. The guru's advocacy of celibacy becomes abrasive, going against your consortium of core beliefs about marriage and sexuality. If you are still hooked on religion, or belonging to one is an upscale value in present day society, you'll find another that advocates abundant children and marital fidelity and provides you with a community to play it out against. Unlike passé vehicles, furnishings, and husbands, children are harder to dispense with. However, with joint custody and fathers having custody, you can drop off the excess youngsters and keep only the acceptable number with you when you change religions again.

Consistently you do not notice yourself repeating the pattern of setting aside what you've embraced and joining with the next available cult. Of course it's not nearly so extreme, making it all the more difficult for you to realize what you are doing. You might be able to teach the Yoga you do so well to those Mormons or Moonies you've recently linked up with.

Channeling   There are three types of channels or psychics. The first type of channel is the sleeping one* who remembers nothing. Any half-baked, unlearned entity can tell the channel anything and they'll say it like a trained parrot without discernment. They cannot tell an enlightened discarnate from a foolish ghost in pajama bottoms. To channel asleep allows the channeler to evade any responsibility for whatever statements she makes.

The second type recalls what he said after he comes back from the sleeping trance but has no way of sifting the information for greater clarity. This type is a bit better because he may ask for verification the next time and will also recognize the difference between a knowledgeable entity and one who only wants publicity. Those who prophesy in trance, not knowing what they say, are not able to question the information they receive at the time it is given. Both of these types have a work span of about two-and-a-half years of actual channeling before the entities become bored with them. From that point forward, if the first type continues, they have to fake it.

The late Edgar Cayce was a notable exception as his remedies and healings were verification of his true contact with a great guide.

The second type, if they are not egotistical about the information or greedy, can get seven or eight years of guided helpers who deliver excellent truthful material. After that point, their health deteriorates. The visiting entities do not keep their heart pumping, or their breath at their body's normal rates during channeling. If the occupying entity hasn't had a body for 700 years, digestion is completely shut down and there are other shocks to the body. If they learn how to work with their guides in an alert type of trance, they turn into the third type of channel.

The third type is the one spirit guides work with for twenty years, or an entire lifetime. They do not sleep while in a mild to deep trance, but channel awake and alert to what is going through them. Astute mediums, psychics, prophets—whatever your culture tends to call messengers—are naturally intelligent and curious. They ask for detailed information and clarification. Discarnates prefer those who are members of their own Clan with Missions on earth that are beneficial to that Clan's projects and purposes.

These are people who are able to ask their guides for clarification in interpreting what they've just been told. They know they might have to sit with a vision for a long time until it's ready to be implemented. Such prophets do not spill all at one time, they wait until people can hear it.

As Murry Hope wrote in her book *Practical Techniques of Psychic Self-Defense:*

> *"When we are born into the physical world each of us is allotted a special frequency with which we may tune in to the cosmic unconscious. When we turn on our radios we scan the frequency spectrum until we find a station we like, and we may choose to stay with that station and listen to no other. But a radio station does not play the same programme over and over; it provides a variety of entertainment. At one time we may tune into a news broadcast; or a symphony; or a play; or a sporting event. All of these may be on the same frequency or station, but each has its own time slot. Perhaps we can be likened to that radio receiver, picking up those cosmic programmes and reports to which we have a special affinity, compatibility or frequency. But, unfortunately, most of our radio receivers are not properly attuned and we hear only an intelligible voice breaking briefly through the static*

which drowns out most of our programmes. More unfortunate, however, are those people whose receivers are not turned on at all, for they drift through life in total silence, wondering . . ."

Channeling is just a form of sharing and caring in the world. Pride in doing the job well is fine, but acting superior or feeling more blessed isn't. You aren't always channeling.

My teacher, shaman Essie Parrish, used to tell me this to help me keep it all in perspective: "You may know all this, do all these things, but you still have to raise your children. You still argue with your husband." In other words, you aren't exonerated from your own problems or being part of the human family.

Readers or channels who see clients do not speak harshly to the client when telling them truths that hurt. Kind rather than accusatory language is chosen to convey what they see. If you are a reader giving a sitting (which is what the English mediums call a channeling) you will deliver messages outside your own knowledge from time to time. It is important that you do not censor these, as they are appropriate to the client. Many channels get some information, but cannot give trustworthy guidance since they aren't able to merge with your Source Self. They throw in their waking beliefs without regard for who you are. Strong personal beliefs or moral outlooks cannot enter into a channeling that comes from spirit.

There are some faddish unprovable themes in channeling that provide comforting outs and evade responsibility. For a channel to tell you that during a prior incarnation you were married to your sister, who is very jealous of your current wife, is a bit of a cop-out and may also be untrue, although it is a nice reassuring pat answer. Cheerily dismissing a family schism as a left-over from a previous life only adds fuel to the conflict, especially if other family members do not share that belief system. Ultimately if a spouse remains firm in their love for mate and sibling and stays out of the fracas, the combatant in-laws will work out their problems. All that is required is a willingness to come to a loving and peaceable solution. A good reader or spiritual healer points the way with the help of her guides.

Some years ago, I was asked to attend a meeting of well known channels who were going to talk to the audience through their guides. I found the distractions they used to be very strange. One had a series of burps, sputters, and body contortions that spun him into trance. Yet not one of his jerking postures was the uncontrollable type where the nervous system is affected as it is in spontaneous out of body experiences. Another kept rolling something on the table while an assistant pushed her elbow. A middle-aged housewife-cum-medium kept rocking back and forth while she referred to every person she spoke to in the audience as entity. These affectations can convince a naive crowd or one that has been trained to see them as bona fide evidence of true channeling, but they aren't. None of them dared to have their guides speak to each other. Every channel communicated solely with their guides, even though the guides are fully capable of interacting with one another in spirit and when in a human host.

A word of caution: exclusive contact with the spiritual portion of your own nature will make you very unbalanced in the world. Balance is the key to a successful life.

Rituals All human beings require rituals to maintain their spiritual lifestream. It can be something as simple as your daily routine, or as elaborate as a ritual you devise for a special occasion. Every society has yearly rituals. Ours has Independence Day (fireworks), Thanksgiving (big dinners of cranberry sauce and turkey), and New Year's to name a few. There are housewarming parties, funerals, baby showers, and weddings all with attendant ritual practices. Then there are times when a person is going through a private passage and needs some help. One way to mark the moment is a ritual. It might be groundbreaking for a new home, turning fifty, getting divorced, a career change that requires some spiritual expression. Trust yourself and the Realm of Creation to come up with an effective ritual.

Ritual works whether you are in a group or alone. The leader can be a lay person, a trained priest, a long experienced medicine person, or yourself.

Symbolism in ritual and ceremonies is a focal point and an expression of piety. The items usually represent fire, air, water, and earth. Herbs or aroma extracts made from them can serve as the element they are linked to, water—jasmine, angelica, rose; fire—tobacco, peppermint; air—sandalwood, thyme, mugwort; earth—sage, honeysuckle, pine. Candles can take the place of an open fire. Feathers can be the air; crystals or a bowl of sand can be the Earth. Water in a bowl is itself. Out of doors, a grove of trees forms a green cathedral, a creek or the ocean is your water, the wind acts as itself. If it is safe, make a real fire. A hibachi works well as an impromptu firepit.

You must be careful never to take back the things you have asked the Universe to remove from your life, or those of a person you have prayed for.

Dance is magical and anyone can participate to symbolically recreate the world. Dance in all primitive, provincial cultures is used to invoke transformative states and to unify the participants. Sacred dances recreate the world. Dance works as prayerful movements combined with musical accompaniment that elevates the watchers and the dancers to altered states of consciousness, allowing them to reach the Realms of Creation and the Source.

You dance in both directions of the circle, counter-clockwise and clockwise, to include all sides of an issue, situation, or every aspect of the Universe. Stand with your hands above your head, out to the side, twirl hands at your sides to invoke all the benefic attributes of the Source. Hand motions and body poses invoke the powers associated with them. Highly prescribed hand movements are known as *mudras* in Sanskrit. Balinese and Hawaiian sacred dances are known for their mudras, each of which have prayers and specific words attached to them.

Sacred   What is actually sacred? Wise ones will tell you everything is sacred. All of life and every second. But most people want sacredness and sacred times to be set aside from ordinary living. Sacred is the reverential feeling that all of life is worth caring for. It is the wonder of it all.

For some, sacred is an action like catching the mistletoe in a pure white cloth to keep it from touching the ground, thereby preventing the precious herb from being contaminated by the earth's vibration. But is our Earth a profane place, dirtied by the foul inharmonic emissions of human beings; or is everything sacred, every action, every thought, every natural thing?

Many religions and spiritual practices admit that everything is sacred, yet they have rituals to restore the sacredness of despoiled, hallowed ground and baptisms for the sin of being born. The latter is a concept too perverted to be given credence. We are always sacred in our souls and in our desire to grow through an incarnation. We come from the Creator and return there when our time is over.

A vast majority of the sacred grounds, sacred for thousands of generations, have been reduced to tourist attractions, or watering holes for farm animals, or submerged beneath concrete and brick. Does this eliminate their sacredness?

Sacred sounds and sites remain holy, despite what conquerors and realtors do with them. Every regime falters at some time. The emanations from a sacred place will remain, even if it is turned into a garbage dump, like Findhorn before it was resurrected. Most Christian Churches were built over the hallowed grounds of Pagan Matriarchal religions. No matter what faith dominates the location, nor how badly a church built there makes a mockery of its principles, the spot goes on being sacred, credited with miracles, as it has been since time out of mind.

Still the religion or spiritual group recapturing an ancestral holy ground, or even borrowing it for a single ceremony, does a thorough cleansing, a rite of purification for the site.

The longer a place has been revered the more likely it is to be noticed in periods of neglect, when it is treated as a curiosity. Glastonbury Plain is one such location. Mount Shasta was sacred to Native Americans long before Europeans invaded the Americas. Any purification done for the location is to the ease of minds of the faithful. Sites will return to their own harmonic level automatically. Believers feel they are assisting that operation. And it's true, for what you have faith in grows in merit and what you only rarely think about decreases.

Delicate places that were trodden on by pilgrims on foot, now have elevators for the physically handicapped or ill. Those who do not have to take the full perilous journey, as seekers did in the past, still can get a measure of healing from the site. But, for the really faithful, who believe they have to offer some sacrifice to achieve a healing or a vision, only a laborious and perhaps dangerous climb, or descent to the sacred spot, will suffice.

Can you get the same cure or depth of vision from taking a car to gather medicinal herbs? Must you take the same journey on foot for three days there and three days back, able to harvest only what you can carry? Many native people have taken trips to their sacred site by van and car. Has doing so diminished the prayerfulness with which they approach their holy grounds? Does a Muslim arriving at Mecca via jet receive less of a blessing than the pilgrim who tramped barefoot? Each came by a means they could afford. Was one more pious than the other?

Death The last of the sacred rites is death, your final touch with the incarnation you've come to revere or loathe. To die consciously, aware of your surroundings as you reach out to your friends and loved ones in the Realm of Creation, is a true measure of sacred experience.

There is no set formula for a sudden death. The only preparation is conscious living. If you've allowed yourself to change and grow and do not fear meeting your maker, then your death can be peaceful. The agonizing and horrified looks we see on the faces of those who die without coming to terms with the circumstances of their death is what frightens survivors. That's the look of struggling to stay alive when the final call has been given. People who die of illness or who have a few minutes to come to terms with their sudden and perhaps violent death wear more peaceful, and sometimes beatific, expressions.

It's always best to have a home death if you can. You always hear stories in families about how, while uncle snored, auntie got out of bed and went to make her husband's coffee. She called to him as she did every morning and he didn't waken. She went to the bedroom, shook him, and found he'd died. The circumstances vary, but this is considered to be a very good way to go.

Many people today suffer from lingering ailments that will cause their body to deteriorate to the point of death. In this kind of death, families can make plans to have a comfortable and loving atmosphere for the family member to take their leave in.

Families are often in denial. Our culture has many ways to ease our frightful feelings surrounding death. Hospices are some of the best help we've devised to face the truth. Our relative is going to die, and we will be required to take an active part.

The account here is not intended to be a prototype, other than to spark some ideas that may assist you in deciding what to do for your beloved family member when their time draws near.

This is the narrative of André Christiaan Cuppen, whose mother chose to die at home. It is one way of facing the truth when there is a death in the family:

> *My mother decided to die. She started to withdraw after her last words; "Wouldn't this be a great day to go?" she said*

noting the fact that it was the seventh and a Saturday. In the old Catholic weekly schedule Saturday is Saint Mary's day, the archetypal mother she had a deep bond with. The number seven was her lucky number. She knew that if she waited one more day I couldn't attend her funeral because of my scheduled flight back to America.

It was one o'clock in the morning and I had just administered her midnight pain medication by injecting it into a plastic tube inserted into a shoulder vessel. She slept in the living room. That night it was my turn to rest on the floor next to her bed. She didn't speak anymore, nor did she open her eyes.

The following day we didn't see her reach for the bowl with ice cubes, the only way she had been able to take liquid. During the afternoon there was a noticeable change in her breathing pattern. I went to the store and bought more flowers in her favorite color, white. I lit several candles in the living room. There was a sense of a sacred stillness. We communicated in a subdued voices while we were making all kinds of necessary preparations.

In the late afternoon I had to interfere with my sister. She walked up to mother's bed and started to call her and asked; "Mama, shall I give you another ice cube?" I told her not to persist since I had the feeling that Mama had already started her journey.

Early in the evening her breathing became heavier and more irregular. Mama hadn't moved one inch from one o'clock in the morning on. Dad and I looked at each other, we were aware of each other's thoughts; "How much time do you think?" We decided to call my two other sisters since they were only a couple of hours drive away. Two days before, my brothers had returned to their jobs after bidding goodbye to Mama. My brothers were in different countries, a day's travel away; we had decided to contact them after she had passed on. Tonight my youngest sister was working the evening shift in a hospital and my oldest sister, a midwife, was participating in a baptism ceremony for a baby she had delivered. Mama appeared stable when she'd left the previous evening.

My arrival a week ago completed the nuclear family reunion, although I missed my wife who had to stay behind. For several days we shared our last time together. Mama was able to see that life went on, food came to the table and everybody enjoyed what was served. During the past few months she had initiated Dad into her household secrets, an important step in letting go.

We talked about the specifics of the funeral ceremony; she wanted a lot of singing and contributed a written word of gratitude to all the people who had been so caring and loving during her last months. She gave clear directives about her possessions. One night, she wanted us to divide all her jewelry, everyone got a share. The final day my brothers were there she sat up in bed and we took our last family pictures. As Dad supported her to sit, we all sang in four part harmony the song she favored most: "Animée de l'amour" (animated by love). It was hard to keep straight tones knowing it always made her feel proud of her offspring, and it was the last time she could enjoy our singing. Tears were shared, Mama knew . . . .

It was around ten o'clock the next step of Mama's departure was noticeable; the process seemed to go faster and faster. We gathered around her bed. Dad on her left side, my sister and me on her right side. We held her lifeless warm hands and followed her breathing, every time there was a little shock noticeable when it stopped for several seconds and picked up again with more and more effort. "Wait mama, don't go, just wait a little bit longer, Mama . . . ," my sister asked her to hold until our sisters arrived. I stayed connected with Mama through my mind's eye and reassured her it was up to her and her spirit companions to decide. I felt Mama was struggling through the passage.

At one moment she stopped breathing again, we waited for about fifteen seconds and thought it was over. Dad covered his mouth and nose with both hands and started to cry. Suddenly Mama inhaled again, making a deep ruckling sound. We knelt back and witnessed Mama working her way through the birth canal. I thanked Mama several times for the privilege to be with her during this transition. We must have sat there for about half an hour, my concept of time was gone. Shortly before eleven o'clock; we were waiting for another breath, but it never came.

We cried and held each other. The doorbell rang. My oldest sister came in, she saw, she knew, she burst out in tears. She passed under a bridge at the moment Mama left and felt suddenly overwhelmed with an intense sadness. She brought with her a big bouquet of white flowers the baby's parents had given to her as a token of gratitude. Several minutes later my other sister and her husband arrived. Sad but relieved. They're both nurses and had commuted for weeks to give Mama the care she needed, so she could stay home.

Shortly before midnight I called Mama's physician to come over to do the postmortem examination and also notified the undertaker. The physician arrived soon and we left him alone for a few minutes. After he finished we all gathered in the living room and drank coffee together. The doctor praised Mama's determination and willingness to try to fight her way out of the disease with the help of alternative healing methods.

I looked at Mama's body, I was grateful that she was still with us. I suddenly noticed that her face looked so much younger, clearly peaceful; the painful, struggling expression disappeared, even the number of lines had lessened.

My sister and her husband decided to lay out Mama's corpse right after the doctor left. Keep in mind that it was a very diseased body and we wanted to keep it at home until the morning of the funeral. They did a great job cleaning and conserving the body. They dressed her in a robe she had chosen and used the right touch of make up to respect the stillness of the body.

The next morning the undertaker arrived, willing to help us in our effort to keep her at home as long as possible. He put the body in a plastic cover, up to the chest and added several hands full of odor absorbing salts, as protective measures to contain the cadaverous smell. He advised us to keep the temperature in the living room as low as possible to slow down decomposition.

Mama was a silent hostess twice a day when we allowed friends and family into the room to pay their respect and say goodbye. The atmosphere was one of lightness, nostalgia and laughter. The coffee and cake went around the circle, while Mama was resting and still part of this social event. Visitors who never had experienced a home death were surprised at their own comfort. Even the undertaker expressed his delight at how natural the whole situation was.

The morning of the funeral the undertaker brought in the white coffin we had chosen for Mama, she must have loved it: simple and real beautiful. We flanked the coffin as it rolled down the aisle to the center of the church. Again we sang Mama's most favorite song, the choir respected her choices and the trumpet honored Mary, her dearest refuge.

At the crematorium, I played my guitar and we sang the Ariadne song; "You are part of the chain, the chain determines the tide . . . ," My oldest brother and sister both gave their retrospective of Mama's life. Mama had decided that she didn't want her ashes to be saved; she didn't want to have a memorial stone or tablet, she only wanted to live on in our spirit.

Taking charge of the death and funeral for and with the help of the family member places you squarely in the corner of truth and the finality of a single human incarnation. Few families would be so united by the death of a parent as this one, since facing the ultimate truth is so difficult.

17

How The Universe Works

The Universe is made up of stories, not atoms.
Muriel Ruckeyser

PETRONIA

Several mornings per week at precisely ten o'clock I would sit down to listen to Petronia, White Eagle, or Raphael. I wrote down what they said until I was tired or until the conversation took a turn I couldn't fathom. Later I would formulate the questions I had for our next meeting. These meetings turned out to be the core of the teachings I was given for the solar spiral.

Petronia is an archangel who appears in lavender glyphs, either round or elliptical. She is neither male nor female. During the life of the patroness (the form in which she appears to me) she took a female form. The center of my being tells me, "She is trustworthy."

Petronia, who lived as a woman in the early time of the Roman Caesars, says life and afterlife are but two sides of the same record. Some souls long to be out of the body. However, there are seven more levels to the graduate soul's journey. A graduate soul is one who has finished physically incarnating. By and large, for the vast majority of ensouled beings, the graduate path begins in the phase between lifetimes, when you may serve as a spirit guide. The levels of development are:

Spirit Guides
Master Guides
Archangels
Spirit Counsellors/Buddhas
Advisors
Gods—the planetary gods,
The ONE—the great mystery, the Great Spirit, the Creator,
  all that is.

"Once you become a god you can have a world of your own with which to experiment." Petronia said. "By world we mean planet."

I wondered if anyone of us could do more than feel oneness with The Creator. I already assumed that no one could become another Great Spirit.

"The energy manifested by spiritual practices focusing on God, manifests as God and increases God. Disbelief does the same in reverse. The more people who believe in a positive God, the more positive the God of the Earth becomes. The more who see him as wrathful, the more vengeance and wrathfulness he manifests. Your God is influenced by and influences you. The duality schema on earth calls up a devil who is feared as a god. In turn, that cosmology manufactures a great amount of negativity.

"Those in human form rarely have any contact with the Source, except through their God concept. Throughout the ages certain enlightened prophets have been contacted by the Source, a brave task to undertake for the knowledge sets them apart from their fellow-beings ever after. The Realm of the Source is slowly being revealed to a wider audience and will continue to show itself as more people are able to accept the information. We will know they are ready for all of it when they demonstrate honor, trust, compassion, respect, honesty, and self-confidence in their human relationships, both public and private.

"The god you have is young, enthusiastic, and appreciative of learning. As gods go he's an adolescent. This is not his first planet, but it is his first planet on his own. Yahweh (Yod Hee

Vay Yee) is dedicated and faithful to the Source much like
Samuel of the Bible. He could be better off (and your world, too)
if his skills in gentle strength, especially influencing the minds of
human beings, were more finely honed. He still thinks of you as
strange and intractable people."

I asked if there are gods above Yahweh (Jehovah). "How
does that work, and what lies beyond the Universe?"

"What Yahweh does is work on mountains, earth minerals,
and plants, to achieve a balance," Petronia answered carefully.
"He could allow the minds of earthlings to do this work as it is
done on other successful planets. He is very fond of fishes of the
deep ocean, and spends time with two enlightened entities experimenting with those.

"Yahweh is insulted that people are destroying his work
quicker than he and the nature devas can fix it. He's a puristic,
perfection-driven god, who never measures up to the standard
he has set for himself. This is one of the reasons love is in short
supply on your planet. He is also hurt about continuing racism
and ill treatment of people classified as undesirable due to ethnic
or religious boundaries societies set. The fallout from exclusion-
ary practices limits the amount of personal, emotionally satisfy-
ing love available to every living thing on Earth.

"Throughout the Universe skin and hair coloration is considered an exciting experiment, without the limitations human
beings place on race and ethnicity. There were once blue people,
who were heavily ostracized.

"Young gods are required to consult with other gods who
have planets like theirs, and with gods who have successfully
reared their planet." Petronia wasn't finished, but I was overcome
by a wave of disbelief. Quickly, a phrase from Genesis popped
into my head, "A million years is but a day to God."

Petronia observed my reaction and continued transmitting.
"Just as institutions are worlds unto their own [ashrams, mental
hospitals, universities, corporations, laboratories, monasteries],
having limited interactions with the outside world, so it is with a
planet that a young god gets to experiment with.

"A young god has to deal with solar systems and the laws of
the Universe and whatever free-willed beings do on their planet.
Your god is not mature enough to control you gently and firmly,
so your world, although not a reform school, is a difficult learning place.

"Yahweh or Jehovah is not the god of this solar system, just of the earth. He is very masculine, with an active female component. His belief in total freedom arose in a lifetime on a planet like Mars where the lifeform had an almost transparent body. In an advanced civilization, living peaceably, working on their planet's structures, he found the value of individual freedom.

"Free will exists on the earth even in the most totalitarian regimes and in all closed societal groups like tribes. Yahweh favors tribes as the format for acculturation and interaction. This giant nation idea is not one he subscribes to, but you're free to follow the experiment with his blessing.

"Freedom in everything you say and do is the rule. As a result no limits are imposed on thoughts, actions, or personal quests. Anyone may reach for the stars or ignore the entire realm of spirit. Jehovah does this so you will learn discretion. And he has the support of many advanced entities, in letting you find your own way.

"At present there are thirteen other planets closely resembling earth, in other solar systems. There are still others approaching your stage of development, using similar structures of socialization and topography. Some planets that were like yours self-destructed. Their gods have been returned to relearn material that will keep their next world in better order.

"Very young gods and those who want to experiment between lifetimes are given old solar systems to rejuvenate or very new ones to form, to see if they can control matter with their thoughts. They do this in tribal groups, under the supervision of a leader.

"You also may belong to a tribal affinity group for a time, or switch groups when you need to. You might remain in your group inconsistently, or forever. This is the only forever there is, by choice.

"Yahweh is superb at physical manifestations. His experiments in diversified insect, plant, and animal forms are renowned throughout the Universe. He is highly respected for this and widely imitated. His mineral forms are rather ordinary, but competent enough.

"When he found his mastery of physical diversification to be so respected, he began his current concentration on the mental. He gave numerous creatures mental powers in a variety of styles. For example an elephant remembers everything as if it just happened. It has total recall but no concept of time. All dolphins and whales use telepathy. Humans could do so too, to a much greater extent.

"Your god gave human beings the capacity for unlimited thinking and reasoning powers, but he failed to put in instinctive safeguards. People use societal beliefs to enforce norms of behavior, but this is a faulty arrangement, requiring more intuition and self-regulation than most people can muster. Until their souls are Adult or Mature level, people are ruled more by their passions than by inner knowing. As is frequently the case, they can get carried away by their emotions and abandon their principles.

"Yahweh himself decided human beings' mental/emotional powers should be greater than those given to souls on similar planets. He finds your mental experiments unsatisfactory for the amount of skill you've been granted. The mental experiments will take a minimum of 500 years to turn the corner, at the current rate of development. Either more advanced individuals must communicate what the populace is lacking to grow more quickly, or you'll have to wait for Yahweh to find out what corrective measures are necessary.

"If you want your world to survive, more people must turn to positive action and peaceful means to create circumstances which allow your god Yahweh to acclimate to that desire.

"We consider his problem to be one of divided attention. The Buddha nature that so many are striving for brings with it emotional detachment. To become more godlike, literally more like your God, you must develop detachment. However, Yahweh has allowed the cultivation of detachment to an extreme. This is an outgrowth of his belief in total freedom.

"On other worlds *doctors* grow up knowing they must care for their planet. That is their job by inheritance. In your world there are all too few such beings."

I understood the word *doctor* to mean master shaman.

Petronia noted the mental notes I had made and went on. "A few tribes once had these skills. On some very advanced planets even the most urban sophisticated beings are always consulting *the doctors* and listening to their advice, for the benefit of the environment and for keeping in harmony with all living creatures. They create matter from atoms when needed and redisperse it once the object is no longer required. There are some individuals on earth who can do this. At this juncture, technology and science, teamed up with the avarice of industrialists, have set the wheels of destruction in motion. This near disaster has happened in spite of the other gods advising your god, as a precaution, to withhold the skill of making ether into matter until the earth has *doctors* of repute and integrity. Greed would cause hoarding until your entire atmosphere is used up.

"For another thing, he is very disheartened at the level of bigotry and hatred. He is hurt that his people of color are so disregarded and mistreated. Skin color, in the Universe, is actually from a people's origin. Not all human beings are indigenous to the earth. Some came from other star systems as much as sixty million years ago. There were at one point five distinctly colored human beings. The blue ones merged with African blacks and are mistakenly thought to be very dark blacks whose skin coloring looks blue/black. These are descendents of what was left of the blue people.

"Irrespective of color, when human beings have offspring there are no mules resulting, no separate, barren species created. Your bodies are equally dense. None of you float on light beams, as do humanoids on other planets. The blood, if it's typed correctly, can be transfused from one person to another regardless of race. In other words, compatible humans irrespective of color, hair, height at maturity, and other factors were the only ones allowed to populate the planet. All are the Source's children, and his consciousness is such that he knows every one of you. People who feel they ought to inherit the earth might be surprised to know they are actually descendents from out of this world."

This was the second time she chose to mention skin coloring to me. I wanted to ask her about gradations of shading and other features but she was not interested in getting into a conversation that others might use to pinpoint differences rather than unifying factors.

I asked, "What makes an Essence Being seek the assignment of being a god over a planet? Who gives this privilege, provides the impetus and the spark for growth of an entire world, constellation, or galaxy?"

"Other planets in your sun's orbit are occupied, but not by humans at this time. Mars, for example, is very much inhabited, preparatory to being a world like yours. Orbits do change. The asteroid belt is actually a planet which went awry like your own, destroying its ecosystem. Mars could be moved into an orbit like the Earth's if the world becomes unlivable or is destroyed.

"Venus is not for mammalian, avian, or reptilian habitation at this time. The life forms are gases, minerals, and other non-vegetables. A huge team of devas is currently working on Venus. They would otherwise be ordinary spirit guides or Master guides; however, this work intrigues them more.

"Devas aren't gods, but they do the work of gods when none is available or if one requires serious thought processors to work in her stead. Deva is a stage of becoming an adept. You must have cleared all the material from all your previous incarnations before undertaking a devic assignment. If you aren't clear, your energy wouldn't be properly focused on the structuring of a planet or galaxy. This work is a form of egolessness. The Deva takes an assignment which can go on between lifetimes, or without a rebirth for millions of years.

"A planetary project is not considered a hideout. From time to time Advisors or Great Helpers tell an individual to become a physical being to iron out something which stymies their Deva or creational work. The lifetime can be as a gardener, a mother of eight, or a murderer, particularly if the Deva cannot let go of a project once it has failed. Attempting to salvage a plant or mineral or animal or etheric form, after it's proven useless or has reached completion, is a big problem among Devas. Some need several human childhoods solely to let go. If the Deva doesn't learn this all-important lesson, the cells or life forms she experiments with can get out of hand and destroy the globe itself. A Deva who cannot give away a project she can't control, or bring it to its logical conclusion, may have a human life where she gets a severe cancer, to learn that growth for growth's sake is not honorable.

"The lesser gods do not permit more advanced civilizations to beset ones without equipment or well developed psychic powers. Your solar system is protected by thought forms that keep out beings alienated from their own culture and hungry for power."

"Are there no warring worlds?" I inquired.

"Yes, there are warring worlds and planets that engage others in war, but these planets do not last long. They self-destruct or are destroyed by enemies. We have no intergalactic peace-keeping force. Every planet learns peace or perishes. There are peaceful means, like force fields, to stop the warmongering worlds from interfering with peaceful planets that do not fight with outward weapons.

"Love is the law of the Universe, love over all. Everyone eventually learns this, which is why planets hardly ever set against each other in vibrational wars. All is forgotten and forgiven and trade resumed once one side has been declared the winner. Rains, constant night, and similar natural means are used in these vibrational fights. Causing crop failures and killing are forbidden. Parts of the biblical exodus from Egypt were orchestrated in this manner. It went too far; smiting of the firstborn has been banned as horribly cruel. These methods of settling feuds are not ones your world is used to or ready for. For one thing, you do not know the antidotes to inundations and wind storms. Besides, your god forbids other planets from interfering in earth's natural development.

"That's why few except Archangels enter it without coming through a human mother. Every so often one or two sneak through to teach talents you're not ready for. They find a small, interested audience, although some are ridiculed and laughed right out of existence. This small audience has grown larger in the last hundred years or so—a steady pace of increase, not monumental, until the last twenty-five years.

"Huge numbers of beings chose birth this time, to eradicate grief on this planet. Those of you who did this have already passed through the gate of initiation to implement the earth changes. You are moving into higher levels of consciousness without much opposition. Some of you are members of Clans that are preparing a planet of their own to work on. Whatever you think is transmitted to some member of your Clan so that they can steer you in the right direction and purify negative karma earth civilization."

On occasion I would stimulate a direction for our session. "How do you see planetary karma?"

Petronia: "The earth is also a living breathing organism, although Western civilization generally regards her as inert and unfeeling, available for endless exploitation. Oil is Mother Earth's joint fluid. Exploiting it to run industry, transportation, and private heating, not only putrefies the air you and she need to stay alive, it's also making her 'arthritic'. As she readjusts her aching 'bones', it's one natural catastrophe after another. Specifically, you do notice a great increase in earthquake activity."

I thought for a moment while she read my mind. "To disregard Earth this way courts disaster. Yet thought forms and activities once limited to Western Europe and North America have been transplanted globally. Rich people in China, a nation that hasn't the electricity to keep refrigerators running, buy them for show, hoping someday they can use them. Whole forests that supply the earth's oxygen are cut down for settlement and farming, in areas where the soil is unfit for agriculture. That's precisely how the American desert has expanded so rapidly since the country was settled by Europeans, who used the savannah for grazing. The karma of believing there's no piper to be paid, has begun to destroy the seas, fresh water, air, and the very fields food grows in.

"Babies everywhere are drinking formula, sold by corporations who lie and say they've ceased while they go on marketing death." I threw out a series of thought forms including a couple of boycotts I had become involved in. "Will these examples do?" I ask Petronia and she lets me see that I understand the underlying truths of her messages.

Raphael then surfaced to talk to me about the deep ocean fishes and rivers. That information was so disheartening I had to begin to look for a way to clean up the oceans. Years later, Oma Ocean surfaced to show me how sound could work to revitalize the seas.

PEACE

As a lifelong pacifist I have had to deal with life in a warring world and in a nation where the warrior is held supreme. For years, as my spirit guides and human friends instructed me, my inner battle raged on. Finally, during my annual vision quest just before the Gulf War, the spirit helpers mercifully showed me how to make the internal lion peaceful. It took me four days to tame it. The first morning of the Gulf War I arrived in Germany to teach a course on Shamanic Wisdom. Large peace demonstrations were happening everywhere. The accumulated wisdom of my own struggles to achieve peace came tumbling out, and that night everything crystalized in a lecture on peace. Achieving peace is real Shamanic Wisdom.

If you want peace and a new world order, you will have to change your world view. In America we come from a warrior culture where someone is the winner and someone has to be the loser. The converse viewpoint is that we all can win.

To come to terms with peaceful means takes a kind of watchfulness and self-examination that encompasses years of one's own lifetime. Master inner peacefulness, and from that world peace is a never ending process. If the culture you live in doesn't conduct its affairs in a diplomatic, honest, and respectful manner it is all the harder to learn noncombative methods for settling disputes.

You are demonstrating *for* peace, not *against* anyone. The enemy is war as a concept, not the latest proponents of it. Hating the politicians, the military, and industrialists who profit from it is far too short sighted. War will cease when a majority of those called to fight it refuse to participate.

Reviling the soldiers is no way to win hearts and minds. Many who have to fight would not do so if they had the courage to resist induction or possessed other skills. How can you be angry with people who are just learning to stand up for themselves?

Demonstrations cannot succeed if we listen to speeches given in the same tone as that of the politicians, with speakers in strident competition with one another. That is the equivalent energy of war. To make a change for peaceful settlement of national and international disagreements, another vibration must be raised. Potential outcomes are seldom foreseeable if we hurry. Let things season. Take no action that causes one side or another to feel it shall never be heard or heeded. The best decisions will come from patient waiting in prayerful silence.

March in a parade, sing and chant unto God, or walk in silence. No talking, no whispering. Nothing important is likely to be said that outweighs the power of silence. The peace in us makes peace in the world.

Make peace with one another. End old feuds and create no new ones. Speak truthfully, with respect, and extend nonpersonal love to all. Show consideration and gratitude. The anger in us makes anger in the world. The Universe has a way to clear negativity using wild wind and rainstorms to disperse it. To those who are violent, throw up walls of universal love. To those who are fearful be centered and serene. If someone moves against you physically, preserve your own life. Self-defense is permissible. Act without fear. Your demeanor is of the utmost importance in sending the signal that you are not to be messed with. Words are so powerful that they can disarm the armed.

In demonstrating for freedom it's better not to throw rocks but to sing songs of peace, freedom, and homage to your native land. When I saw the people of Lithuania singing in the streets, I knew they would win freedom for their land.

Peace Sound   In our lifetimes we can never work hard enough to create peace without getting help from the Realms of Creation and the Source. Call the twelve guardians of peace by singing the ah sound in the note of G below middle C twelve times. The note is toned breathy and light for as long as you can hold it. After you have sung it twelve times, bask in the vibration of peace. You can use this sound to kindle world peace or peace among a few people.

To create a new world order requires a sacrifice. To open the way for peace also takes sacrifice. It can be personal or regional, but do not abstain from making it until others join you. Be a beacon, let them follow your example. Your sacrifice can be as simple as riding your bike to work rather than taking your car. It can be attending a weekly peace vigil without fail. You might change jobs because the one you do is war-related. It could involve lobbying the government, which would be a great personal sacrifice in terms of frustration and length of commitment. You could refuse to pay your taxes because the money supports war when you do not. Whatever your sacrifice, do not force your spouse and children to take part unless they are willing.

Sacred Fire   Edison Chilaquin, a Native American from Oregon, decided that the government's offer to pay for his tribal land was unacceptable. From time out of mind the land had belonged to his tribe, the Plaigore, and he as leader would not give away his portion of their sacred place. No amount of government lobbying worked. He steadfastly refused to cash the check, and built a fire to convince the government to give him title to his land. This fire he burned for four years, tending it at all times. He lived and slept in a tipi close to his fire. His granddaughter spelled him, some friends came from time to time to help him keep it burning day and night. He used long logs, pushing them into the center of the fire as they burned. Keeping the fire going in winter was a formidable task. Once, due to severe rainstorms, the fire almost went out. He called friends in Eugene to come and help him. People believed in his cause. After many years he won and the government gave in.

This fire worked magically since it was a sacrifice to keep it going and it took constant vigilance. It was a meditation, a prayer, and a peaceful way to challenge the byzantine United States laws regarding Indian rights.

Fire can be used to create world peace. Do an all night fire with a group. Do fire meditations. Organize a fire to be kept burning until the governments of the world agree to live peaceably. Organize fires to burn for years and years.

The "new age" or Aquarian Age demands the consignment of greed, both corporate and private, to the rubbish heap. Instead, a worldwide celebration of sharing and community will become the norm. The three obstacles to worldly happiness, famine, disease, and war, will be eliminated as the people of the world progress through the heart chakra to another dimension of universal love and compassion. Ever growing numbers of people find war to be an unacceptable method of settling differences. Should we fail to accomplish the changes Adult, Mature, and Old souls are charged with implementing, an abundance of dire predictions will come true and human life on this planet will end.

Heed this message. Take it to heart.

WHITE EAGLE

White Eagle, my special guide, and I had numerous interchanges one summer in the early Eighties when I fasted for seventeen days. Various guides belonging to the Archangel class chose the opportunity to teach me portions of the material contained in "Forty-nine Steps: The Source Self's Journey" (Chapter 4), "Rootman/Rootwoman" (Chapter 6), and the four parts of the soul explained in "Who's Who" (Chapter 3). White Eagle told me:

"About the Mission, you go through incarnations in all phases of learning in every possible position. You will be a sage of an appropriate developmental level from time to time, in a variety of cultures as a maturing process. You will be a scholar, just as you must be a servant. There are many ways you can be a servant, from simple milkmaid to power brokering politician. The choice is always yours. The assignment may be to learn to deal with power; however, it is always your ideas that determine the form it takes.

"You're following in a cloud, Laeh, waiting for concrete examples. There are no illustrations your statement about patchwork quilts won't cover."

I usually tell students, "Life is like a patchwork quilt, you have your Mission to accomplish. How you do it is your business. To make a quilt, you can use any pattern you like. You can sew it of whatever fabric scraps you have on hand, or buy totally new material. All that is required is that you make a quilt and do it well."

The information White Eagle gave me was at times so revolutionary, such a challenge to my belief system that I wouldn't meet with him on the appointed day to hear it. Sometimes White Eagle would remove the top of my station wagon's closed metal roof, as I was driving, and I would see the sky as he spoke to me. He wanted me to do rituals for world peace. And I began with some reluctance and disappointment. As the years moved along I began to invite more and more people to these rituals held on equinox, solstice, and fixed full moons.

I retreat annually to seek a vision on the anniversary of receiving final transmission from my living teacher Essie Parrish. One year White Eagle chose to introduce the following concept at that time.

"One of the purposes of the Earth is as a training ground for fighters of all kinds. On Earth we teach the art of fighting to make you strong and ready for your future missions.

"More advanced forms of fighting are being learned by two main groups, those who build greater and bigger weapons, using science, and those who are learning the mastery of inner communication and the power of thought in defensive or compassionate outreach. Love being the most powerful force in the Universe, the next lesson is learning to defuse fighting or war (ritualized fighting) with it. Later you will fight with the strength you gain in ways not frequently realized on the earth plane. Some of this love is to forge new universes before you ascend to Deva status, or much later if you decide to become the god of a planet.

"Volunteers and those who've graduated from the type of physical incarnation you're familiar with employ love as a tool for strength, courage, and other attributes you can only dream of during your stages of reincarnation.

"The majority learn love is the only true resource to escape the brutality. Humanity devised the method, and it has worked throughout the ages. If this sounds a little provocative, remember you were the ones who had problems with concepts of love everywhere. This is just part of the apprenticeship each of you chose. You could have gone on as before, but you requested this daring Mission (the levels of the soul) to stimulate your growth and advance yourselves in the Realm of Creation.

"The questioning ones among you do the best. It may appear that there are two teams at the moment in the fighting process I have been revealing to you. In fact there are many middle grounds where new teams arise, each with their own segment of the lesson. These groups each give the members something to strive for. As they play with weapons, money, power, hoarding of any kind, each learner comes to the conclusion that outward weapons are of no use. There is no true winning in that way.

"As you already surmise, even a person who avoids their true path and plays cards will receive the assignment through the cards, playing situations, players, and the human dynamic of the game. It seems petty when people take their fighting lessons to that level, and it is, for they were meant to have greater examples to learn from. But if they're playing to avoid life, we bring life to the card table.

"We sent thousands like you to earth, on a Mission to remake the world as an equal zone for racial, ethnic groups, and women of all classes. We are about to change the world, but it must come through the thoughts of human beings. This Mission undertaken to increase the depth of your own essential nature is in addition to your personal Missions.

"Through the mother come thirteen genes, which are from her mother and her mother before her. This is the legacy of the grandmothers. No cultural tradition of male superiority can alter this universal plan. Sons may be important socially because they carry the family name, but daughters carry the lineage. A man ought to be very careful whom he blends his seed with, for through her come attitudes, abilities and racial memory, spiritual identity, and depth of personality. A bland woman will not make interesting children. A man of little consequence can have geniuses, or those with an inborn concept of beauty, through the genetic energy of his wife's bloodline. Some talents are ambilineal: musical gifts, capacity to heal, mental acrobatics, artistic bent."

Our Choice   "We want something new to happen. And, as you know, many have been sent on this Mission, most in female form. We have chosen you because it is your dearest wish that the Earth shall prevail. You are one of our devas who put it together millions of years ago. You love this planet, demonstrating repeatedly that it is one of your favorite places. We give you this task because you are no forecaster of doom, prophesying holocausts or nuclear destruction. You do see human beings doing stupendous acts of violence and unleashing their baser selves. Your belief in humans as better than they appear is likely to aid their emergence, at the millennium, into a more spiritual, philosophically oriented, caring world, where they are their brother's keeper. As you know, in the interim it'll be just plain wild, untamable, acts of no moral fiber committed by the unwise. At the same time, others will strive ever more deeply and soundly for peace, love, compassion, and justice. Teach people to know their own Mission and stick to their principles. Many call their Mission, The Path.

"This time there will be a new vision for humankind that supports spiritual longings maturely and patiently. It won't be a paradise on earth, but very likely the world will have come of age. We prefer that set of ideas to permeate rather than fearsome annihilating ones.

"Fortunately you see the world and the Universe of nonphysical beings as much more friendly than the major religions do. The fear of negative entities makes one a receptacle for them. A balanced state is the way to experience realms wider than the physical one.

"Churches have espoused an exclusive position on who will or won't be saved. Most organized religions claim only those of their own persuasion have valid souls and are therefore worthy. Saved is to follow your own path no matter what. That's what salvation is."

He let me sit with this teaching for a long time before he brought the subject up again. I wondered how masses of people could learn to realign their thinking and take up the way of the spiritual warrior within the framework of their secular lives. Will people ever take responsibility for what happens in the world? Will they make the necessary sacrifices to attain the peaceable kingdom? The answer lies in you. By your actions, or lack thereof, you shall decide if the world goes on.

18

Transmission

Faster
　　the drum sounds
　　　　as the spirits move closer
　　　　the rattle shakes
　　　　　and we dance.

Chief Dan George

A great deal of confusion surrounds the concept of transmission. Many students covet it, yet do not know what kind of commitment they are entering into. Participants in shamanic, mystical, esoteric, or healing workshops incorrectly believe a few months of study will confer total knowledge and wisdom in the field. People label themselves capable in the shamanic tradition simply because they've made a drum, a mask, or purchased a pipe. These are only the accouterments of the trade, not bonafide for empowerment.

　　Knowing a few shamanic skills does not necessarily qualify one to be a shaman. It is a long path, best done with a teacher of great ability and patience. The path requires dedication, selfless-ness, and commitment. It is a fierce mistress, which will take all your time, waking or asleep. Additionally, it demands the strength and courage to reckon with and work out all your own emotional baggage. For being with a real shaman, or seeking to become one, will cause the Cosmos to throw you back on your-self continually, until you crack or become completely balanced. You will never rest easily unless you do all the things the Creator and your spirit helpers ask of you. Native people know this and many hope not to be chosen, so they won't have to face the bur-dens and responsibilities of a shaman.

Shamanism is not an instant pathway offering a quick fix system of rewards. It takes approximately eight years for an ap-prentice to master the basic knowledge and wisdom a shaman must have. Should you receive transmission from a teacher with real power, it will take you a good ten years afterward to realize your own full capacity for prophesy, journeying, healing, and serving the human community. Wisdom and a sense of propor-tion is a prerequisite, otherwise the power can get ahold of you and use you, if you don't know how to handle it correctly. To quote Essie Parrish, my teacher, "If a shaman doesn't do right, it can kill her."

The learning will go on for years and years. Once you be-come proficient in the first level of enlightenment, symbolized by the moon and the raven, the Universe will introduce you to the second level of enlightenment, known as the solar level. It is rep-resented by the eagle. The third stage of enlightenment is the star, and its bird is the swan, which represents transmigration of the soul. Commitment, a seldom understood concept, is neces-sary to even begin the steps along the shaman's way.

Healing is an important part of the shaman's path, but not the only one. Prophesy, singing, dance, and artwork are in-cluded. Some shamans make their own rules without interfer-ence due to their exceptional powers, while others must follow the old way strictly.

One part of shamanism involves empowerment or transmis-sion, which is occasionally spontaneous.

People seem to ask the same questions about transmission over and over. The format for this chapter may answer many of your own queries related to extra help given by the master to an apprentice, whose life will forevermore be changed. These questions are taken from classes and private sessions with students of mine, so that many of them are addressed to me, rather than generally stated.

Q—What exactly is transmission?

A—In the oral tradition, an introduction to the powers occurs. Transmission literally makes the truth come alive for you. An empowerment is an initiatory process, the mastership to come is within you. You must reach inside your own subconscious and bring it forward. The empowerment comes from the Source to the great teacher, and is in turn given to the true seeker, a student/apprentice.

The more entrenched a religion becomes, the more crystallized the methods for bringing about enlightenment get. The easiest way is when a master grants you an initiation. The most difficult is to seek it alone, finding your own methods by trial and error.

Empowerment is passed from master to apprentice by word, breath, deed, touch, thought, and intention.

There are often conditions that go with transmission. You adopt the entire package, not just the parts that suit you. Therefore, if your teacher asks you to abstain from imbibing alcohol, become a vegetarian, say certain prayers as you've been instructed, or places restrictions upon your behavior, it is due to the lineage that is being bestowed upon you. That lineage has its quirks and works best when those rules are observed. Wise teachers refuse to take students they feel will be unable to restrain themselves, since by breaking the rules of empowerment you can kill yourself.

Q—What happens when someone agrees to go through an initiation or empowerment and then breaks the rules by having an occasional glass of wine, or smoking when the spirits haven't told them to?

A—That depends upon the student and the circumstances. A Jewish woman who observes the Sabbath by having a ritual draught of wine is following the path she must, in addition to the empowerments she may have taken from her master. If you are empowered and you go to a communion where sips of wine are customary, or to a pipe ceremony, although you ordinarily abstain from the substances, it is acceptable to join with others for the occasion as these are bonding experiences. You can participate freely, knowing that human beings need to accept one another's spiritual journeys in order to break apart the barriers previously used to keep us at odds.

If your best old buddy has just returned from the Himalayas and it was always your special treat to go to Joe's Bar and have a few, this is out. In truth and in fact if you disobey the rules, the power will get ahold of you, rather than you holding onto it and it will destroy you.

Q—Can people accept transmission and ignore what they're told?

A—Yes, and with disastrous results. Many teachers have a sorcerer's apprentice story. This one is included in detail so you can comprehend what vanity and denial can do to those who accept the power but not the responsibility.

Years ago an enthusiastic woman, named Babe, approached a teacher she perceived as gifted and compatible. Babe had all manner of visions and dreams and quite a bit of personal mystical experience. She wanted an apprenticeship. But the teacher held Babe off, explaining that she'd have to dream on her to see if it were right. The morning after their talk the teacher had to throw Babe out of her dream, as the erstwhile student was pleading with her in it. The teacher informed Babe that she'd felt her interject herself into the dream, and this was not a true sign. The student was to wait patiently until one came, if it did.

Several weeks later the teacher had a dream. She wrote Babe instructing her to go to an isolated place in the mountains and remain three weeks. She was not to speak to anyone during this time. It was the dead of winter, deep in snow, and Babe was to soak up the silence. She was to wait for a vision. Once it came, she was to sit with it awhile before returning home. After the three weeks were up, Babe could leave. Within the allotted time Babe had her vision and departed from her retreat.

Several months later, determining that Babe was prepared for her first empowerment, the teacher gave her transmission. The teacher delivered strong admonitions that nothing but tobacco and a legal sacred herb were to be smoked, and those only "when the spirits tell you to." Above all, the newly inducted apprentice was never to drink alcohol.

A few months went by. Babe and the teacher spent a couple of days together. The teacher noticed Babe was distracted and rather flaky. This is a frequent occurrence in the year following transmission. It happens to those who haven't cleared out a sufficient amount of their personal trash. Babe's husband inquired of the teacher if it was possible to love someone like crazy, yet be unable to live with them. The teacher laughed. All too often the husband or wife of an apprentice goes through many extremes with them, as the student readjusts to seeing several realities at once.

During the summer Babe had gone to a Sun Dance and placed herself in the midst of the energy reserved for the dancers, where she ought not to have been. She became separate from her body for two days. The medicine man who ran it had to bring her soul back. When Babe described the experience to her teacher, the teacher was shocked at her behavior and even more upset that Babe didn't recognize the danger she'd put herself in. Babe waved off her teacher's counsel.

A year after transmission, another student informed the teacher that Babe, who'd never been overweight, was fasting extensively and drinking a strong mix of coffee and brandy every evening. The teacher confronted her. Babe denied it. Unfortunately, there would be nothing she could do to help, unless Babe quit drinking. Babe's behavior led the teacher to believe she was at least mildly alcoholic, thus without will power to cease drinking. Babe had to recognize her alcohol dependency and go into a self-help program to help her grow beyond it.

As the year progressed Babe was dropped from her doctoral program for failing to fulfill the requirements. Her husband unilaterally decided to return to his home state. Babe and her family moved to his former home town. She hated it. Her husband filed for divorce. He was not the father of her children and owed her nothing. She couldn't support her teenagers without a job, so temporarily they lived with her mother. After quite a search, Babe found a quality position that measured up to her education and previous employment. Her children were reunited with her. She seemed to have reestablished her equilibrium, but her teacher wasn't ready to advance her training, opting for a wait and see attitude.

As part of her job, Babe traveled to deliver a lecture series. Her employer called, demanding she cut short her trip and return at once. She complied. They'd found massive incompetence and gross negligence, and Babe was terminated on the spot. Within weeks, as if the Cosmos was giving her another chance, she found a prestigious position on the west coast, far from home. Her children longed for more familiar terrain. They were sick and tired of their mother's emotional ups and downs, and went to live with their father whom they hadn't seen since they were preschoolers. Babe complained that they rarely called her.

There's more, but it doesn't get any better. All kinds of medicine people have advised her, but years later Babe is still drinking and bouncing from one thing to another, as a regular Calamity Jane.

Q—If you are born into a people, such as Gypsies, Jews, Indians of the Americas, both North and South, and you fail to be initiated into their rites, are you still bound to them?

A—How can you live under laws you barely know or willingly practice? If you have had no confirmation, no initiation, no instruction, you are only making yourself feel guilty for the lack of knowledge. If you want, you must dedicate yourself to locating a worthy teacher and become a devoted and respectful practitioner of the way your people follow.

You can, if you feel you were under family pressure to take on the rites of your church or ethnic group, let it go at any time. Walk away from it, recognizing that family and friends who still adhere to the tenets of the religion will be disappointed in you, ostracize you, and generally register disapproval for your honesty.

You can leave any path, in the clear knowledge that the Almighty is not waiting around to strike you dead for seeking another way. You have to ask to be freed from the vows you made or accepted which no longer satisfy your spiritual longings.

Q—I feel like we're in a new time and I am eclectic with the way I put my spiritual life together. Is there any harm in this?

A—That depends upon what you are a part of. If you have a strong Protestant background that you still feel a connection to, it won't disappear when you layer other teachings over it. You can make certain kinds of amalgams as many people do when switching traditions; however if you have a spiritual teacher you cannot ignore the teachings you are being given.

Whatever tradition you are part of has rules. The rules have a purpose. Do not bring rules from other cultures into your spiritual practice unless you know them to be universal and true. Around the world tribal women are forbidden to participate in rituals when they are menstruating. However, in some traditions like the Hopi they do not incorporate the restriction. If your teacher bans vision quests and attendance at rituals while menstruating, you do not go off and do your own vision quest or ritual. There may be other rites you are permitted to perform.

In the tradition I come from, you do not go to running water (creeks, waterfalls, rivers) during your period. I tell many stories about this prohibition so that the students will understand the danger they can place themselves in.

A rather headstrong woman who accompanied us on a trip into the spectacular, sacred, and powerful Grand Canyon began menstruating. Disappointed that she couldn't have a vision quest, she went off to the creek and had one of her own. Earlier her guides had shown her the entire group around the fire, and led her away from the fire. A clear sign that she was to stay by herself and let the group go on with its mission. Misinterpreting the vision with a proud and self-righteous attitude, she decided it meant she should no longer take teachings altogether. She believed she was on her own to learn solely from the guides. Shortly thereafter she began offering shamanic workshops and exorcisms in her brochure. She ran into some difficulties and began to call other longtime students for information. If she had been in a less belligerent frame of mind she would have remembered that the taboo provided protection for her and the group, and saved herself much emotional turmoil.

Q—Should you carry a Biblical name or a legendary name from a non-western religion, like Helen for the beautiful woman of Troy, or Adam of the Bible, is that your personal myth for transformation? Is it by the same token transmission of the powers held by that name?

A—No. Not all women named Rachel are subdued, patient, gentle, barren, or wives. The legend can influence you if your name provokes comments about the myths associated with your namesake. For instance, Helen of Troy had a face that launched a thousand ships. A woman who is of the same name, although remarkably ungainly and homely, might do the deed as well but for opposite reasons. A man named Solomon can be extremely unwise and even ignorant about human nature. So it's possible to adopt either polarity from the name.

How many realize that Sarah, wife of Abraham in the Bible, was a sea goddess born of the sea, the same as Aphrodite? In her mature years she was a healer, just like Aphrodite. In her elder years Sarah, like the aged Aphrodite, was a woman of wisdom. She laughed over being granted a child long after menopause had sealed her fate as forever childless. "Sarah was a laughing goddess and her progeny was to be like the sand of the seashore . . . ," Robert Graves, *The White Goddess*.

Q—How do you decide who to give transmission to and what does it cost?

A—Transmission is never for sale. It belongs only to those who ought to have it. I give it when I know it is to be conferred. There are three stages to transmission. The first is the healing capacity and the protection needed for the voyage through the deeper parts of the first level of enlightenment. The second is the opening of the heart to allow compassion to become the norm of behavior. The third is for total empowerment on all points of the inward journey. It is only given to true seekers after a long and arduous journey.

Q—I've been lovers with a couple of shamans. Does that mean that I have something like transmission?

A—No, it is not transferred by bodily fluids. More than likely you were feeding him power rather than receiving it. What is true, particularly of males who have been through an initiatory process and were then dropped by their teachers, or of those who never really had any power, is that they gather it by sucking the shakti out of women lovers during intercourse. This is a very old technique and the basis of tantra. Any man can live off of a woman's energy. He might even require several fixes per day to keep going.

The seducer exists within all traditions, Hindu, Amerindian, Tibetan, Christian, whatever types are available will have men and sometimes women who take advantage of their student's gullibility. Several famous teachers on the guru circuit have left many dozen children to be raised as best they can by their single mothers, who chanced to be the lover of the moment. The woman gets to feel she has some sort of elevated status. However, it is temporary, since he will be on to the next luscious flower once he's depleted your juices. If you become the one and only spouse or consort of your teacher, your life will not be an easy one. You will work hard to support their quest, and if you aren't cautious may abandon your own path for the role of helpmate to the famous teacher.

Q—I'm skeptical about spiritual teachings as an avenue of growth. My boyfriend has gone to lots of workshops and long retreats given by famous people. He returns elated and then the whole thing fades.

A—There are people who are workshop junkies. Hungry ghosts, internally vacuous, ever trying to fill themselves with experiences and information, albeit second hand. The growth tourists hunger eternally, sitting with the Zen master, attending Sun Dances, taking Tibetan initiations, going to peace gatherings, learning Tai Chi or Yoga from enlightened teachers. They go to seven weekend workshops in ten weeks, yet absorb little since they take no time to make the practices their own. It's a lick and a dab and they're on to the next Primal Scream, Men's Gathering, NLP, Adult Children of Alcoholics, or Geomancy course. And they buy the books, tapes, and latest spiritual geegaws from pyramids to crystals purveyed by this week's leader, all in a futile effort to find themselves.

It's a vainglorious attempt to purchase enlightenment and spiritual wisdom. Ultimately, it's spiritual consumerism with the same kind of false high that alcoholism, drug dependency, and sexual conquests produce for the non-seeker.

These are people who go to couple therapy on Tuesday night, gestalt with their co-workers on Wednesday morning, see their own counsellor Thursday evening, and attend a couple of self-help therapeutic groups a week. Nothing helps them, for they are into the illusion of growth and won't get out there and really give of themselves. Some are into therapy as a lifestyle, as a shield from actualizing their potential. Others are terribly selfish parents and partners whose preoccupation with their own imagined growth shuts out meaningful intimate interactions. Literally they are shamanic tourists, spiritual babes in the woods, unable to perform their own salvation. Something out there, the next fad or trend, will do it for them. Then it'll really click. And it does for a while, until they hit a hard place, when they abandon that for the next "spiritual high."

Q—What's it like to have transmission?
A—It's different for everyone. One apprentice told me she heard sound more acutely following the second stage. The quote below is from Yona Ash who received all three stages of transmission.

"To be given transmission on any level, to be involved with a person who can give transmission is a special relationship not often found in our society. It involves the active conscious participation of the giver and the receiver.

"A teacher, especially a 'real' one, unlocks possibilities inside the student's soul. Our culture locks wonderful treasures away from us and our lives become robotized, separated from breath and life.

"To begin to look for connections to this more 'real' world takes a person with inner direction and conviction. It is a path that needs support and guidance from another level. A mentor is necessary in either physical or spiritual form.

"The transmission itself is not from the mentor to the initiate in terms of vision, but transfers an ability for the initiate to unlock personal understanding, healing, and visionary powers.

"It was a rainy winter evening when Laeh gave me my first transmission. I had no idea what it was about or what to expect. I was instructed to shower completely and wear a fresh set of clothing. The act of bathing became a new holiness in myself. As I waited for Laeh who was on the phone in a lengthy conversation, I wondered how we'd have time to do the ritual. It turned out to be a deceptively short, simple action. Laeh checked to see that I'd received it and said, 'Good.' I thought 'What, I missed it.' But immediately the quality of color began to steadily change. There was a glow and distance to the world around me. My bones felt as though their molecules were rearranging themselves. It took the full three days for the empowerment process to set completely. (To set, the requirements are: no love-making, no visitors, no telephone calls, no showers or bathing. Rest and be quiet for 72 hours afterward.)

"Each of the transmissions affected me in a totally different way. The second stage of transmission, sometime later on, went through my blood. The third empowerment was preceded by a vision quest. During that quest I'd been worked on by non-physical entities. The night after, Laeh performed the ritual of final transmission. It was almost an exact duplicate of what my guides had done to me in my vision. It went to my soul center, traveling from crown chakra to perineum. I felt the lineage of initiates that had passed before me. The connection gave me a new relationship to life, past and future.

"To be on such a path you must be ready to submit, prostrate yourself. This is not on a physical or simplistic level, but to be open to energy washing over and through you so that at points you are egoless or disassembled totally. There remains no room for lies, hate, or negativity. You have nothing to cling to, no material distractions or protections. This takes deep faith and centeredness. You are being totally reshaped and there is little in your daily secular life that will validate this other life."

Q—What chance is there that someone might misuse mystical knowledge?

A—This is the old duality principle. How far can the dark side go with this knowledge? You're really asking if they can obtain the same benefits and go as far as the good side. Usually after a certain point they have no capacity to understand the knowledge, and the people who use it for negative purposes exceed their bounds. At that point the power gets ahold of them, using them. They then fall and fail the test of life.

Spiritually, no difference exists between good and evil. The power is only there to be used. It is how you use it that makes it good or evil. Your intention is what makes the magic be good or not. Practitioners of the black arts who send curses or cause others to have misfortune, know that if they ever let down their guard it'll all come back on them.

Q—Do I have to be a perfectly honest and trustworthy person to be able to seriously undertake a spiritual path?

A—Many people believe they are only worthy if they are absolutely perfect in every single way. Their acceptance/rejection material is so strong that the example they hold themselves up to is an impossible standard. Saints in real life were people who laughed, cried, got frustrated, and dealt with the mix of reverence and mundane in life. Feeling unworthy of being in or taking a leadership role in a ceremony, or thinking your prayer is not good enough, profanes your own access to divinity. You must always honor yourself and seek the inner journey wherever you are. Not to see yourself as a Divine creation is definitely profane.

Q—What is Karma?

A—There are two kinds of karma. The type we in the West usually mean is in terms of fate either predestined or created by our actions in our current lifetime. The Eastern philosophies have the doctrine of Karma which is simply that of causality and is common to all Hindu and Buddhist philosophies. This quote, one of the best on the topic, is from *Buddhism: Its Doctrines and Its Methods,* by Alexandra David-Neel:

"In the same way, your words, your thoughts, the teachings which you propagate, the examples you set, are so many sparks that spring forth, and fall on others. Sometimes they penetrate into your neighbor's mind, or into the mind of a soul whose very existence is unknown to you, or who receives them at the other end of the world, through an account that they hear, or a book they read, or like Tibetans say: through the power of the 'waves that our actions and our thoughts create in the ether.'"

Q—Would you explain what power is?

A—There is a vast difference between people attracted to explore the spiritual realm for knowledge, wisdom, and enlightenment, and those who seek it only for self-aggrandizement. In German there are two words for power. *Macht* is power given by inheritance, or in ruling others. It is political. It is granted by others and means control over people. *Kraft* is strength, abilities, power in the sense of forces spiritual and self-contained. *Kraft* means being able to manage force fields, energy, to put concepts and things into operation or deactivate them.

Power is correctly sought to give service, to gain knowledge and abilities, and its proper wielding is to do no harm. Power over others, or to show off, gained to make up for your own insecurities, will never satisfy and leads to all manner of damage to yourself and others. The use of power for control over others breeds fear, not only in others, but in the person who is in power. Medicine people who use power for the benefit of society need only the protection of the Creator when traveling or out among people. Those who use it for their own means take body guards and an extensive entourage to buffer them from the supposedly adoring masses.

There is power in persons, objects, places (geological locations or buildings), movements (dance), sounds (music or utterances), images and transempirical entities, deity, or abstract principle. Power is the goal of rituals. Manipulation of power means performing the myths and actions of a spiritual format, using power for promoting good and averting evil. Power resembles an invisible creative force which benefits (or sometimes harms) both spiritual and worldly affairs.

As an example of non-physical power, monks chanting in unison can bring rain when there is none, or install a cloudless sky for several holy day observances.

Q—Why do you forbid your students to drink alcohol?

A—You can easily fool yourself, or be fooled by the forces you've contacted. Although this quote, by Grace Cooke in *The New Mediumship,* White Eagle Publishing Trust, addresses would-be mediums, her answer is valid for healers, visionaries and spiritual seekers of all stripes.

> *Certain agents can stimulate the solar plexus centre, alcohol being one. Astonishing communications can take place when drugs or alcohol are used. Any would-be medium under the influence of drugs or alcohol is in the position of a child set down in a power-house, who turns on a switch, but cannot turn it off. People sometimes so long to get into touch with the other side that they will do anything to achieve their object; and being aware that their natural psychic gifts seem to be stimulated by alcohol, they open themselves to various astral broadcasting stations and through ignorance of the laws of mediumship become obsessed by a conglomeration of simultaneous voices and sounds from the astral plane.*

Confusion, lack of discrimination and discretion, as well as an inability to stop the voices or continuing to be upset by the information gained, once sober, is the real problem when you drink.

The other reason is that my teacher Essie Parrish forbids alcohol completely and I have followed her directive.

Q—What kinds of rituals do you recommend for taking drugs or herbs in a sacred manner?

A—With sacredness, reverence, and infrequency, spiritual paths restrict use of their "medicine" to specific ceremonies. In the right season pilgrimages are made to gather and use the plant. Songs sung, prayers made, they celebrate their visions together. An entire community visions together led by one or more wise leaders who act as their guide.

After you've been invited to and have taken part in a number of rituals, you and your mentor, whether a spirit companion or a living person, will know you are ready and initiate you into one or more ways to ingest the substance that is to be your sacred practice. To do so you'll have to know how to prepare a nonlethal dose, in sufficient quantity to attain a vision that is both mystical and clear.

It is hard to believe people who use chemically synthesized substances on a regular or prolonged basis, when they tell you their MDMA (ecstasy) or Thorazine is a sacred drug. In whose tradition are these pharmaceuticals a sacrament? Persian, it was whispered to me, was special, by a person hooked on that derivative of heroin. Cocoa leaves are a holy substance to some South American tribal people; however, in the form of cocaine or crack they are nothing but drug abuse.

Mother Nature made narcotic plants to soothe pain or lift you beyond your everyday mirage to the world of the spirit. It's the nonchemical kind that can be called sacred; nothing else qualifies as bonafide irrespective of its current vogue. Herbs are a natural part of our existence, but only in their natural form, which can include fermentation, taken as tea, dried to smoke, or cooked whole for eating.

You must be extremely careful with substances traditionally taken for spiritual endeavors. The intake of alcohol as a relaxant, or to socialize or to deaden psychological and emotional pain, diminishes its effectiveness as a spiritually enlightening essence until it has power over you. Imbibing becomes not a planned event but a subconscious desire and later on the body craves it so that you are unable to resist.

The Druids used small quantities of alcohol as a sacrament on feast days or for specific group magic. Their intake was on a limited basis and the times of the year for taking alcohol were severely limited, half a cup, no more, once every few weeks to solemnize an occasion such as solstice, equinox, Hallowmas, Lammas, or May Day.

Peyote is taken by various tribal groups in an all night ritual where everyone stays awake. There is a roadman to guide the people along their way, making certain all return ready to function from their individual contacts with the Creator. One medicine man may mix wild oregano with his Peyote, to cut the nausea, while another may have his followers tough it out. Yet the plant is intact, ingested as non-chemically-altered substance. The frequency of the ceremony varies among groups from a single time in the year, to thirteen times per year, to bi-weekly observances as done by some members of the Native American Church.

Peyote grows wild in the Southwest, Nevada, or lower desert of California. It's illegal, but mother nature grows it abundantly anyway. The scientific name is *L. Williamsi.* This plant is a powerful psychotropic. Taken without a roadman to guide you it can frighten or enlighten you, depending upon your interpretation.

Marijuana has a long history of sacrificial usage. Marijuana taken with coffee is mentally stimulating. Smoking confers a very different mystical experience than eating it. Proper methods of preparation must be learned, so that leaves and seeds are totally absent from the food it is mixed with. As a daily or weekend treat, its consumption hardly qualifies as anything besides an addiction.

My own teacher instructed me to smoke the root of an herb that grows in the western part of California and Oregon. She repeatedly said, "Smoke only when the spirits tell you to." The herb brings absolute clarity and spiritual understanding.

If prayer is strong, prayer itself becomes the "medicine." No ingestible substance is required, if one strong praying doctor is available to teach you how to pray. You may stumble upon powerful conditions for prayer, or practice praying until you have mastered the art by remaining concentrated, centered, and positive.*

Prayer is covered in Chapter 12 of Sound Medicine, *by Laeh Maggie Garfield*

RECOMMENDED BIBLIOGRAPHY

Amerindian
Barbara Means Adams, *Prayers of Smoke*, Celestial Arts.
John Redtail Freesoul, *Breath of the Invisible*, Quest Books, 1986.
Malcolm Margolin, *The Way We Lived, California Indian Reminiscences, Stories and Songs*, Heyday Books, 1981.

Astrophysics
Stephen W. Hawking, *A Brief History of Time*, Bantam Books, 1989.

Buddhism
Ngakpa Chögyam, *Rainbow of Liberated Energy*, Element Books, 1986.
Alexandra David-Neel, *Buddhism: Its Doctrines and Its Methods*.
Pierre Delattre, *Tales of the Dalai Lama*, Creative Arts Book Company, 1971.
Sogyal Rinpoche, *Dzogchen and Padmasambhava*, Rigpa Fellowship, 1989.

Christian Mysticism
Elaine Pagels, *Gnosis*.

Dreams
Strephon Kaplan Williams, *The Jungian-Senoi Dreamwork Manual*, Journey Press, Berkeley, California, revised 1985.

Enneagram
Margaret Frings Keyes, *Emotions and the Enneagram: Working Through Your Shadow Life Script*, Molysdater Publications.
Helen Palmer, *The Enneagram: The Definitive Guide to the Ancient System for Understanding Yourself and the Others in Your Life*, Harper and Row.

Jewish
Penina V. Adelman, *Miriam's Well: Rituals for Jewish Women Around the Year*, 1986, Biblio Press, Fresh Meadows, New York, 11365–0022.
Rabbi Aryeh Kaplan, *The Light Beyond: Adventures in Hassidic Thought*, 1981, Maznaim Publishing.

Love:
Susan Peabody, *Addiction to Love: Overcoming Obsession and Dependency in Relationships*, 1989, Ten Speed Press, Berkeley, California.
Carlotte Davis Kasl, Ph.D., *Women, Sex, and Addiction*, 1990, Harper and Row.

Sexuality
Andrew Ramer, *Two Flutes Playing*.
Richard Alan Miller, *The Magical and Ritual Use of Aphrodisiacs*, Destiny Books, 1985.

Sound
Hans Cousto, *The Cosmic Octave*, published by Liferhythm.
William David, *The Harmonics of Sound, Color and Vibration: A System for Self Awareness*, De Vorss & Company, 1980.
Kay Gardner, *Sounding the Inner Landscape: Music as Medicine*, Caduceus Publications, 1990.
Laeh Maggie Garfield, *Sound Medicine*, Celestial Arts, 1987.
R.J. Stewart, *Music and the Elemental Psyche: A Practical Guide to Music and Changing Consciousness*, 1987, Destiny Books.

Spirituality
Grace Cooke in *The New Mediumship*, White Eagle Publishing Trust.
Laeh Maggie Garfield & Jack Grant, *Companions in Spirit*, Celestial Arts, 1984.
Joan Hodgeson *Why On Earth*, White Eagle Publishing Trust, England, 1979.
Murry Hope, *Practical Techniques of Psychic Self-Defense*.

Women:
Robert Graves, *The White Goddess*.

Yoga:
books by Baba Hari Dass—
Silence Speaks
Fire Without Fuel
A Child's Garden of Yoga
Ashtanga Yoga Primer, 1981

All books, Sri Rama Publishing, P.O. Box 2550, Santa Cruz, California.
Namkai Norbu, *Yantra Yoga: Yoga of Movements*, Verlag TSAPARANG Graz, Austria, 1988 (in English).

GLOSSARY

Adult souls begin to view their life not just in terms of comforts and power but in terms of more important values, such as compassion, love, grief, kindness.

Advisors are from the star level. They are not assigned or attached to a single solar system. Series of Advisors undertake guardianship for a galaxy and work in consort with other Advisors who oversee other galaxies. A pair of Advisors who have no other duties oversees each Clan.

Ahimsa—"The yoga of Ahimsa consists in the devising of means and doing of acts . . . . to check the evil effects . . . . of such acts from human society," **M. Gandhi.**

Arthi—a fire ceremony using cotton dipped in ghee.

Astral travel is either the movement of the psyche to other realms or planes of existence or travelling with your nonphysical body to distant geophysical locations.

Big heads are mentioned in Elizabeth Haich's Initiation.

Blow doctoring—A shamanic healing method using breath as the revitalizing force. Literally resetting the breath pattern of an individual. Someone can be brought back to life by this method or restored to full health.

The breathing place—The spot where the impetus to breathe is located directly under the shoulder blade.

Chapter Test—Once you have examined your behavior whenever a specific issue arises, or seen how you have created your own reality and have successfully demonstrated your ability to function in a new manner, an equivalent situation comes back on you as a final exam that you either pass or fail.

Clan—An affinity group related to each other as a family is but larger and more diversified.

Co-beings are souls from the same Source Self. Often referred to as past lives.

Creator—see God's Breath.

The Creator—The Source. All That Is. The Eternal One. God. The Universe.

Death is a cessation of the winds of change within the life that was being lived. The entire soul not only chooses the time to die, but has lots of latitude in resetting the moment.

317

The Death Sound—A sound never heard anywhere else. It is whirling whistling, like a lasso, with a sireny overtone. A captivating, droning sound, that leads you on a swirling tricolored umbilicus, out of your body.

Dismemberments is a form of reconstructing your life by throwing everything away and taking back what you need. These usually take place unbidden as a mental/spiritual rather than a physical experience.

Dreamtime—Entering a mythological time frame centergirding a culture through dreams and visions. Experiences can come from a special trance dream, a vision, or an abrupt departure from standard reality while in the midst of an otherwise normal day. There's a type of dozing that produces a memorable form of dreamtime.

dZog Chen—Mystery school of Tibetan Buddhism.

Empowerment is passed from master to apprentice by word, deed, touch, thought, and intention.

Eternal Time—Time that always is, where all events in all places occur without limitations.

Essence Being—see Source Self.

Essence Self—see Source Self.

God's Breath is your inner spark of the divine. This is the final component of the soul to enter an infant's body. It does so at the moment the emerged neonate takes its first breath.

Grandmother Ocean—The ocean and seas each have their own grandmother guardian who oversees the energy.

The Holy Spirit is literally "breath."

Human Soul has four components, each of which serves a separate function, together forming a distinct one-of-a-kind self.

Infant souls may seem to be innocent and too much of the spirit world. Unlike Old souls, whom they resemble in this respect, they seem naive rather than wise.

Ley Lines are a path of power extending around the globe. They are marked at megalithic sites on the earth by buildings and structures, which accent the mysterious powers that occur where Ley Lines intersect each other.

Life cord/chord—Death comes first, then life. There's a point inside the anus, below the first chakra and attached to it, that holds the cord (braided tri-color of red, blue, and yellow) and the chord (sound) that grounds you to earth.

The Mansions or houses of growth number seven in the dimension known as physical life.

Master Guides are spiritual beings who strive to plant seeds of cosmic knowledge on the earth plane. They rarely channel for the sake of one individual, choosing those who will go on to teach others.

Mature souls work on projects associated with the fifth chakra. They are concerned for the common good, often pacifists, with a look-the-other-way attitude toward activities they don't care to participate in and don't quite approve of.

Mission—The work you have agreed to do before incarnating. For your life to be successful you must complete all of it.

Moon Spiral—Knowledge is gained, especially the discovery of the self, in the transition through the first level of enlightenment represented by the moon. The skills associated are healing, visioning, journeying, working with spirit allies, uncovering your unconscious, and your own godly potential at the same time as you apply the knowledge gained to everyday life.

Old souls live by their own rules, desires, and principles regardless of the society they enter. These are the world's successful mavericks. They listen clearly to their own intuition.

Oversoul is the advisor and guardian to a group of Source Selves.

Passing Time—see World Time.

Past Lives—see Co-Beings.

Personality is the third component of a living soul. It enters the body anywhere from the time the mother feels life until birth. The underlying code of your personality is a string of thought forms, requirements of your Source Self for developing its overall character.

The Physical Realm is also known as the manifesting realm, or realm of motion, which encompasses every point, water, wind, fire, molecule, chemical, and geophysical location in the Universe.

Racial memory is the accumulated knowledge of millions of lifetimes lived by all souls who have incarnated. Everyone has access to it.

Ray—Your Ray is the color that is always with you. The color tonal quality remains steady irrespective of illness, emotional trauma, age, or steps to spiritual growth taken or avoided. The ray's tint or density is a good indication of the soul level you are operating from.

Realm of Creation is the world of pure mind, mind beyond intellect. This quality of mind is the power to grasp and express with genuine inner understanding, to create as well as to register and absorb knowledge.

Realm of Formation is home to immaterial guardians who oversee the development and the safety of land formations such as mountains or sacred places. Elves, Devas, fairies, leprechauns, tree spirits, animal spirits, all belong to the Formation Realm.

Rootman and Rootwoman are internal guides and partial co-beings for a particular lifetime. Chapter 6 is devoted to this special and very private relationship.

Shakti—the energy current that runs the world. My teacher Essie Parrish said it was like electricity but it wasn't electricity.

Sitio—small personal power site.

The Source is the dwelling place of the Almighty, ruler of our Universe. It is the home of planetary gods, of ascended beings, of Star-level enlightenment. Everything known and unknown in the entire cosmos emanates from the Source.

Source Self is the first component of the soul and is present at the moment of conception. It is your essential nature and the essential nature of all the other lifetimes you have been privy to.

Sun spiral of enlightenment—The second degree of enlightenment is the solar level represented by the Sun. Five areas of wisdom and illumination are contained within this step: Death, Decay, Love, Birth, Time, Truth.

Star spiral of enlightenment is the entryway to "The Great Mystery," the wisdom known in all times and in all places. Through this doorway space becomes an integral part of your knowledge. Here you work with transformation, electromagnetism, gravity and its opposite, vacuums, and nuclear and molecular structure.

Synesthesia is the intermingling of two unrelated phenomena paired in a single individual, such as taste and touch, or smell and sight. Synesthesia of color and sound, touch and smell, form and memory, smell and/or sight, are common phenomena to those who retain the ability of sensory crossover.

The Take Away Person—No one is permitted to make the passage from life to death unaccompanied. A take-away person is assigned to assist you on your journey.

Teenaged Souls—No matter what chakra the individual is working on, the lifetime is perceived through the route to power and influence. They make plans and carry out their goals.

Toddler Souls—Often pedantic, demanding, obstinate, or overly sweet, this series of lifetimes deals with acceptance and rejection or outright abandonment.

Transmission—The passing of powers by touch, sight, word, deed, intention, and thought. Transmission itself is not from the mentor to the initiate in terms of vision; however it transfers an ability for the initiate to unlock personal understanding, healing, and visionary powers.

Tumo is the art of warming yourself without any fire.

Vision Quest—The seeking of a spiritual direction, usually personal. Two formats exist for vision quests. The inner, usually referred to as journeying, and the outer kind, wherein the body is stressed to its endurance by fasting, sleeplessness, and exposure to the elements. The more popular route is the inward quest.

Volunteer souls have attained full status as graduates of ordinary life. They relate to life chiefly through the seventh chakra. They are born with access to all memory everywhere in the universe and are the master builders.

Wildcraft—To hunt and pick plants in their natural habitat that nature herself planted and grew. Herbalists consider these plants to have the most vital force.

Witness—The second component of the soul is an archangel who watches over several hundred incarnated Source Selves at one and the same time.

World Time—Calendar time and the time we set our watches by.

INDEX

Page numbers in italics indicate illustrations.

For cassette tapes, workshop schedules, meditations and other material in *HOW THE UNIVERSE WORKS*, send $13.00 US postpaid to:

<u>North America:</u> Make checks payable to: Inward Journeys
(U.S. Funds please)   P.O. Box 891
Occidental, CA 95465

<u>Europe:</u> Make checks payable to: Inward Journeys
(Swiss Francs please)   Hauptstrasse 54
CH-8455 Rudlingen
Switzerland

Other books of interest from Celestial Arts:

☐ *Sound Medicine* by Laeh Maggie Garfield
Music, single tones, singing, chanting, even silence—all of these can be focussed and used for healing. This book explains the philosophies and metaphysics behind "sound medicine," then shows how it can be applied to everyday situations. $8.95 paper, 192 pages

☐ *Companions in Spirit* by Laeh Maggie Garfield and Jack Grant
A step-by-step introduction to every phase of working with a spirit guide or helper, with a special emphasis on grounding and preparing yourself for the initial contact. $8.95 paper, 192 pages

☐ *The Art of Ritual* by Sydney Barbara Metrick & Renee Beck
A guide to creating and performing personalized rituals for growth and change. The authors discuss the importance of ritual in traditional cultures, and show how to integrate it into modern life, celebrating births, achievements, special friendships, and the like. $11.95 paper, 152 pages

☐ *Prayers of Smoke* by Barbara Means Adams
A Native American writer form the tribe of Black Elk presents the traditional myths and rituals of the Makaha people in this fascinating cultural document. $9.95 paper, 172 pages

☐ *The Common Book of Consciousness* Revised Edition by Diana Saltoon
A beloved sourcebook, newly revised and updated for the 1990s. This guide to leading a whole and centered life shows how to use meditation, exercise, and nutrition to gain a higher consciousness and a full, balanced daily life. $11.95 paper, 160 pages

Available from your local bookstore, or order direct from the publisher. Please include $1.25 shipping & handling for the first book, and 50 cents for each additional book. California residents include local sales tax. Write for our free complete catalog of over 400 books and tapes.

Ship to:

Name_____

Address_____

City_____ State ____ Zip _____

Phone _____

Celestial Arts
P.O. Box 7327
Berkeley, CA 94707
For VISA or
Mastercard orders
call (510) 845-8414